STAR WARS

COMPLETE LOCATIONS

STAR WARS

COMPLETE LOCATIONS

WRITTEN BY
KRISTIN LUND (EPISODE I), SIMON BEECROFT (EPISODE II),
KERRIE DOUGHERTY (EPISODE III), JAMES LUCENO (EPISODES IV–VI),
AND JASON FRY (EPISODE VII)

CONSULTATION BY
CURTIS SAXTON

ILLUSTRATED BY
RICHARD CHASEMORE, HANS JENSSEN, AND KEMP REMILLARD

ADDITIONAL ILLUSTRATIONS BY
ROBERT E. BARNES, JOHN MULLANEY, RICHARD BONSON,
GREG KNIGHT, CHRISTIAN PICCOLO, CHRIS TREVAS, ALEX IVANOV,
MASAHIKO TANO, ROGER HUTCHINS, BILL LE FEVER, AND JON HALL

FOREWORD BY
DOUG CHIANG

FOREWORD

Since I was eight years old, I have been fascinated with creating fantastic worlds and understanding how they are built. My earliest drawings were filled with diagrams of structures and rocket ship constructions. All of my spaceships had interiors. It wasn't enough just to draw the outside. I needed to make sense of the inside. Little did I know that this fascination with details would lead to a long career in film design, where I would have the opportunity to create and shape the worlds and locations of *Star Wars*. That career has now spanned more than 25 years.

I grew up in the suburbs of Michigan, in a new residential development that was surrounded by acres of wild woods. Those woods were a playground that fueled my growing imagination. I spent entire weekends exploring them. A fallen tree became an ancient city. I imagined that the layers of decaying wood were buildings of alien construction. During the winter months, I would explore the frozen creeks behind our house. The layers of thick ice, when held close to my eyes, formed complex shapes that became a miniature crystalline metropolis. Later, at home, I would draw the things I had seen and embellish them even further, inventing stories and crafting exotic reasons for why they were built.

When I wasn't outside, I would spend hours inside looking through an encyclopedia, marveling at its cut-away view of the pyramids. Or getting lost within NASA illustrations of space stations and future moon bases. One of my fondest memories during this time was building a model kit of a cut-away submarine. I had often wondered where the bathrooms were on a submarine. Or where the crew's beds were.

That summer, construction began across the street on several new homes. Over the course of several months I saw foundations dug and skeletal frames of houses erected. Before my eyes, in slow motion, I learned about the different parts of a house. That was my first real-life cross-section experience, and it transformed how I approached my drawings. I realized that the inside was just as interesting as the outside, and perhaps more important.

Twenty-three years later, I found myself working on the new *Star Wars* films with George Lucas. My childhood fascination to figure out how things functioned was about to pay off. That first year at Skywalker Ranch was the most significant for me. Because I didn't know how the environments and locations that I was designing would be used in the film, I imagined them as real, believable places, places that worked from the inside as well as the outside. That year of early exploration gave me the opportunity to design locations in their entirety. I didn't approach them as movie sets. Instead, I wanted the sets to have a logic for why they looked the way they did.

One of the keys to designing successful film environments in this manner was to take a real location and twist it by 20% to make something new. This approach to cinematic design turns the ordinary into the extraordinary, while anchoring it in reality. The podrace course was a wonderful example. George wanted each terrain to be recognizable and distinct. To achieve this, we combined and condensed real locations and exaggerated the scale to add that 20% extra to make it unique. Topographical maps were made for George to stage the race. Canyons and plateaus were configured to create memorable landmarks. Using this map, we timed out the race to see how many laps could be completed in eight minutes at speeds of up to 600 miles per hour. This determined the length of the course. Obstacles were then added to dull sections while other areas were simplified for visual clarity.

Other times we built detailed cardboard models to work out a location. These simply constructed card models were very elaborate in form. For the Naboo starfighter hangar, the card models allowed us to figure out how the hangar would be connected to the power generator room. That connection became important when George staged his climactic fight between Darth Maul and Qui-Gon Jinn. For *Star Wars: The Force Awakens*, we made many detailed card models of Starkiller Base, the Resistance base, and Maz's castle, as well as Rey's AT-AT desert home.

Sadly, these models are rarely seen by the public. However, with *Star Wars: Complete Locations*, the sets and locations are revealed in even greater detail in these remarkable illustrations by Hans Jenssen, Richard Chasemore, and Kemp Remillard.

In *Star Wars: Complete Locations*, the locations come to life in exquisite detail. Not only have the artists remained faithful to the film designs, they have expanded upon them, often improving the designs by resolving discontinuities and errors that we didn't figure out. Hans, Richard, and Kemp have taken fragments of sets and transformed them into real places. Their extraordinary illustrations are accurate, or as accurate as they can be for "a galaxy far, far away." Looking at their work, I marvel at their ingenuity and admire their clever solutions. We can see where Watto sleeps, or what's inside the Yavin rebel base. Of course there would be a communications center at the top of the Naboo hangar, giving it its distinct dome shape.

This book stands as the definitive blueprint for *Star Wars* locations. I delight in them today. Even though I'm familiar with many of these locations, I still enjoy immersing myself, getting lost within these pages for hours. I am that eight-year-old kid again, exploring the woods behind my house.

D. CHIANG

Doug Chiang
Production Designer, Episodes I–III and VII

CONTENTS

INTRODUCTION

THE *STAR WARS* SAGA is the story of the Skywalkers—a family whose members hold the fate of the galaxy in their hands and whose destiny is played out against a background of political upheaval, revolt, and rebellion. Old institutions crumble and harsh new tyrannies arise as Anakin Skywalker, slave and Force-sensitive, seeks his destiny as the Chosen One of the Jedi Order, only to succumb to the dark side of the Force and become an instrument of evil. His children, Luke and Leia, born of his overpowering love for Padmé Amidala, must save their father and the galaxy from the darkness of the Empire, in order to restore true balance to the Force and democracy to the star systems.

REPUBLIC AND EMPIRE

With more than a million inhabited worlds, the galaxy is divided into varying alliances and power blocs, the most important of which is the Galactic Republic. The Republic endures, in one form or another, for millennia, but eventually collapses from internal corruption and Separatist movements. Adroitly manipulating this disorder, Supreme Chancellor Palpatine seizes emergency powers and converts the Republic into the Empire to achieve his Sith revenge. The Empire absorbs and controls many star systems but does not bother with small fringe worlds and alliances that represent no danger to it. Eventually, the Empire in turn collapses in the face of a determined rebellion, and a New Republic rises to inherit the galaxy. But the descendants of the Empire will not forgive or forget what they see as a despicable betrayal, and beyond the Republic's borders they ceaselessly plot their return to power.

THE CLONE WARS

The brutal civil war that comes to be known as the Clone Wars erupts in the aftermath of a political upheaval in the Galactic Senate. A Separatist Alliance of disaffected star systems attempts to withdraw from the Republic, triggering a vast and deadly conflict that rages for three years. In its final stages, the Jedi Order is accused of treason and wiped out, the Separatist leaders are destroyed, and the Republic is transformed into the Galactic Empire.

THE GALACTIC CIVIL WAR

After years of tyrannical Imperial rule, scattered sparks of rebellion across the galaxy combine into a full-scale revolt. Dubbed the Alliance to Restore the Republic, but better known as the Rebel Alliance, this group of brave freedom fighters wages desperate battles against the mighty Imperial military. The Alliance's first great victory sees the destruction of the Death Star—the Empire's most powerful weapon— and after many years of struggle and hardship, the rebels finally succeed in overthrowing the Empire and its evil ruler.

THE RISE OF THE FIRST ORDER

For a time, there is peace. The New Republic attempts to reconstruct a scarred and traumatized galaxy. But in the Unknown Regions, dark forces rise again, determined to destroy all that the rebellion had fought so hard to achieve. Those who see this threat for what it is are branded delusional or warmongers, and are driven to create a new force willing to do what the Republic is not, known as the Resistance. The Republic will soon discover that its attempts to maintain peace have failed, and a new war is inevitable.

1 Endor	**11** Yavin	**21** Hosnian Prime
2 Takodana	**12** Moraband	**22** Tatooine and Geonosis
3 Jakku	**13** Felucia	**23** Ryloth
4 Starkiller Base	**14** Malachor	**24** Naboo
5 Coruscant	**15** Kuat	**25** D'Qar
6 Ord Mantell	**16** Onderon	**26** Malastare
7 Dantooine	**17** Kashyyyk	**27** Utapau
8 Ithor	**18** Lothal	**28** Sullust
9 Dathomir	**19** Corellia	**29** Dagobah
10 Mandalore	**20** Nal Hutta	**30** Bespin and Hoth

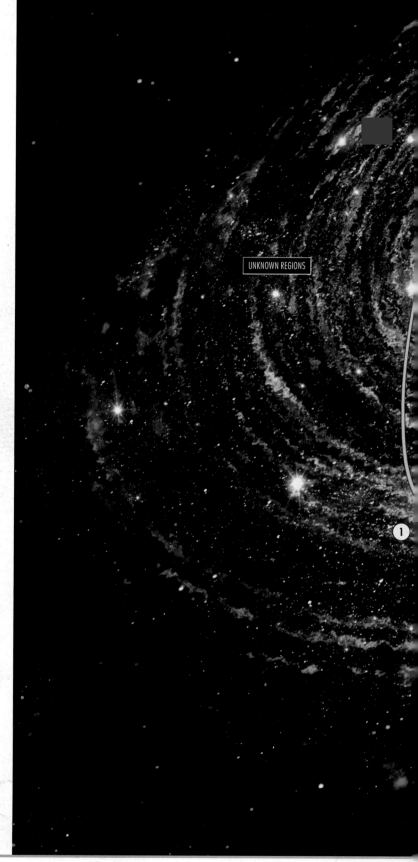

UNKNOWN REGIONS

THE GALAXY

PLANET PROFILES

THE GALAXY IN WHICH the Republic and its successors exert their sway teems with life, both human and alien. There are hundreds of millions of worlds harboring intelligent life and countless millions more where intelligent life is now extinct or never arose. An almost bewildering assortment of planetary environments—from frozen wastes to blistering deserts, from swamp-and-forest worlds to volcanic hells and verdant paradises, from world-oceans to world-cities—form the backdrop to the Skywalker saga and the battle for control of the galaxy. This struggle for peace and justice thrusts some worlds into prominence because of the events that take place there or the heroes and villains they produce.

NABOO

Naboo has long been an enigma to astrophysicists. Its porous, plasma-rich interior and lack of a molten core is an extremely rare phenomenon. It is generally thought, however, that the plasma (a naturally occurring form of intense energy unique to Naboo) is the key to many of the planet's secrets.

Galactic Region: Mid Rim
Diameter: 12,120 km
Principal Terrain: Mountains, plains, swamps
Number of Moons: 1
Length of Year: 312 days
Population: 600 million

TATOOINE

A desert world located in the Arkanis sector of the Outer Rim, Tatooine was settled by corporations seeking mineral wealth that turned out not to exist. Fossils bear testament to an ocean-covered formative period, although today Tatooine is all but waterless.

Galactic Region: Outer Rim Territories
Diameter: 10,465 km
Principal Terrain: Desert
Number of Moons: 3
Length of Year: 304 days
Population: 200,000

CORUSCANT

Coruscant orbits relatively far from its small sun, varying from 207 million to 251 million km (128 million to 155 million miles) and thus does not have a climate particularly suited to many species—a problem overcome by technological means and the vast heat generated by the massive, multi-level cityscape covering the planet. The first foundations of this ancient metropolis were built over a historic battlefield where long-vanished civilizations fought for control of the world. On Coruscant, wealth increases with altitude: the lowermost levels are lightless and abandoned; above them are lawless underlevels; countless blocks inhabited by billions of middle-class workers; and finally soaring towers that are home to the super-rich.

Galactic Region: Core Worlds
Diameter: 12,240 km
Principal Terrain: Urban
Number of Moons: 4
Length of Year: 365 days
Population: 1 trillion (estimated)

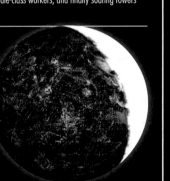

KAMINO

Kamino is a stormy world in a system of 13 planets circling an aging star that straggles south of the Rishi Maze, an irregular dwarf galaxy in a close and decaying orbit about the Galactic Republic. Climatic changes have long since submerged the planet's continents beneath a global ocean. Immense storms lash the surface, with powerful lightning bursts visible from orbit.

Galactic Region: (Extragalactic)
Diameter: 19,270 km
Principal Terrain: Ocean
Number of Moons: 3
Length of Year: 463 days
Population: 1 billion

GEONOSIS

The nearest inhabited neighbor of Tatooine, Geonosis is the second of five rocky worlds orbiting in a nondescript part of the Outer Rim. Geonosis' four surviving outer moons and an array of inner moonlets act as tidal shepherds to a spectacular and recently formed ring system; as a consequence, the planet suffers from frequent asteroid showers. Geonosis has a large diameter, light gravity, and a dense atmosphere. Flash floods and groundwater eruptions carve a precipitous terrain of highland canyons. As Geonosis' weak magnetic field leaves it vulnerable to harsh storms of solar radiation, the most persistent surface organisms are humble red rock-algae and creatures that can sense when to shelter underground.

Galactic Region: Outer Rim Territories
Diameter: 11,370 km
Principal Terrain: Canyons, deserts
Number of Moons: 15
Length of Year: 256 days
Population: 1 billion (none in Imperial era)

UTAPAU

Utapau is a windswept world, whose bleak and riven surface conceals its habitable areas and the mineral wealth of its underground ocean. Extensive oceans once covered the surface but leaked away through the easily eroded calcareous rocks of the crust into vast caverns that were originally massive magma chambers. This water now forms the sub-crustal world-ocean.

Galactic Region: Outer Rim Territories
Diameter: 12,900 km
Principal Terrain: Plains, sinkholes
Number of Moons: 9
Length of Year: 351 days
Population: 95 million

KASHYYYK

Covered in vast forests dominated by mighty wroshyr trees, Kashyyyk is a benign world of wide continents with a tropical ocean belt dotted with strings of islands and long coral reefs. Lacking an axial tilt, and with a perfectly circular orbit, Kashyyyk has no seasons.

Galactic Region: Mid Rim
Diameter: 12,765 km
Principal Terrain: Forests, seas
Number of Moons: 3
Length of Year: 381 days
Population: 56 million

MUSTAFAR

Tiny Mustafar is suspended in a tug-of-gravity between its neighboring planets, gas giants Jestefad and Lefrani. Jestefad is the nearer planet and is constantly trying to capture Mustafar as a moon. Lefrani's gravitational field stops this happening by pulling Mustafar the other way. Mustafar's hellish volcanic world is the product of this battle, which causes tidal forces that heat the planet's interior. Its environment is one of the harshest known in which native intelligent life has evolved.

Galactic Region: Outer Rim Territories
Diameter: 4,200 km
Principal Terrain: Mountains, volcanoes
Number of Moons: 0
Length of Year: 412 days
Population: 20,000

YAVIN 4

The largest of 13 moons orbiting the giant gas-planet Yavin, Yavin 4 is distinguished by interconnected continents and inland seas. Turbulent rivers plunge from volcanic heights to meander through endless tracts of pristine jungle. Here, the purple-barked Massassi tree thrives, named for the ancient civilization that once inhabited the moon and that left behind towering stone monuments. Yavin 4 has extreme wet and dry seasons, the former of which often gives rise to violent storms.

Galactic Region: Outer Rim Territories
Diameter: 10,200 km
Principal Terrain: Jungle
Number of Moons: N/A
Length of Year:
4,818 days
(planet)
Population: None
(no permanent
settlements)

HOTH

The sixth planet in a system of the same name, Hoth is an isolated, desolate, ice-bound globe that circles a blue-white sun. It is also a perpetual target for meteors spun off from a nearby asteroid field. Daylight temperatures rarely exceed freezing point even in Hoth's relatively temperate equatorial zone, and much lower readings are not uncommon at night. One third of Hoth consists of open ocean, and the remainder is either ice-covered continents or sea areas under ice shelves. The planet's massive glaciers are riddled with caverns, and crystalline geysers punctuate the frigid surface.

Galactic Region: Outer Rim Territories
Diameter: 7,200 km
Principal Terrain: Frozen plains, mountains
Number of Moons: 3
Length of Year: 549 days
Population: None (no permanent settlements)

DAGOBAH

Mysterious, mist-shrouded Dagobah in the remote Sluis sector has neither cities nor an indigenous population of sentients. However, the near-fabled swamp planet is a veritable cauldron of life, brimming with exotic fauna and flora, such as the gnarltree, which begins its life as a pale, slender shoot and then grows to such size that its buttressed roots fashion themselves into enchanting living caves. Dagobah's continental and oceanic crusts are only vaguely defined, and there is little in the way of volcanic activity or earthquakes. The surface is relatively flat, with water distributed in countless shallow lakes and lagoons.

Galactic Region: Outer Rim Territories
Diameter: 14,410 km
Principal Terrain: Swamps, bogs
Number of Moons: 0
Length of Year: 341 days
Population: None

BESPIN

Bespin is one of the few gas giants in the galaxy that is capable of harboring a wide variety of life. Separated from its two sister worlds by an asteroid belt known as Velser's Ring, the planet rotates every 12 standard-hours, orbits its sun every 14 standard-years, and is a primary source of naturally occurring tibanna gas. Bespin has no landmasses, but its upper atmosphere of billowing clouds hosts an envelope of breathable air, within which float exquisite orbital cities and sleek gas-mining facilities.

Galactic Region: Outer Rim Territories
Diameter: 118,000 km
Principal Terrain: Gas giant
Number of Moons: 2
Length of Year: 5,110 days
Population: 6 million (located entirely on hovering gas mining facilities)

ENDOR MOON

Largest of the nine moons of a gas giant in the inaccessible Moddell sector, the Endor Moon—known variously as the Sanctuary or Forest Moon—is a temperate world of woodlands, savannas, and mountain ranges. Many native life-forms thrive in the moon's relatively light gravity and hospitable climate.

Galactic Region: Outer Rim Territories
Diameter: 4,900 km
Principal Terrain: Forests, savannas, mountains
Number of moons: N/A
Length of Year: 402 days
(planet)
Population: Unknown

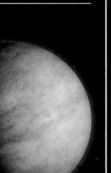

JAKKU

Jakku was once a verdant world, but some past calamity turned it into a barren globe of scorched badlands and marching dunes. Located in the galaxy's Western Reaches near the uncharted frontier, Jakku was all but uninhabited during the war between the Empire and the Alliance; few knew that the forlorn planet was the site of a secret Imperial research base used as a jumping-off point for exploring the galaxy's Unknown Regions. A year after the destruction of the second Death Star at Endor, an Imperial task force engaged a New Republic fleet above Jakku, with wreckage from the battle crashing onto the planet. The surviving Imperial forces then vanished into the unknown.

Galactic Region: Inner Rim
Diameter: 6,400 km
Principal Terrain: Desert
Number of Moons: 2
Length of Year: 352 days
Population: Unknown (less than 25,000)

TAKODANA

Located on the border of the galaxy's Mid Rim, the forested world of Takodana has long been a crossroads for bold scouts traveling beyond the frontier, and a base for treasure hunters and prospectors... as well as pirates who prey on them. For centuries Maz Kanata has run a legendary bar and hostel in an ancient castle by the shores of a Takodana lake, collecting travelers' tales and turning a profit from all who pass through her doors.

Galactic Region: Mid Rim
Diameter: 12,100 km
Principal Terrain: Forests, plains, seas
Number of Moons: 0
Length of Year: 215 days
Population: Less than 1 million

D'QAR

A lush jungle planet located in the Outer Rim, D'Qar was discovered by Alliance scouts in the final days of the Galactic Civil War and briefly housed a rebel outpost. But the war moved on and D'Qar was all but forgotten—which made it perfect when Leia Organa broke with the New Republic and sought a secret headquarters for her Resistance movement. From D'Qar, Leia keeps tabs on the First Order, employing the service of daring fighter pilots, a network of droids programmed as spies, and sympathetic politicians and military officers within the New Republic.

Galactic Region: Outer Rim Territories
Diameter: 10,400 km
Principal Terrain: Jungles, plains
Number of Moons: 2
Length of Year: 415 days
Population: None (No permanent settlements)

STARKILLER BASE

During the height of the Galactic Empire, Palpatine demanded deep space exploration of the Unknown Regions, using ancient navigational routes uncovered in the captured Jedi Temple as the backbone of such expeditions. It was in this manner that the Empire secured a small, frozen world with a natural abundance of energy-focusing kyber crystals. The Empire mined these crystals to create focusing arrays for the Death Stars' superlasers. When the First Order fled into the Unknown Regions, it turned this world into the heart of its secret holdings. A massive engineering project transformed it into Starkiller Base, a weapons platform of terrifying destructive power and range.

Galactic Region: Mobile
Diameter: 660 km
Principal Terrain: Forests, snow, mountains
Number of Moons: 0
Length of Year: Variable
Population: Unknown (classified)

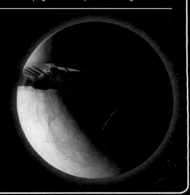

GRAVEYARD OF GIANTS
The eerie wrecks of crashed starships lie scattered across the dunes of Jakku—all that remains of the final battle of the Galactic Civil War.

EPISODE I
THE PHANTOM MENACE

Turmoil has engulfed the Galactic Republic. The taxation of trade routes to outlying star systems is in dispute.

Hoping to resolve the matter with a blockade of deadly battleships, the greedy Trade Federation has stopped all shipping to the small planet of Naboo.

While the Congress of the Republic endlessly debates this alarming chain of events, the Supreme Chancellor has secretly dispatched two Jedi Knights, the guardians of peace and justice in the galaxy, to settle the conflict....

NABOO

NABOO IS A BIZARRE, GEOGRAPHICALLY UNIQUE WORLD LOCATED along a major galactic trade route near the Outer Rim. The planet's serene surface of sweeping hills and rolling seas is deceptive: beneath it lies a shadowy underwater world of winding caverns and tunnels inhabited by gigantic, ferocious sea creatures. This immense labyrinth runs through the entire planet, becoming increasingly rocky and dense in the lower strata. The planet's center seethes and bubbles with eruptions of exotic plasmic energy. Over millennia these eruptions form new caverns and tunnels, and influence surface features such as mountains. The planet's two primary civilizations, the Naboo and the Gungans, rely on this plasma power, although they collect and use it in different ways.

The Naboo royal residence, Theed Palace, perches on top of a tremendous cliff with panoramic views of the surrounding countryside.

SECRETS OF OTOH GUNGA

When the amphibious Gungans were forced to retreat underwater in a fierce struggle for territory thousands of years ago, they stumbled upon a secret that enabled them to live there permanently. In deep waters, they came across a strange life-form known as locap that burrows into porous rock and siphons out plasma. The Gungans found that they were able to extract plasma from the plant using special harvesting bongos (Gungan submarines) equipped with a front-mounted siphon. This natural source of energy has many uses in Gungan life, including the creation of their unique bubble cities. Plasma-based technology allows powerful hydrostatic fields to be generated around basic frameworks, keeping water out but allowing individuals to pass through.

CULTURED CITY

Chancellor Palpatine's shuttle hovers over the elegantly domed buildings of Theed, his home city and the capital of Naboo. From this vantage point Palpatine can admire the city's unified, harmonious style, the result of extensive rebuilding after the upheavals of the ancient past. Theed's sophisticated culture has produced many able and admired galactic politicians, not least of whom is Palpatine himself, who learned much about the mechanics of government and the subtleties of power during his early years here. Naboo's reputation for peace and tolerance in the moral wilderness of the galaxy's rim lent Palpatine credibility as a young politician. The Naboo now feel secure in a galaxy ruled by this willful individual, however remote and inscrutable he has become.

NABOO LOCATIONS

THE DIVERSE TERRAIN OF NABOO teems with luscious plant and animal life. Whether it's the rich, green plains and insect-ridden swamps of the surface or the dark, fish-rich depths of the oceans, Naboo offers fruitful existences to those inhabitants who live in harmony with the planet. Several Gungan and Naboo chroniclers have advanced the theory that the mysterious and now long-dead civilization whose ruins dot the countryside failed to respect this balance and were destroyed by their greed.

The Gungan capital city of Otoh Gunga is hidden deep in the Naboo swamps, in the depths of Lake Paonga.

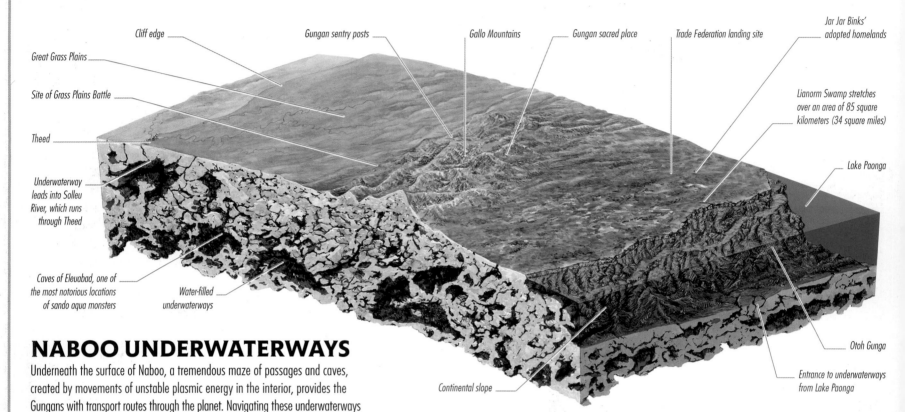

Cliff edge

Gungan sentry posts

Gallo Mountains

Gungan sacred place

Trade Federation landing site

Jar Jar Binks' adopted homelands

Great Grass Plains

Site of Grass Plains Battle

Lianorm Swamp stretches over an area of 85 square kilometers (34 square miles)

Theed

Lake Paonga

Underwaterway leads into Solleu River, which runs through Theed

Caves of Eleuabad, one of the most notorious locations of sando aqua monsters

Water-filled underwaterways

Otoh Gunga

Entrance to underwaterways from Lake Paonga

Continental slope

NABOO UNDERWATERWAYS

Underneath the surface of Naboo, a tremendous maze of passages and caves, created by movements of unstable plasmic energy in the interior, provides the Gungans with transport routes through the planet. Navigating these underwaterways requires immense skill since they are home to ferocious creatures. A single wrong turn can spell certain death. In spite of the risks, fleets of Gungan trading subs constantly voyage through these routes; overland travel on fambaas or kaadu is slower and more arduous for this amphibious species.

SACRED PLACE

Hidden in the swampy foothills of the Gallo Mountains, the sacred place is a haven of worship for the Gungans and a sanctuary in times of trouble. Scattered around are giant statues and a vast, crumbling temple, relics of a long-extinct race of Naboo inhabitants. The Gungans acknowledge this race as their planet's elders. Yet archaeologists are mystified as to the relevance of these crumbling remnants: are they giant representations of the race themselves or are they massive icons devoted to their gods?

Dense foliage cuts off site from outside world

Temple ruins

Tangled roots of cambylictus trees

SOLLEU RIVER

Although the cultures of the Naboo and the Gungans are different in many ways, both share a close relationship with water. The Naboo capital, Theed, is virtually a floating city, nestling on the banks of the mighty Solleu, a river fed by underground tributaries flowing through the planet interior. However, unlike the amphibious Gungans, the Naboo believe the meditative and restorative qualities of flowing water are best appreciated from dry land.

FUNERAL TEMPLE

The Theed Funeral Temple is located in a tranquil spot on the edge of the city. Its open-air design and numerous windows frame a magnificently carved stone platform. Nearby stands the Livet Tower containing an eternal flame, whose never-ending light reminds the Naboo of their own mortality and their duty to lead harmonious lives. Naboo funeral custom dictates that the body of the deceased be cremated within two days of death. In this way, it is believed, the life force of the dead is returned to the planet. Once the ashes are collected, they are carried onto the bridge between the temple and Livet Tower and cast into the Solleu River before it plunges over the cliff.

TURRET ROOM

As active members of the Galactic Republic, the Naboo regularly entertain dignitaries from other worlds in lavish, hand-crafted suites of rooms within Theed Palace. When the Jedi High Council arrives for the funeral of Qui-Gon Jinn its members make use of a turret room in which to mourn privately and celebrate the life of their fellow Jedi. This serene chamber is attached to a small temple where Naboo monarchs pay homage to the great rulers of the past. The temple and chamber were built by the first ruler of the Great Time of Peace, King Jafan, who helped reestablish peace on Naboo. It is here that Yoda warns Obi-Wan of the grave dangers he forsees in training Anakin as a Jedi.

Grazing kaadu

Gungan sentry

Anakin

GUNGAN SENTRY POST

The huge statue heads that dot the edges of the Lianorm Swamp at the foothills of the Gallo Mountains provide lookouts for Gungan sentries. These soldiers scan the Great Grass Plains using *farseein* (Gungan electrobinoculars). Before the Battle of Naboo, a sentry spies the Naboo Head of Security, Captain Panaka, and a group of volunteers crossing the Great Grass Plains from Theed.

OTOH GUNGA

ANCHORED TO AN UNDERWATER CLIFF DEEP IN LAKE PAONGA, Otoh Gunga is home to nearly one million inhabitants. Like all Gungan underwater cities, Otoh Gunga's central district is a dense cluster of bubbles made up of elegant city squares, noisy cantinas, oval-shaped sacred bubbles, and an Ancient Quarter, with fragile bubbles that now glow only faintly. Radiating outward are the Otoh Villages, where most Gungans live and work. At the furthest edges are satellite clusters, some of which have been cast out from other cities and are trying to attach themselves to Otoh Gunga.

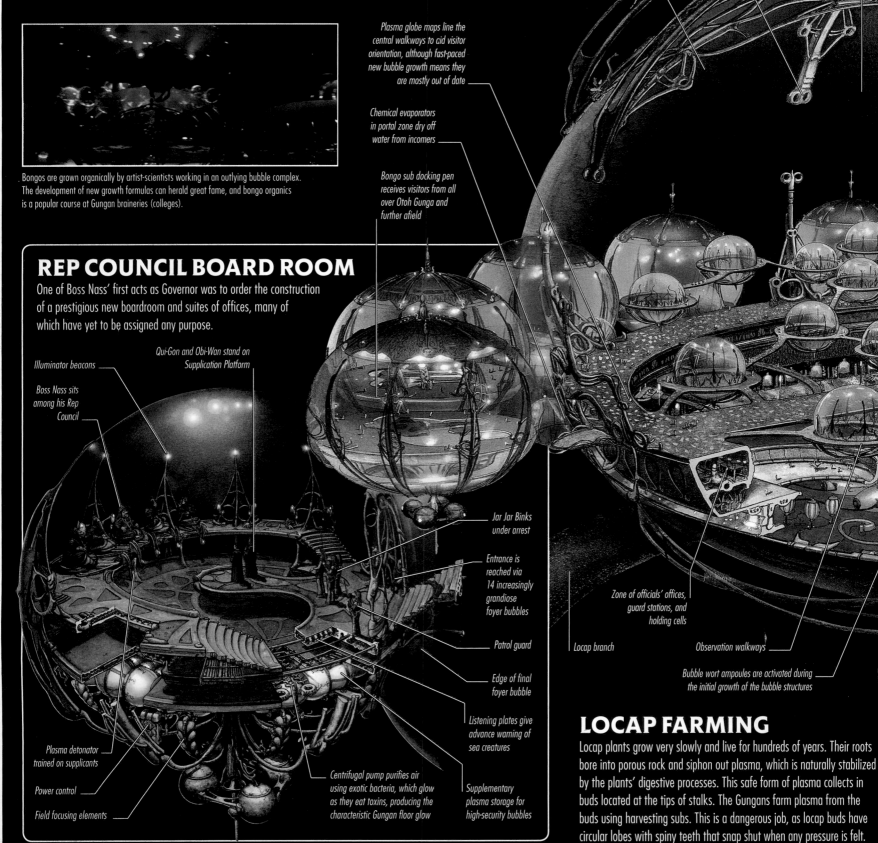

Bongos are grown organically by artist-scientists working in an outlying bubble complex. The development of new growth formulas can herald great fame, and bongo organics is a popular course at Gungan braineries (colleges).

Hydrostatic bubbles keep water out but allow individuals to pass through at special portal zones; the bubbles close up behind, like organic membranes

Utanodes project hydrostatic bubble field

Bubbles are partly lit by their own natural glow

Plasma globe maps line the central walkways to aid visitor orientation, although fast-paced new bubble growth means they are mostly out of date

Chemical evaporators in portal zone dry off water from incomers

Bongo sub docking pen receives visitors from all over Otoh Gunga and further afield

REP COUNCIL BOARD ROOM

One of Boss Nass' first acts as Governor was to order the construction of a prestigious new boardroom and suites of offices, many of which have yet to be assigned any purpose.

Illuminator beacons

Qui-Gon and Obi-Wan stand on Supplication Platform

Boss Nass sits among his Rep Council

Jar Jar Binks under arrest

Entrance is reached via 14 increasingly grandiose foyer bubbles

Patrol guard

Zone of officials' offices, guard stations, and holding cells

Locap branch

Observation walkways

Edge of final foyer bubble

Bubble wort ampoules are activated during the initial growth of the bubble structures

Plasma detonator trained on supplicants

Power control

Field focusing elements

Centrifugal pump purifies air using exotic bacteria, which glow as they eat toxins, producing the characteristic Gungan floor glow

Listening plates give advance warning of sea creatures

Supplementary plasma storage for high-security bubbles

LOCAP FARMING

Locap plants grow very slowly and live for hundreds of years. Their roots bore into porous rock and siphon out plasma, which is naturally stabilized by the plants' digestive processes. This safe form of plasma collects in buds located at the tips of stalks. The Gungans farm plasma from the buds using harvesting subs. This is a dangerous job, as locap buds have circular lobes with spiny teeth that snap shut when any pressure is felt.

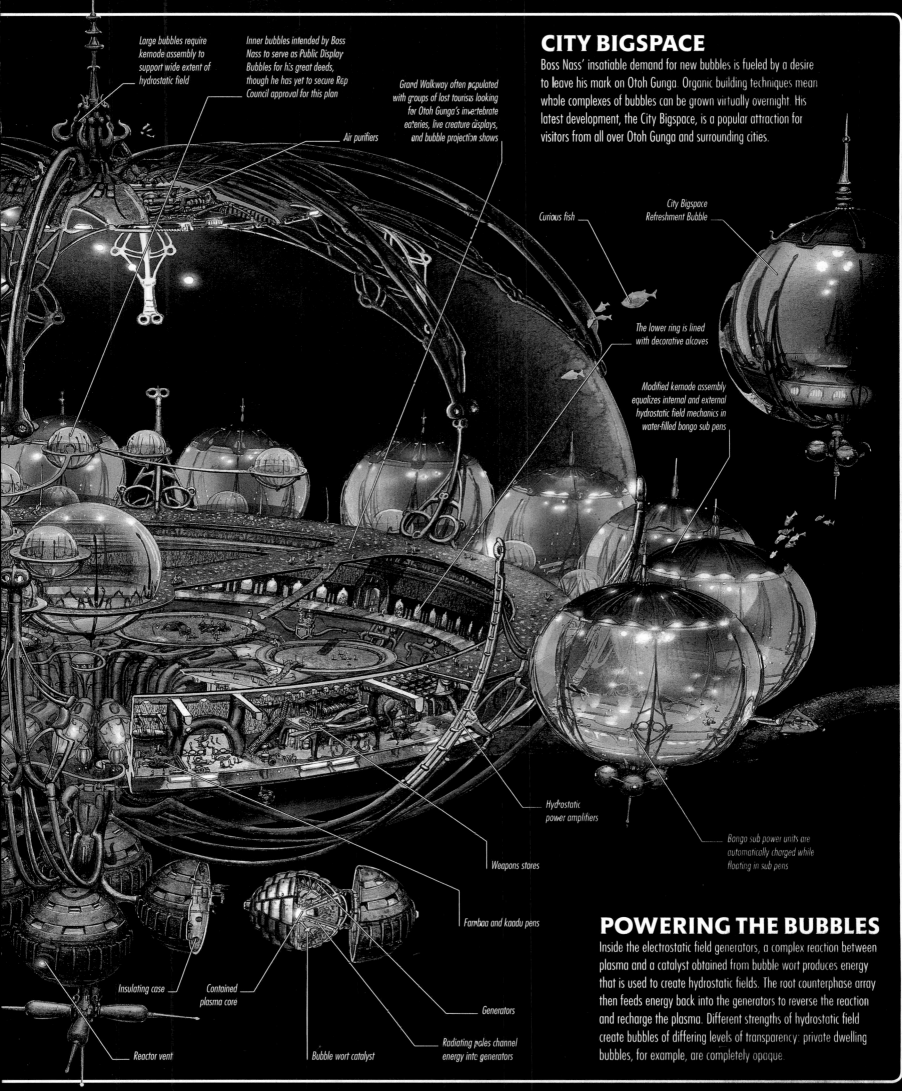

CITY BIGSPACE

Boss Nass' insatiable demand for new bubbles is fueled by a desire to leave his mark on Otoh Gunga. Organic building techniques mean whole complexes of bubbles can be grown virtually overnight. His latest development, the City Bigspace, is a popular attraction for visitors from all over Otoh Gunga and surrounding cities.

Large bubbles require kernode assembly to support wide extent of hydrostatic field

Inner bubbles intended by Boss Nass to serve as Public Display Bubbles for his great deeds, though he has yet to secure Rep Council approval for this plan

Grand Walkway often populated with groups of lost tourists looking for Otoh Gunga's invertebrate eateries, live creature displays, and bubble projection shows

Air purifiers

Curious fish

City Bigspace Refreshment Bubble

The lower ring is lined with decorative alcoves

Modified kernode assembly equalizes internal and external hydrostatic field mechanics in water-filled bongo sub pens

Hydrostatic power amplifiers

Weapons stores

Bongo sub power units are automatically charged while floating in sub pens

Fambaa and kaadu pens

Insulating case

Contained plasma core

Generators

Reactor vent

Bubble wort catalyst

Radiating poles channel energy into generators

POWERING THE BUBBLES

Inside the electrostatic field generators, a complex reaction between plasma and a catalyst obtained from bubble wort produces energy that is used to create hydrostatic fields. The root counterphase array then feeds energy back into the generators to reverse the reaction and recharge the plasma. Different strengths of hydrostatic field create bubbles of differing levels of transparency: private dwelling bubbles, for example, are completely opaque.

DROID CONTROL SHIP

FOR THE TRADE FEDERATION OFFICIALS who live in it for months on end, the huge Droid Control Ship is an entire world in space. Confinement aboard the converted cargo ship causes frayed nerves and petty backbiting among these merchants of greed. Neimoidians rarely stray far from the command bridge for fear that a colleague will gain some advantage in their absence or form an alliance against them. Equipped with a computer powerful enough to remotely control an entire droid invasion force, this ship is set to launch a determined act of aggression against the virtually defenseless planet of Naboo.

The signal to begin activation of the droid army is given via the pilot's manual controls.

Control signal computer relays commands to droid army

Pilot in navigation station controls ship systems via datagoggles and hand-operated instrument panels

CONTROL SHIP BRIDGE

Dominated by the throne-like pilot navigation station, the control ship bridge is a well-guarded location on a tower at the heart of the spacecraft. Droid pilot operatives are stationed at navigation computers on an underfloor. In this small, confined environment, Trade Federation officials frequently seek the relative privacy of the shadowy corners to scheme against each other, nominally out of earshot (though actually inviting and welcoming attention and suspicion). They communicate with trade partners via a viewscreen situated in a port at one side of the bridge.

Jedi emerge from circulation vent

SECRET ARMY

Usually piled high with cargo, the cavernous hangars in the control ship have been cleared to allow for the transport and mobilization of a droid invasion army in complete secrecy. The most recent customs officials from the Galactic Republic to venture on board the ship were persuaded that the suspicious-looking components they saw had no military function, but were a shipment of the latest, expensive binary load-lifters. However, the Jedi who emerge from a circulation vent are under no illusions about what they are witnessing.

CONFERENCE ROOM

The control ship's centersphere contains 50 conference rooms. As these rooms are used for trade negotiations, they are specially adapted to place clients at a disadvantage. The adaptations include variable gas emitters and remote-operated "concentration deficit" chairs, which make it difficult for customers to think clearly.

AIR TRAFFIC CONTROL

The flow of traffic in and out of the ship is monitored from droid stations that overlook the hangars. Despite their slow reaction times, droids now oversee many ship functions. Replacing paid employees and expensive protocol droids with low-maintenance droid "slaves" partially offsets the massive costs of assembling the droid army.

BLAST DOORS

While the Jedi face fearsome droidekas, the Neimoidian viceroy and his aides cower in the bridge behind triple blast doors. In status-obsessed Neimoidian society, even doors assert social standing, and these bridge doors are particularly elaborate—reminding ship employees of the superiority of its high-level occupants. However, the doors are not as impenetrable as they look, as Qui-Gon proves when he burns through them with his lightsaber.

Cargo bay

Row of MTTs (Multi-Troop Transports)

Cargo containers moved aside to make space for droid army

THEED HANGAR

SITTING ATOP THE CLIFF EDGE in the city's central district, the elegant Theed Hangar is a well-guarded military airbase for the N-1 starfighter fleet and Queen Amidala's Royal Starship. The neighboring power generator supplies the spacecraft in the hangar with plasma energy through underground conduits. Equipped with air traffic control, tactical computer stations, and a secret subterranean tunnel link to the palace, the hangar will play a pivotal role in the Battle of Naboo and become a rallying point for the eventual uprising.

Anticipating no resistance from the peace-loving Naboo—let alone two experienced Jedi—battle droids leave the Royal Starship operational and ready to fly.

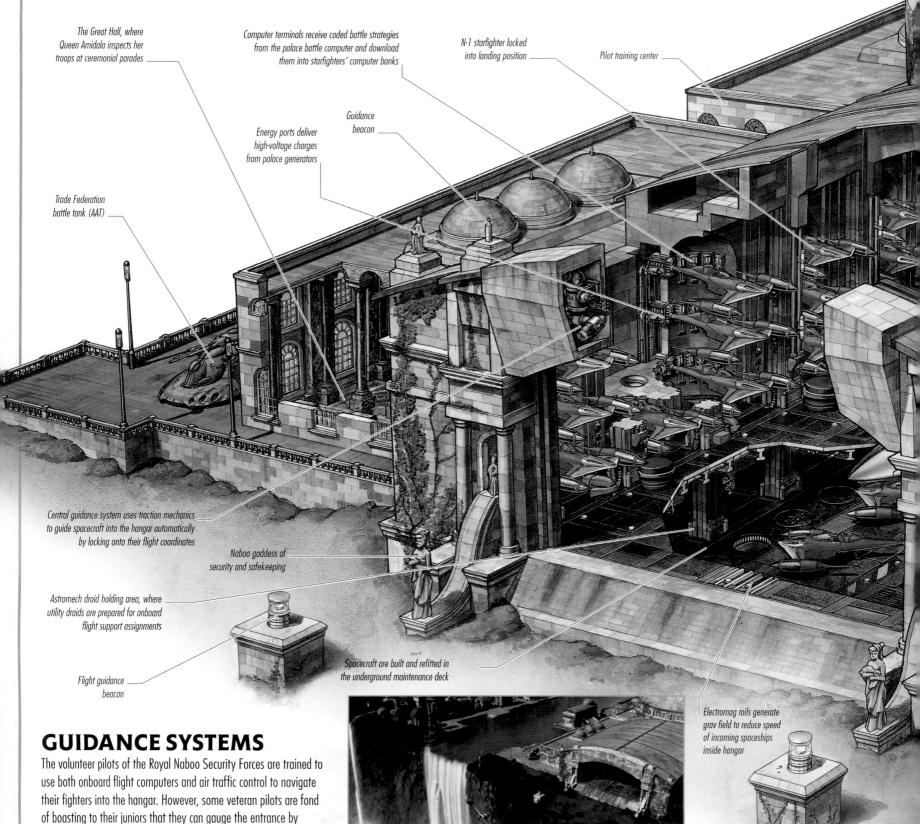

The Great Hall, where Queen Amidala inspects her troops at ceremonial parades

Computer terminals receive coded battle strategies from the palace battle computer and download them into starfighters' computer banks

N-1 starfighter locked into landing position

Pilot training center

Guidance beacon

Energy ports deliver high-voltage charges from palace generators

Trade Federation battle tank (AAT)

Central guidance system uses traction mechanics to guide spacecraft into the hangar automatically by locking onto their flight coordinates

Naboo goddess of security and safekeeping

Astromech droid holding area, where utility droids are prepared for onboard flight support assignments

Spacecraft are built and refitted in the underground maintenance deck

Electromag rails generate grav field to reduce speed of incoming spaceships inside hangar

Flight guidance beacon

GUIDANCE SYSTEMS

The volunteer pilots of the Royal Naboo Security Forces are trained to use both onboard flight computers and air traffic control to navigate their fighters into the hangar. However, some veteran pilots are fond of boasting to their juniors that they can gauge the entrance by observing how the wind is affecting the nearby waterfalls.

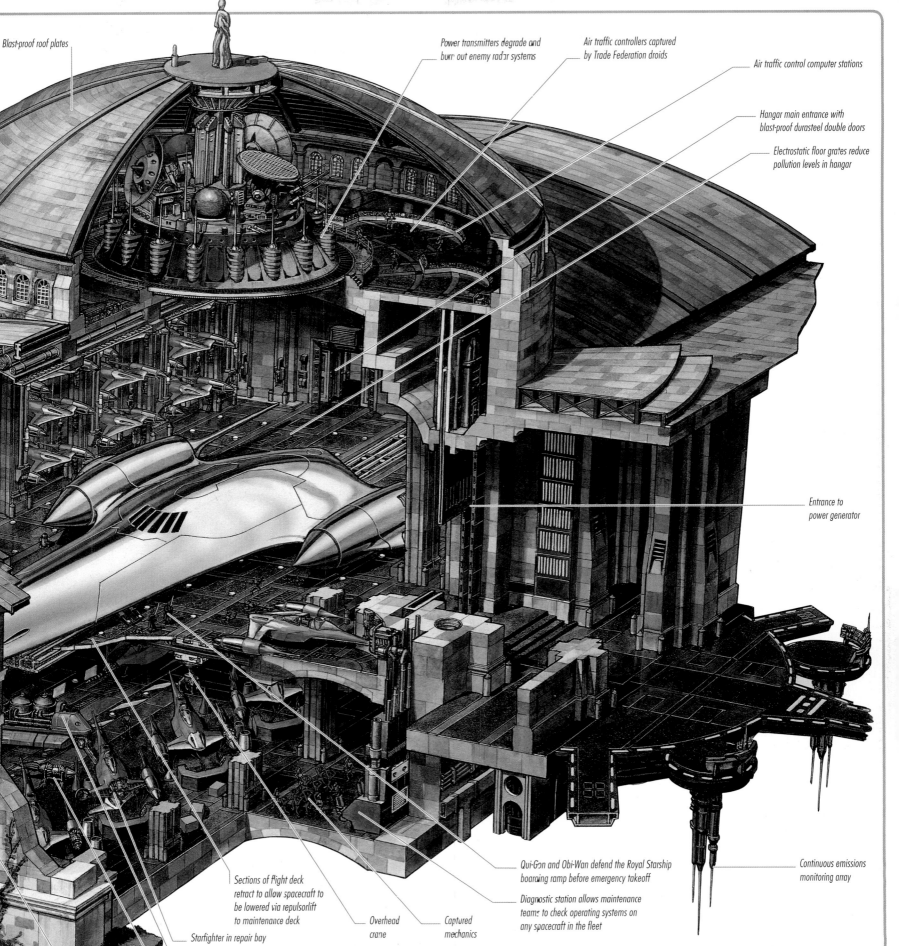

Blast-proof roof plates

Power transmitters degrade and burn out enemy radar systems

Air traffic controllers captured by Trade Federation droids

Air traffic control computer stations

Hangar main entrance with blast-proof durasteel double doors

Electrostatic floor grates reduce pollution levels in hangar

Entrance to power generator

Continuous emissions monitoring array

Qui-Gon and Obi-Wan defend the Royal Starship boarding ramp before emergency takeoff

Diagnostic station allows maintenance teams to check operating systems on any spacecraft in the fleet

Captured mechanics

Overhead crane

Sections of flight deck retract to allow spacecraft to be lowered via repulsorlift to maintenance deck

Starfighter in repair bay

Maintenance and refueling vehicle

Malfunctioning sublight engine from starfighter

Brick sections of the hangar are embedded with high-tensile durasteel support webbing to protect the building from blast damage

DETECTING THE INVASION FORCE

Naboo's powerful sensor arrays immediately detected the arrival of the Trade Federation's landing ships, which did not even bother to use their stealth systems. Having only experienced simulated attacks before, the Space Fighter Corps radar operators were shocked by the scale of the Trade Federation forces and the speed with which they advanced on the Naboo cities. Yet the pilots remained steadfast, waiting for the order from their monarch to attack. However, even as tanks rolled along the main avenue of Theed, Queen Amidala remained convinced that peaceful negotiation was possible. When battle droids were dispatched to capture the pilots, Amidala ordered her people not to resist—for the time being.

TATOOINE I

A VAST YELLOW GLOBE, baked by the heat of its twin suns, Tatooine is a testament to the tenacity of life. Its native life-forms, from dewbacks, eopies, and krayt dragons to Jawas and Tusken Raiders, must all find ways to survive in the harsh desert wastes. More recent immigrants have found a way to eke out a living as well: the first settlers were poor laborers employed by mining corporations that believed Tatooine was rich in ore and minerals. It wasn't, and when the mining venture failed, the workers and their equipment were abandoned—but their descendents and more recent arrivals have survived through moisture farming and trade. Tatooine sits at a nexus of Outer Rim trade routes, and is a frequent stopover for smugglers moving goods to or from Hutt Space, as well as outlaws, mercenaries, and those seeking to disappear. Much of its economy is controlled by the Hutt clans, and Republic law is but a rumor.

TOWN AND COUNTRY

Tatooine's few settlements are separated from each other by vast expanses of desert. The poor standards of living and harsh conditions on Tatooine mean that little distinguishes one town from another. Yet Mos Espa's location near Tatooine's famous podrace arena gives it a distinctive feel. Along with the usual spacers, its cafés and cantinas buzz with podrace crews, visiting fans, and professional gamblers. By contrast, rural Tatooine is a lonely world of small moisture farms. These use simple vaporators to collect the tiny amounts of water in the air, which is sold as a commodity and used to irrigate underground plantations.

Tatooine is so fiercely lit by its twin suns that it appears from a certain distance to be a star itself. The planet is uninhabitable save for one relatively cool area of its northern hemisphere.

THE SECRETS OF THE STONES

Characterized by gigantic, top-heavy rocks that rise eerily from the sand, Mushroom Mesa is one of the most astonishing features of Tatooine's desert wasteland. Many observers have noted the humanoid faces that appear in some of the stones: a freak accident of wind erosion or ritual objects carved by alien hands—no one knows. Some observers believe the secret lies with the Sand People, who, they note, avoid the Mesa as if it were cursed. Tatooine's more recent settlers are less superstitious: Mos Espa's famous podrace circuit now runs directly through the stones.

The activities of Tatooine's settlers disrupt the traditional hunting patterns of the indigenous Sand People. This has resulted in intense periods of frustrated savagery, with the fearsome natives attacking other species in random raids, and taking potshots using stolen blasters as weapons.

MOS ESPA

INHABITED MOSTLY BY POOR SETTLERS and controlled by powerful gangsters, Mos Espa is a rough, lawless town and one of Tatooine's largest spaceports. Its inhabitants eke out a living by scavenging, trading, stealing, or gambling. The wealthiest citizens openly disregard the Republic's laws by owning slaves, an illegal practice. Slaves are housed on the outskirts of Mos Espa in cheap lodgings originally put up by mining corporations for their workers. Since local authorities stay away from the slave quarters, enterprising slaves regularly provide safe houses for outlaws on the run—for a price.

Although the food is guaranteed to be undercooked and stringy, Sebulba often hangs out at Akim's Munch, a street café where his fans can see him and pay their respects. However, the hot-tempered Dug is just as keen to meet opponents and enemies.

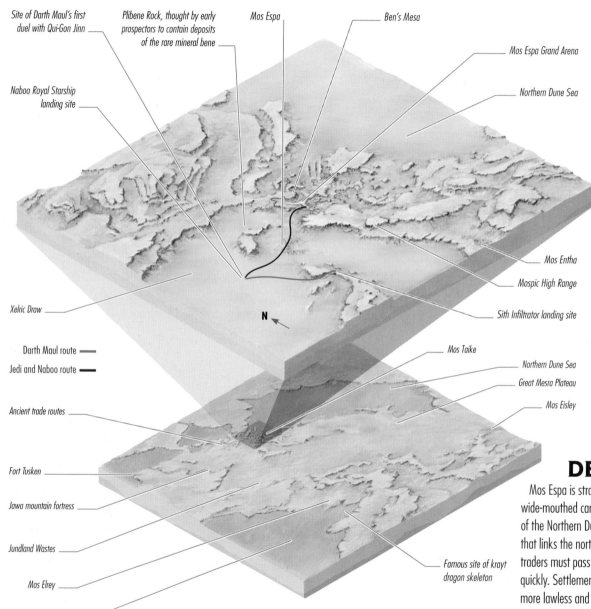

Site of Darth Maul's first duel with Qui-Gon Jinn

Plibene Rock, thought by early prospectors to contain deposits of the rare mineral bene

Mos Espa

Ben's Mesa

Mos Espa Grand Arena

Northern Dune Sea

Naboo Royal Starship landing site

Mos Entha

Mospic High Range

Sith Infiltrator landing site

Xelric Draw

N

Darth Maul route

Jedi and Naboo route

Mos Taike

Northern Dune Sea

Great Mesra Plateau

Mos Eisley

Ancient trade routes

Fort Tusken

Jawa mountain fortress

Jundland Wastes

Mos Elrey

Western Dune Sea

Famous site of krayt dragon skeleton

DESERT SETTLEMENT

Mos Espa is strategically situated in the Xelric Draw, a shallow, wide-mouthed canyon that splits the Mospic High Range on the edge of the Northern Dune Sea. The Xelric Draw is an ancient trading route that links the northern settlements to those further south. Since all traders must pass this way, Mos Espa's marketplace developed quickly. Settlements off the main trade route tend to be even more lawless and hostile toward traders of any species.

HOVEL BACKYARDS

Anakin works on his podracer behind the slave quarters safe in the knowledge that Watto never ventures here. As a slave owner, Watto is expected to maintain slave hovels. However, repairs are usually left undone until structures actually begin to collapse—then they are hastily patched up by one of Watto's most expendable droids.

MOS ESPA ARENA

Many off-worlders from the Outer Rim associate Mos Espa with its famous podraces, held at the enormous arena in the desert outside the city. The thrill of the races can be addictive, and fans new to the sport soon find Tatooine-style gambling to be an expensive pursuit.

DESPERATE SELLING

Mos Espa's market stalls are busy with salvage dealers selling ill-gotten used parts for all manner of vehicles and vessels. An off-worlder who neglects to leave his ship under guard will almost certainly find parts missing on return!

URBAN MUDDLE

Mos Espa's domed, mostly windowless architecture is intended to protect settlers from the burning heat of Tatooine's suns—and from each other. With the absence of any discernible building codes, new streets and buildings are tacked on whenever needed. Shacks stand shoulder to shoulder with cupolas; vendors with overhead awnings do business next to climate-controlled trading houses. Only longtime residents are able to make their way through the labyrinth of dusty streets without a map—visitors are at a distinct disadvantage, and risk losing their way and their valuables at every turn.

CHANGING LANDSCAPES

Tatooine's cities are frequently blasted by severe sandstorms and the market vendors of Mos Espa seem to know instinctively when one is approaching. At the first sign, outdoor traders cover their wares with faded tarps while shopkeepers close their doors and plug vents. In a sandstorm, even seasoned inhabitants lose their way within city limits, mistaking one sandswept building for another. Adding to Tatooine's ever-changing landscapes are mirages and heat hazes: the dark cantinas are full of haunting stories of lost travelers and the desert apparitions they have seen.

WATTO'S JUNKSHOP

EVEN AMONG MOS ESPA'S ODD ASSORTMENT OF BUILDINGS,

Watto's junkshop stands out. Originally a simple, squat dome, the money-minded shopkeeper added the unusual bell-shaped top himself after his first highly successful deal (with a wealthy Hutt clan leader). Recalling the muck nests of Watto's native Toydaria, the distinctive top attracts customers and provides Watto with a safe perch.

SUCCESS STORY

Watto's shop is one of the most successful parts dealerships in Mos Espa. His secret is simple: inflated prices, stolen stock, slaves, and no questions asked. Watto spends little time behind the counter these days, letting droids do much of the work.

Durasteel habitat main support ring

Jawa R1-type shopkeeping drone

Astromech relaxing in a droid lubrication bath

Moobian torsion valve

Anakin and Padmé meet for the first time

Coolth grid within wall

Passing Rodian

Pipes convey coolth and shisha oil from private underground tanks

Toydarian clan bell signifying noble family (purchased)

Air vent

Polyfiber netting helps contain Toydarian muck lake atmosphere

Circular perch

Security viewscreen connects to anti-theft weapons in shop

Egg-seed dispenser

Nest

Heat reflector for use at night

Built-in shisha pipe

Power generator

Entrance portal

Spare parts rack

Vaporators extract precious moisture from the air

TROPHY SHELF

One wall of Watto's nest is given over to his treasured collection of podrace memorabilia. Some trophies are gifts from famous podracers and pit crews. Other items were purloined from podracing museums or purchased by Watto's agents on the illegal markets traditionally held immediately after races involving spectacular crashes.

Grand Trophy from race at Ando Prime Centrum course

Twi'lek siren whistle

Glove recovered from crash site of famous podracer Bekk Tunit

One of Sebulba's victory chains (stolen)

Antigrav bracket supports shelf

Durasteel box with unidentified contents

Disintegrator staff

Toydarian N'Omis flower

Bendine XR12 Satellite Liberator

Nacelle from Huulian starfighter

STAYING COOL

The junkshop's plain adobe outer shell covers durasteel double walls with a layer of coolant flowing between them. Micro-elements embedded in the dome's power grid force by-product warm air out through slots in the skirt and the top.

Whenever the shop is running smoothly, Watto flies up to his nest to rest, think, or just count his money

Gonk power droid storage bay

Dome-stabilizer re-inforcer ring

Surplus coolth conduit

Repair and maintenance pod of unknown origin

Arched portal into junkyard

Welding droid

Corellian freighter cargo containers

Landspeeder turbine engine

Qui-Gon and Watto haggle over the price of a T-14 hyperdrive

Unopened gift from anonymous admirer

Durasteel double wall

Jar Jar meddles with a pit droid

Illegal alta-wave calibration device

Main brace from a Corellian drop ship

Rock infill wall

JUNKYARD

Watto stores the bulk of his merchandise in the yard behind his shop. Many of his (so-called) bargains are the result of insider trading information received from Jawas who owe him large gambling debts. Security is provided by two customized agricultural droids wielding motion detectors and blasters.

Useless parts left out for Jawas to scavenge

Exclusive private casino that fronts as an arms dealership to keep out uninvited guests

Burned-out podracer engine plating

ANAKIN'S WORKBENCH

When Anakin isn't repairing droids for Watto, he spends his precious spare time tinkering and inventing. He works on his podracer engines outdoors due to their size. When it gets dark, Shmi calls Anakin inside and he works at his workbench on the protocol droid he is building for his mother.

Half-finished scanner Anakin is inventing to detect hidden slave implants

Power coupler

Antistatic toolbox

T3 web comber

C-3PO

Gausser (broken)

Murchason ring stress analyzer

Anakin shows Padmé his room

Woven rug takes its pattern from rock paintings found in Tatooine's interior

Box left by previous tenant

Bed alcove

Karmova drum

Noeu sphere racquets

Dried poonten grass bedding

Rough, poor-quality blankets on Anakin's bed

Thick adobe walls offer cool protection from Tatooine's harsh twin suns and fierce sandstorms

Stone infill mined locally at Ebe Crater quarry

POWER FROM WASTE

Slave hovels on Tatooine are cooled and heated by archaic bio-converter power generators. These machines receive liquid sludge composed of animal and municipal waste via underground pipelines. The liquid is then converted into natchgas. The Skywalkers' oversized generator also serves four adjacent hovels.

Diagnostic screen on workbench

Storage cupboard fabricated from a gutted jukebox from Mos Espa's first cantina

Strange statue of alien pirate Anakin picked up from passing trader

ANAKIN'S ROOM

Filled with the clutter of an active nine-year-old's life, Anakin's bedroom houses his mechanical projects, spare parts, and tools, as well as his homemade toys and games.

Coolth inflow pipe leading to second level of hovel

Clothing storage

R2-D2

Repulsor-operated door

ANAKIN'S HOVEL

ANAKIN AND SHMI SKYWALKER share a hovel in Slave Quarters Row on the edge of Mos Espa. They have been fortunate to have a home to themselves ever since Watto won them in a gambling debt from the fearsome Gardulla the Hutt. When the Skywalkers belonged to Gardulla, they were forced to share quarters with six other slaves. Their good fortune is not due to Watto's generosity, of course. He reluctantly lets them live alone until he can afford more slaves—a threat he uses against the Skywalkers whenever he is displeased with them.

Stairs to upper level and refresher

The hovels are stacked on top of each other to save space.

MOS ESPA CIRCUIT

HOST TO THE EAGERLY AWAITED Boonta Eve Classic and countless other races, Mos Espa podrace circuit weaves around a broad, flat-topped mountain called Ben's Mesa. Its cliff-like sides help ensure that scheming racers stick to the official course. Nevertheless, pilots continue to experiment with new shortcuts through the desert wilderness—no pilot or fan has ever agreed which route guarantees a spectacular win.

BEGGAR'S CANYON

On non-race days, Tatooine youngsters sneak into the section of the course known as Beggar's Canyon. Here, in the winding channels of this dry river bed, they push their souped-up landspeeders and super-fast skyhoppers to the limit, dreaming that one day they might be hometown heroes.

2 Ben Quadinaros is one of many pilots who stall on the starting grid. Usually, they are moved quickly to avoid collision with pilots returning at the end of lap one. In Ben's case, however, his podracer explodes before pit droids can get to him.

Seasoned racers have come to believe that the faces that can be discerned in the stones of Mushroom Mesa change expressions when viewed from different angles

MUSHROOM MESA

EBE CRATER VALLEY

Dead Man's Turn

Diablo Cut

The Notch

Stone Needle

BEGGAR'S CANYON

Ben's Mesa, named after Ben Neluenf, the first great Tatooine-born racer, who lost his life in a spectacular attempt to scale the central mesa

Service ramps provide race personnel with access to valley floors when they need to scavenge for parts or make occasional repairs to cam droids

B E N ' S   M E S A

The small houses in Beggar's Canyon are inhabited by hermits who were chased out of Mos Espa (and bounty hunters on the run)

The sudden drop into Ebe Crater Valley causes many crashes; in the third lap, Sebulba bumps the ground but quickly regains control

3 Total concentration is needed in Mushroom Mesa, where shadows and harsh sunlight play tricks on pilots' depth perception. Mawhonic's dreams of winning are dashed when he focuses on his competitors rather than the course in lap one.

D E S E R T   P L A I N

Lesser races than the Boonta Eve avoid the perilous Arch Canyon, routing pilots over the Dune Sea instead

JAG CRAG GORGE

LAGUNA

4 No pilot has yet managed to race up the steep gradient of a service ramp, keep control of the machine as it flips beyond its maximum repulsorlift altitude, and descend safely further along the circuit. Yet Anakin makes podrace history by doing just this.

THE WHIP

D U N E   S E A

5 For Jawas, podraces are fabulous scavenging opportunities. These cloaked Tatooine natives work in teams to cover as much of the circuit as possible, competing with P-100 Salvage Droids to pick up scrap engine parts from crash sites.

6 Sebulba treats the long, flat Desert Plain as light relief from the more demanding and difficult sections of the circuit. Inevitably, it is here that his vile mind turns to dirty tricks—and here that he brings down Mars Guo in the second lap.

7 In lap one, Ratts Tyerell crashes into a stalactite in Laguna Caves. Even if he had survived, he could have expected no help from rescue teams, who avoid the caves from fear of the krayt dragon that inhabits them.

MOS ESPA ARENA

THE IMMENSE GRANDSTANDS of Mos Espa Arena are cradled within a natural canyon amphitheater on the edge of the Northern Dune Sea. Constructed of sandrock and ditanium over durasteel supports, the arena seats more than 100,000 fans—though many more squeeze in for major events like the Boonta Eve Classic. While high-priced tickets for podraces are widely sold to gullible off-worlders, Tatooine's regulars simply turn up on speeders and push their way into the barely regulated stands.

FROM LOCAL CULT TO GRAND SPECTACLE

For a long time before the arena was built, Tatooine's thrill-seekers held free-for-all, no-holds-barred races here, first on animal-drawn carts, then on hanno speeders (a precursor to the landspeeder), and, finally, on podracers. The era of modern podracing was instigated on Malastare by a fearless alien racer called Gustab Wenbus, who entered himself on a virtually untested, super-fast prototype podracer that had been designed for him by a rogue mechanic called Phoebus. As use of these death-defying podracers became standard, podracing on Tatooine quickly began to draw fans from far across the space lanes.

Gambling Hall

History of podracing exhibit

Race viewing gallery

Bo Charmian Racing School

Trophy Room

Holding cells for debtors

The Grand Stairway, a popular place for spotting famous podrace pilots

Arena employees watch race from roof

Coolth cells in domes ventilate buildings

Arena citadel with betting floors

Refreshment booths employ vendors to work the crowds

After a number of spectators died from overheating, floating canopies were put up in a bid to prevent further adverse publicity; in fact, the canopies give very little protection

Spectators constantly jostle each other for extra room on the overcrowded seats

Shaded seats reserved for children are generally appropriated by gangsters and bounty hunters

Security watchtowers

ROYAL BOX

With an entourage of aides, bodyguards, sycophants, and hangers-on, the wealthy gangster Jabba the Hutt presides over the Boonta Eve Classic from the best box seats in the arena. Podracing has proved a lucrative racket for Jabba; he financed the construction of the grandstands and makes an immense profit from controlling the betting. However, aside from his passion for gambling and crime, the races bore Jabba: his depraved senses are not stimulated by screaming, high-speed vehicles.

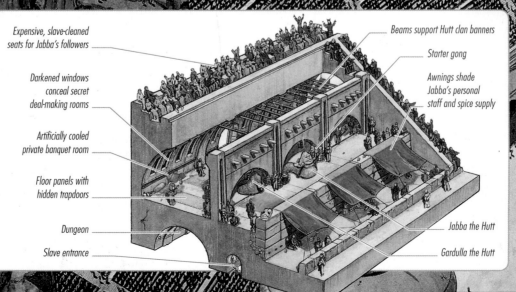

Expensive, slave-cleaned seats for Jabba's followers

Darkened windows conceal secret deal-making rooms

Artificially cooled private banquet room

Floor panels with hidden trapdoors

Dungeon

Slave entrance

Beams support Hutt clan banners

Starter gong

Awnings shade Jabba's personal staff and spice supply

Jabba the Hutt

Gardulla the Hutt

Race officials' building

Sebulba in first place

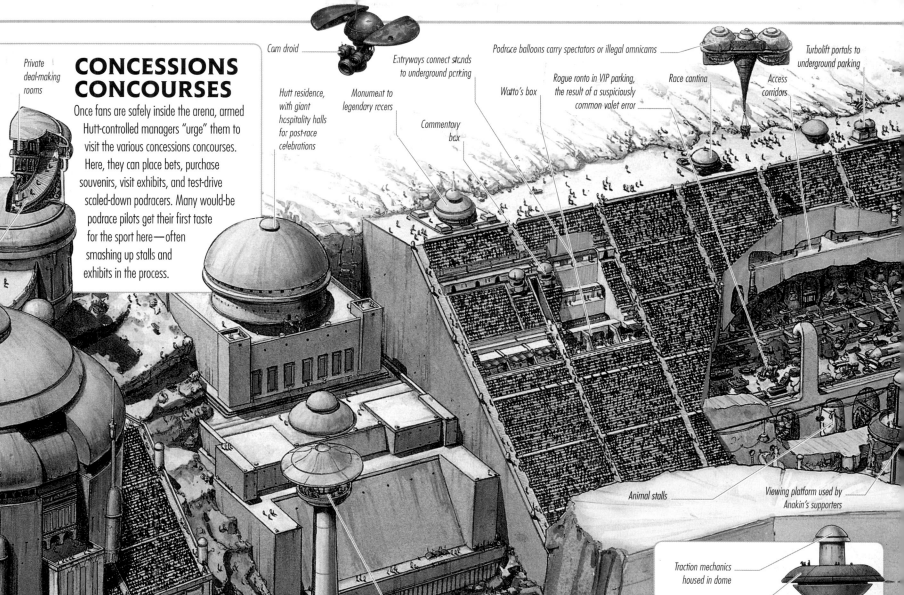

CONCESSIONS CONCOURSES

Once fans are safely inside the arena, armed Hutt-controlled managers "urge" them to visit the various concessions concourses. Here, they can place bets, purchase souvenirs, visit exhibits, and test-drive scaled-down podracers. Many would-be podrace pilots get their first taste for the sport here—often smashing up stalls and exhibits in the process.

Private deal-making rooms

Cam droid

Hutt residence, with giant hospitality halls for post-race celebrations

Monument to legendary racers

Entryways connect stands to underground parking

Commentary box

Watto's box

Podrace balloons carry spectators or illegal omnicams

Rogue ronto in VIP parking, the result of a suspiciously common valet error

Race cantina

Access corridors

Turbolift portals to underground parking

Animal stalls

Viewing platform used by Anakin's supporters

Viewing platform

Box for visiting Hutt clan leaders

Jabba's royal box

The Pinnacle

SPEEDWAY

Numerous crashes and accidents occur at the start of a race because swirling sand blinds the drivers or clogs engines. This hazard, though avoided in more civilized podraces through grit-free race arenas, is integral to Outer Rim racing and makes front-row seats more desirable.

Expensive tourist accommodations

Finish line

Anakin

Press building makes good use of location near the officials' building to gain inside information, scandalous gossip, and malicious hearsay

Hospitality platform

Traction mechanics housed in dome

Repulsorlift platform with entry door

Tower constructed of high-tensile material

Ascension track

VIEWING TOWERS

The family and friends of some privileged racers watch the race from viewing towers. Low-energy traction systems are now in force around the perimeter following incidents of hysterical family members throwing themselves off the top—either from the excitement of the race or from distress at losing a loved one.

SLAVE QUARTERS

The hovels were built by the mining companies that originally settled Tatooine. Desiring cheap, temporary housing for their workers, they piled arched, windowless, adobe chambers on top of one another. The only way to enter the top levels is to climb up the outside on uneven stone stairways.

Sludge intake duct

Bio-converter power generator

Qui-Gon and Shmi discuss Anakin's future

Thermo-static cleaner (beneath panel)

Jar Jar Binks thinks about food

Heavily glazed louvered windows diffuse the harsh desert light

Thermic baster

Polta bean pan

Old-style bread oven

Slave quarters brazier

Upper story

Door entry device

Main door into hovel

Static sand-trap flooring

Shmi's workstation

Sealed doors indicate that the Skywalkers' home was once three smaller hovels

Shmi's bedroom

Sonic welder

CORUSCANT I

CAPITAL OF THE REPUBLIC, seat of government, and home of the powerful Jedi Order, Coruscant is the most important planet in the galaxy. One of the original Core Worlds that grouped together at the birth of the Republic, Coruscant outmaneuvered its early rivals to become the economic and cultural engine of civilization as it expanded along newly charted hyperspace lanes. As these grew into well-traveled trade routes, and scouts explored increasingly far-flung planets, large numbers of alien species made the return trip to Coruscant, swelling its population. Though not located at the geographic center of the galaxy, Coruscant's status as the effective center of the Republic led to it being awarded the coordinates 0-0-0 on standard navigation charts. Many born on backwater worlds or beyond the frontier dream of reaching the galaxy's brilliant heart and proving themselves here, for whoever rules Coruscant is truly master of the galaxy.

Shuttle terminal

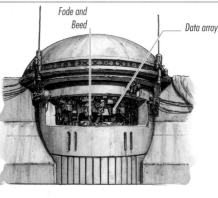

Fode and Beed

Data array

COMMENTARY BOX

The two-headed Troig, Fode and Beed, commentates on the race in Huttese and Basic. This celebrity announcer appears only at the most prestigious podraces, and commands an excessive fee.

NO SAFETY IN

The pit hangar was originally constru
serviced. As the sport's popularity gre
increasing number of podracers in eac
hangar allow plenty of opportunities
a race, mechanics sleep in the upper
some racers even employ spies, disgu

Racers who stop for servicing or refueling at th
starters' grid, run the risk of overactive pit droid

Power substation (hangar has independent
power supply to prevent arena overloads)

Former storage rooms act as a
cantina; legend has it that if you
don't know where the podracers'
cantina is, you shouldn't go there

Medcenter deals with crowd
injuries; serious cases are taken
to a medcenter in Mos Espa

Pit droid work and storage areas

VIP parking

Toughest fans sit in rows most likely
to be hit by podracers turning into
arena at top speed

SACRED PINNACLE

Centuries ago, the rock pinnacle in the middle of Mos Espa Arena was a sacred site for tribes of Sand People, or Tusken Raiders. In rock-hewn caves, this indigenous species performed sacrifices and rituals intended to promote successful hunting seasons. Tusken spiritual leaders retold sacred stories to the next generation in saga rooms. Long since chased away from their hallowed rock by screaming podracer engines and tourists, modern-day Tusken Raiders regularly shoot at podracers during competitions to avenge their ancestors.

Electrostatic repellers in
walls to prevent buildup
of sand inside

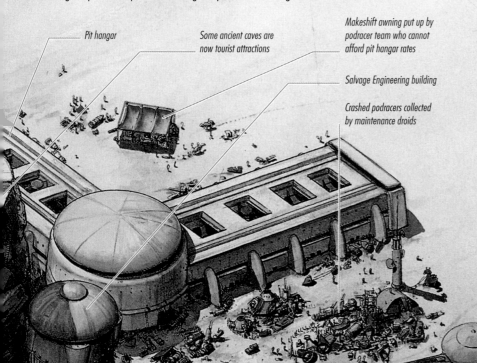

Pit hangar

Some ancient caves are
now tourist attractions

Makeshift awning put up by
podracer team who cannot
afford pit hangar rates

Salvage Engineering building

Crashed podracers collected
by maintenance droids

Access corridor, ideal for making
quick getaways with stolen parts

Entrance for podrace pilots,
mechanics, and some lucky race fans

Ventilation portals

The distinctive engine bay struts are typical of the
famous podrace hangars on Malastare; in an
ostentatious, fan-pleasing gesture, Jabba actually
shipped this hangar from Malastare in blocks

Central section of hangar is usually
reserved for podrace pilots who
compete in warm-up races that
take place earlier in the day

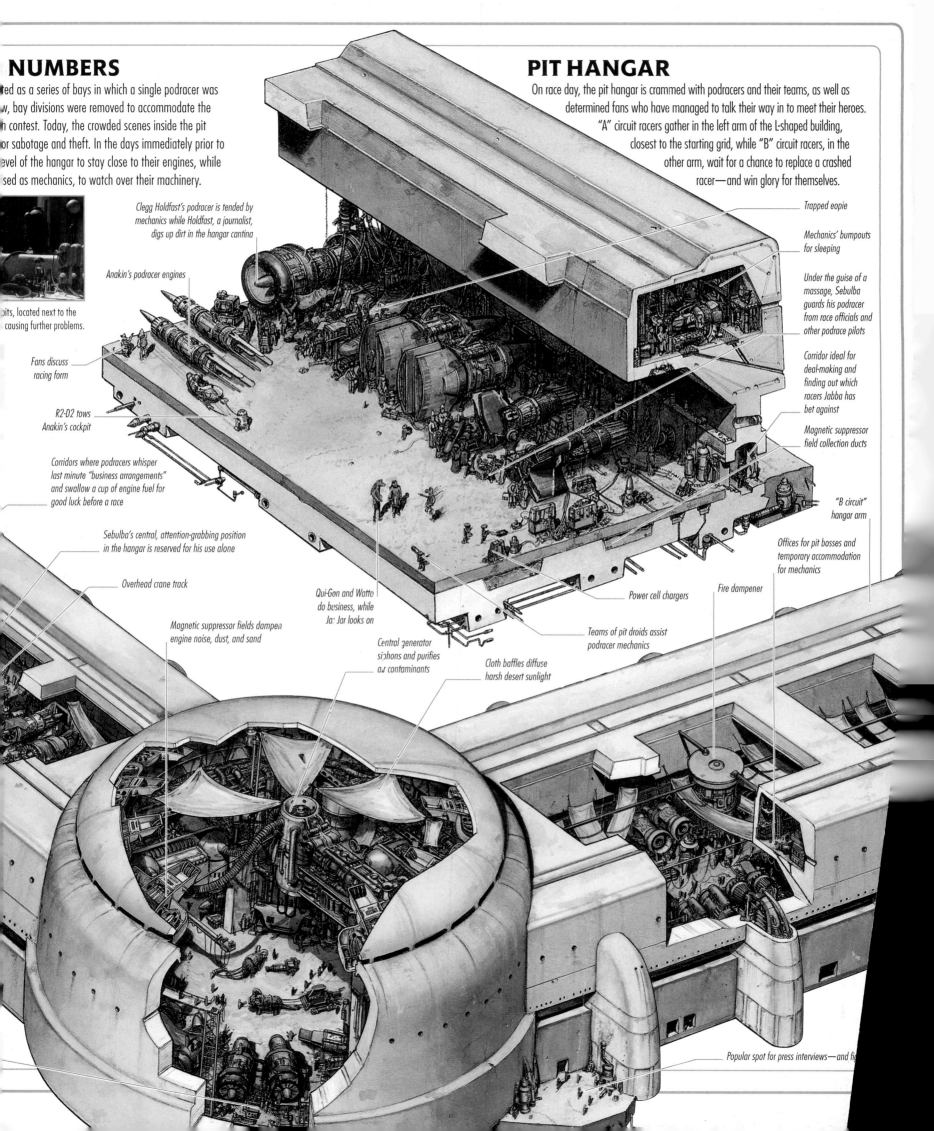

NUMBERS

...ed as a series of bays in which a single podracer was ...w, bay divisions were removed to accommodate the ... contest. Today, the crowded scenes inside the pit ... sabotage and theft. In the days immediately prior to ...evel of the hangar to stay close to their engines, while ...sed as mechanics, to watch over their machinery.

...its, located next to the ...causing further problems.

PIT HANGAR

On race day, the pit hangar is crammed with podracers and their teams, as well as determined fans who have managed to talk their way in to meet their heroes. "A" circuit racers gather in the left arm of the L-shaped building, closest to the starting grid, while "B" circuit racers, in the other arm, wait for a chance to replace a crashed racer—and win glory for themselves.

Clegg Holdfast's podracer is tended by mechanics while Holdfast, a journalist, digs up dirt in the hangar cantina

Anakin's podracer engines

Fans discuss racing form

R2-D2 tows Anakin's cockpit

Corridors where podracers whisper last minute "business arrangements" and swallow a cup of engine fuel for good luck before a race

Sebulba's central, attention-grabbing position in the hangar is reserved for his use alone

Overhead crane track

Magnetic suppressor fields dampen engine noise, dust, and sand

Qui-Gon and Watto do business, while Jar Jar looks on

Central generator siphons and purifies air contaminants

Cloth baffles diffuse harsh desert sunlight

Trapped eopie

Mechanics' bumpouts for sleeping

Under the guise of a massage, Sebulba guards his podracer from race officials and other podrace pilots

Corridor ideal for deal-making and finding out which racers Jabba has bet against

Magnetic suppressor field collection ducts

"B circuit" hangar arm

Offices for pit bosses and temporary accommodation for mechanics

Fire dampener

Power cell chargers

Teams of pit droids assist podracer mechanics

Popular spot for press interviews—and fig...

Race circuit

--- Underground section

0   500 FT

0   150 M

1 When the podrace pilots line up on the starting grid, the crowd erupts with a deafening roar. This is the last chance for thousands of gamblers to size up the pilots and their podracers before placing their final bets.

MOS ESPA
ARENA

	BOONTA EVE CLASSIC—RESULTS		
1	ANAKIN SKYWALKER (Tatooine)	Time 15.42:655	(average speed 858 kph/536 mph)
2	GASGANO (Troiken)	Time 15.48:557	(average speed 850 kph/531 mph)
3	ALDAR BEEDO (Ploo II)	Time 15.52:108	(average speed 845 kph/528 mph)
4	EBE ENDOCOTT (Triffis)	Time 16.04:994	(average speed 827 kph/517 mph)
5	ELAN MAK (Ploo IV)	Time 16.10:737	(average speed 819 kph/512 mph)
6	BOLES ROOR (Sneeve)	Time 16.42:473	(average speed 781 kph/488 mph)
X	BEN QUADINAROS (Toong System)	No laps	Engine stalled at start
X	MAWHONIC (Hok)	Lap 1	Crashed in Mushroom Mesa
X	RATTS TYERELL (Aleen)	Lap 1	Accelerator jammed in Laguna Caves
X	ODY MANDRELL (Tatooine)	Lap 2	Engine burned out on circuit after pit stop
X	CLEGG HOLDFAST (New Plympto)	Lap 2	Crashed in The Notch (suspected sabotage)
X	NEVA KEE (Xagobah)	Lap 2	Left circuit at Hutt Flats (still missing)
X	MARS GUO (Phu)	Lap 2	Crashed in Desert Plain (suspected sabotage)
X	TEEMTO PAGALIES (Moonus Mandel)	Lap 2	Vaporized in Canyon Dune Turn
X	WAN SANDAGE (Ord Radama)	Lap 3	Collided with Jawa sandcrawler off-course
X	DUD BOLT (Vulpter)	Lap 3	Collided with Ark Roose in The Coil
X	ARK "BUMPY" ROOSE (Sump)	Lap 3	Collided with Dud Bolt in The Coil
X	SEBULBA (Malastare)	Lap 3	Crashed in Hutt Flats

Hutt Flats is the bed of prehistoric Lake Anre, which once ran to the Northern Dune Sea via underground tributaries

H U T T

F L A T S

11 The final section of the circuit, Hutt Flats, brings out the worst behavior in pilots. Accelerating to top speed, it is their last chance before the finish line to fight for position. This time, however, it is Sebulba who is blown out of the race.

Pilots must flip their vehicles on their sides to pass through Devil's Doorknob

WALDO
FLATS

WALDO'GRADE

BINDY BEND

Pilots are forced to keep to the outside of the large stone spindle as they make the turn around Bindy Bend; the jagged rocks on the nearside are not worth risking

THE CORKSCREW

THE COIL

JETT'S CHUTE

DUNE TURN

9 In lap three, Anakin's engines overheat in Jett's Chute, a seriously hazardous section of the circuit. Spectators come to blows over which strategy is faster—weaving in and out of the arches or "threading the needle" (slipping right through them).

...alies is hit by Sand People taking pot ...e Canyon Dune Turn. Anonymous ... officials have come to nothing as the ...g has become a popular attraction!

10 In the final lap, the dastardly Sebulba attempts to force Anakin out of the race using the sheer weight and size of his massive podracer. It is a tactic he has used in the past to crowd-pleasing effect.

Repulsorlift

Re-grav plates in holding arm carry as much as 500 kg (1,100 lb) of scrap

Omnidirectional homing mechanics locate distress beacons in downed podracers

Hold stores three pick-up droids with legs folded

Pick-up droid released from underside of P-100

The mechanic who worked on this podracer before the race removes his own "unique modifications"

CRASH CLEAN-UP

Before the dust even settles around a crashed podracer, P-100 Salvage Droids arrive to remove the valuable parts. Pilots have just two hours to claim their junked vehicles before they are auctioned off or sold, usually to Jawas.

Remote pick-up droid transports crash debris to holding arm

CITY SKYLINE

Coruscant's dazzling skyline is a potent symbol of the power and authority concentrated in the city. Many of its buildings reach 6,000 meters (20,000 feet) into the atmosphere, with sleek, transparisteel edifices standing next to older duracrete structures. Negotiating a landing path through these towering skyscrapers is not a task for the fainthearted. Tour operator pilots demand high fees for taking wide-eyed off-worlders on breathtaking cruises over the planet's surface. Coruscant's air traffic is constant and busy, with large passenger ships traveling along autonavigated skylanes and smaller air taxis crisscrossing these routes to take high-paying passengers directly to their destinations.

JEDI TEMPLE

Below the towers of the Jedi Temple, the surface of Coruscant is a dense sprawl sliced through with deep, canyon-like thoroughfares. The Temple itself is reached via a long, broad promenade, which provides a symbolic and physical transition from urban tumult to Jedi tranquility. The Temple's serene exterior hides a more pragmatic interior, with many hundreds of rooms where the Jedi train, practice, meditate, and debate the problems of the Republic.

GALACTIC SENATE

The Galactic Senate stands out at the heart of Coruscant's densely packed Federal District. Here, thousands of elected senators represent their worlds in a vast, arena-like chamber. Statues adorning the entrance concourse depict the Republic's Core World founders. As the Senate swelled over time with representatives of a bewildering variety of intelligent life, the point is occasionally raised that the Core Worlds' humanoid statues are no longer characteristic of the present-day, multi-species Republic.

FEDERAL DISTRICT

MORE THAN 1 TRILLION INDIVIDUALS of diverse species live on Coruscant, the most overpopulated, multifarious megatropolis in the galaxy. Most of them aspire to work for the institutions of galactic government located in the Federal District. Yet for many, life on Coruscant is a room in a low-level sector with artificial light and air, anonymous neighbors of unknown species, and a data-input job in a government sub-office. In this fast-paced, artificial world, few focus on anything outside their own ambitions. Now the institutions of government are in decline, with corruption, nepotism, and negligence decaying the Republic's ideals.

Seen from space, Coruscant's brilliance is only slightly dimmed by the planet's hazy cloud cover. Weather patterns are affected by the troposphere-piercing buildings that cover the planet surface. Inside the tallest buildings, enormous differences of temperature and air pressure from bottom to top produce unusual and unpredictable microclimates.

SENATE APARTMENTS

Senator Palpatine resides in Coruscant's prestigious Federal District. Inhabited by citizens of incredible wealth (and some fame) who demand and receive complete privacy, *500 Republica* offers private turbolifts and clandestine security armaments. The building's stepped design incorporates 53 skydocks and can accommodate even the largest air taxis as well as private vessels.

SENATE LANDING PLATFORMS

Private repulsorlift landing platforms can be reserved for the thousands of sectorial representatives, aides, and visiting dignitaries who arrive and depart daily on Coruscant. Other visitors must make do with municipal landing platforms, which are many kilometers wide and usually severely overcrowded. Vehicles are routinely forced to maintain a holding pattern for several hours until a landing spot becomes available.

MULTILEVELED CITY

The skyscrapers of Coruscant cover the entire planet surface, dwarfing all the original natural features, including mountains and (now dry) seas, which lie somewhere in the depths. Lower levels have been abandoned to mutant species and fearsome scavengers.

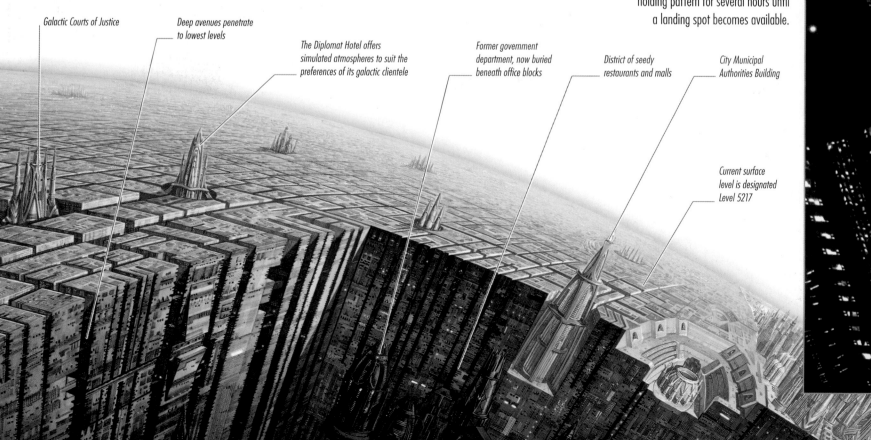

Galactic Courts of Justice

Deep avenues penetrate to lowest levels

The Diplomat Hotel offers simulated atmospheres to suit the preferences of its galactic clientele

Former government department, now buried beneath office blocks

District of seedy restaurants and malls

City Municipal Authorities Building

Current surface level is designated Level 5217

ATMOSPHERES

In the top levels of Coruscant, the richest citizens breathe their preferred choice of gas in high-grade, purified form. Their buildings are routinely scanned for impurities, and problems are dealt with by teams of quality-control droids. In the dirty underworld of tunnels and corridors at the base of the massive buildings, inhabitants struggle to exist on barely breathable combinations of waste gases. Many regular visitors to Coruscant choose to bring their own air supply to last the length of their stay.

PALPATINE'S GUEST APARTMENTS

When Queen Amidala travels to Coruscant, Senator Palpatine insists that she and her retinue stay in apartments in his own building. The expansive suite of rooms is thoughtfully decorated in Palpatine's preferred colors and fitted with remote bugging devices to ensure the complete safety of its regal guest during her stay. Armed guards at the door have been instructed to keep Palpatine fully informed of the Queen's every move.

CLANDESTINE MEETINGS

The architecture of the Federal District is ideally suited to the duplicitous machinations of the political classes that inhabit it. Hidden in the shadows and winding corridors of the megastructures are innumerable balconies, secret rooms, and abandoned buildings, many of which are used by clandestine organizations. In the anonymity afforded by this immense labyrinth, Darth Maul meets with his shadowy mentor, Darth Sidious, on a balcony, unnoticed by the teeming metropolis around them.

GALACTIC SENATE

THE GALACTIC SENATE BUILDING replaces a smaller, more intimate debating chamber instituted in the earliest days of the Republic. Reflecting the success of the expanding Republic, the enormous domed exterior of the modern structure is two kilometers (1.25 miles) in diameter. Inside, the debating rotunda accommodates platforms for more than 1,000 senators who represent the member worlds. The building's internal dynamics are designed to aid efficiency and the speed of decision-making. In fact, the convoluted network of private turbolifts and secret inner sanctums invites misuse, serving to facilitate underhanded dealmaking and avoidance of public accountability.

Receiving no natural light or air, the artificial atmosphere and illumination of the Senate's Great Rotunda is regulated to diminish senators' sense of time. This is intended to allow important debates to continue without being affected by nightfall.

CHANCELLOR'S PODIUM

The focus of the entire Senate rotunda, the Supreme Chancellor's 30 meter (100 feet)-tall podium is symbolic of both authority and, increasingly, vulnerability. The podium itself retracts into the Chancellor's office, which lies beneath the rotunda. Here, Valorum and his staff prepare before they are lifted into the debates raging above.

Chancellor Valorum

Mas Amedda, Vice Chair of the Senate

Galactic Republic crest

Journal Clerk

Data screens identify senators, translate speeches, and show the results of votes

Sei Taria, Administrative Aide

Security systems

Parliamentarian advises on Senate procedure

Sergeant-at-Arms supervises message droids, pages, and other Senate workers

Official Reporter records the verbatim proceedings of the Senate

Laser transmitters control information flow between podium and senatorial platforms

SENATORIAL BUSINESS

The Senate is responsible for creating laws, regulating commerce, mediating disputes, and making treaties. Decision-making is increasingly affected by powerful business interests such as the Trade Federation.

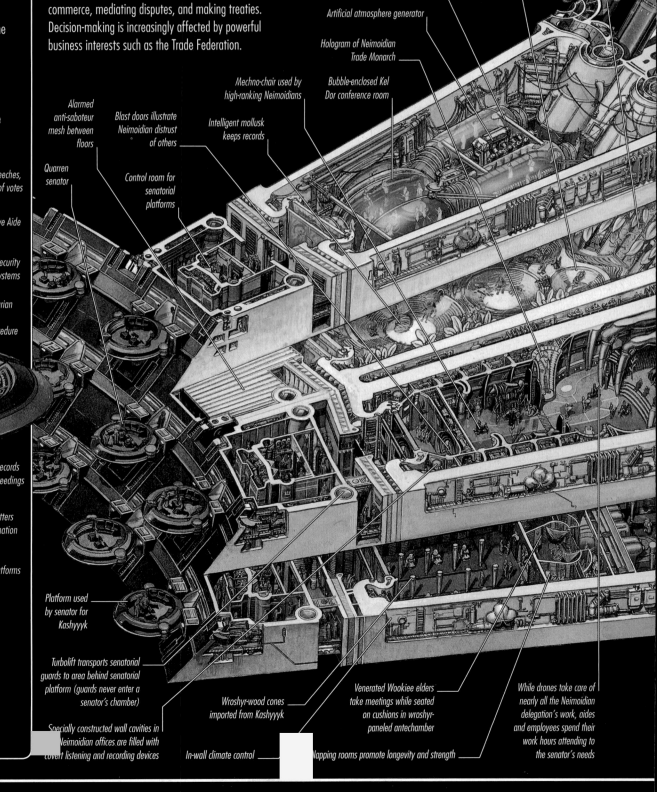

Atmosphere-regulated meeting rooms allow Kel Dor to move about freely without their breathing equipment

Heavy water pools mimic deep water habitat

Imported luminescent and aromatic coral vegetation

Artificial atmosphere generator

Hologram of Neimoidian Trade Monarch

Mechno-chair used by high-ranking Neimoidians

Bubble-enclosed Kel Dor conference room

Alarmed anti-saboteur mesh between floors

Blast doors illustrate Neimoidian distrust of others

Intelligent mollusk keeps records

Quarren senator

Control room for senatorial platforms

Platform used by senator for Kashyyyk

Turbolift transports senatorial guards to area behind senatorial platform (guards never enter a senator's chamber)

Wroshyr-wood cones imported from Kashyyyk

Venerated Wookiee elders take meetings while seated on cushions in wroshyr-paneled antechamber

While drones take care of nearly all the Neimoidian delegation's work, aides and employees spend their work hours attending to the senator's needs

Specially constructed wall cavities in Neimoidian offices are filled with covert listening and recording devices

In-wall climate control

Napping rooms promote longevity and strength

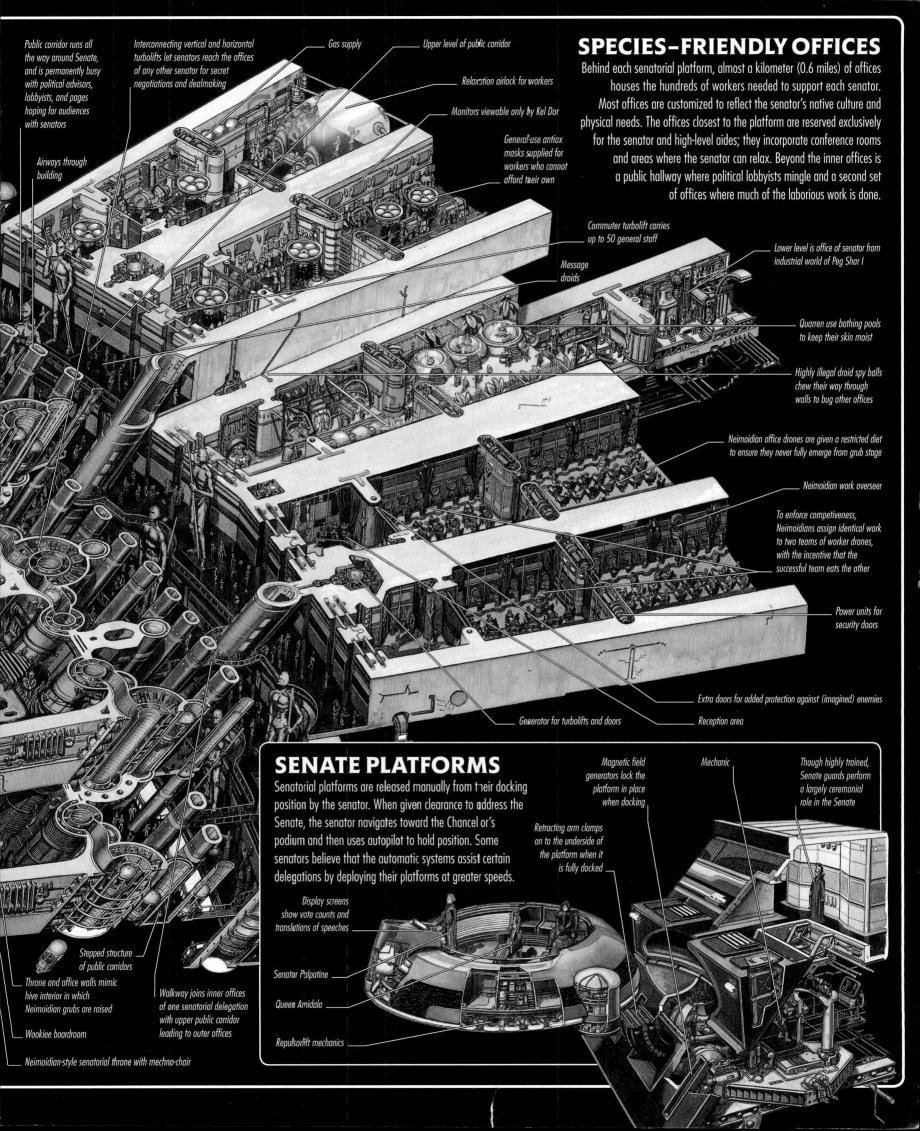

Public corridor runs all the way around Senate, and is permanently busy with political advisors, lobbyists, and pages hoping for audiences with senators

Interconnecting vertical and horizontal turbolifts let senators reach the offices of any other senator for secret negotiations and dealmaking

Gas supply

Upper level of public corridor

Relaxation airlock for workers

Monitors viewable only by Kel Dor

Airways through building

General-use antiox masks supplied for workers who cannot afford their own

SPECIES-FRIENDLY OFFICES

Behind each senatorial platform, almost a kilometer (0.6 miles) of offices houses the hundreds of workers needed to support each senator. Most offices are customized to reflect the senator's native culture and physical needs. The offices closest to the platform are reserved exclusively for the senator and high-level aides; they incorporate conference rooms and areas where the senator can relax. Beyond the inner offices is a public hallway where political lobbyists mingle and a second set of offices where much of the laborious work is done.

Commuter turbolift carries up to 50 general staff

Lower level is office of senator from industrial world of Peg Shar I

Message droids

Quarren use bathing pools to keep their skin moist

Highly illegal droid spy balls chew their way through walls to bug other offices

Neimoidian office drones are given a restricted diet to ensure they never fully emerge from grub stage

Neimoidian work overseer

To enforce competiveness, Neimoidians assign identical work to two teams of worker drones, with the incentive that the successful team eats the other

Power units for security doors

Extra doors for added protection against (imagined) enemies

Generator for turbolifts and doors

Reception area

SENATE PLATFORMS

Senatorial platforms are released manually from their docking position by the senator. When given clearance to address the Senate, the senator navigates toward the Chancellor's podium and then uses autopilot to hold position. Some senators believe that the automatic systems assist certain delegations by deploying their platforms at greater speeds.

Magnetic field generators lock the platform in place when docking

Mechanic

Though highly trained, Senate guards perform a largely ceremonial role in the Senate

Retracting arm clamps on to the underside of the platform when it is fully docked

Display screens show vote counts and translations of speeches

Senator Palpatine

Queen Amidala

Repulsorlift mechanics

Stepped structure of public corridors

Throne and office walls mimic hive interior in which Neimoidian grubs are raised

Wookiee boardroom

Neimoidian-style senatorial throne with mechno-chair

Walkway joins inner offices of one senatorial delegation with upper public corridor leading to outer offices

JEDI TEMPLE I

TOWERING ABOVE A LOW-RISE SECTOR of the Federal District to a height of a kilometer (0.6 miles), the Jedi Temple is the focus of Jedi life, the place where Jedi Knights are trained and housed. Its unobstructed position is not mere show, but a necessary aspect of its function. The five towers are each topped by powerful reception/transmission antennas, which use a wide range of broadcast systems, the most sophisticated of which tap into the superluminal eddies of hyperspace itself for instantaneous galactic transmission. Isolated by its height from the teeming city's electromagnetic fields, the towers' powerful communications array maintains contact with Jedi on far-flung missions.

CONTEMPLATION STATIONS

Around the circumference of the High Council holomap room, a spacious, graceful balcony with three stations provides a space for calm contemplation and reflection. High-ranking Jedi are briefed in the holomap room before being sent on missions, and are encouraged to walk the balcony to focus their Force energies before leaving. It is also used by Jedi awaiting a sitting with the High Council.

HOLOMAP ROOMS

Central to the organization of Jedi activities throughout the galaxy is a pyramid system of holomaps. At the lowest level, 12 teams monitor in detail specific galactic areas. Potential problems are transferred to larger-scale holomaps for the attention of more senior Jedi. In this way, only the most serious issues reach the Jedi High Council and are plotted on their galaxy holomap.

Natural and circular motifs in floor mosaic symbolize harmony and balance

Eeth Koth

Yarael Poof

Adi Gallia

Internal corridor

Qui-Gon and Obi-Wan wait on one of the tower's three Contemplation Stations

Depa Billaba

Anakin is tested by the Jedi High Council

Turbolift utilizes Force-inspired internal dynamics to transport Jedi of vastly different sizes and shapes

Door security panel

Each antenna transmits and receives data at different frequencies and with varying coverage

Crowded lanes of air traffic carry Coruscant's ever-moving population around the planet

Topmast is a powerful transmitter incorporating a multi-frequency eradicator/scrambler

Plo Koon

Mace Windu

Yoda

Ki-Adi-Mundi

Masonry construction supported by high-tensile magnite

Saesee Tiin

Even Piell

Yaddle

Permeon in windows helps balance gravity effects and maintain artificial air supply

Multi-field receiver assembly feeds multiple signals into holomap array

Oppo Rancisis

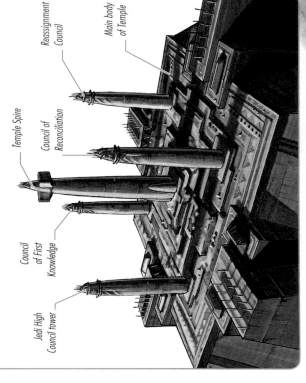

ANCIENT ECHOES

Unlike the surrounding modern buildings, the ziggurat base and slender spires of the Jedi Temple are of an ancient design. Its distinctive stepped appearance derives from very early Jedi architectural styles, and is intended to symbolize the Padawan's path to enlightenment.

Galaxy holomap

Coruscant's largest air buses can carry up to 1,000 passengers

Air taxis dart in and out of bus lanes carrying passengers to specific destinations

Projection array constantly updates map from antenna signals

Collimating dish mechanics automatically focuses signal beam to compensate for power variations

Power signal stabilizers

Wave modulator

Receiver converts signals from antennas into holodata

Holomap indicates galaxy-wide hotspots, including disturbances in the Force and areas of unusual Force concentration

Communication bundles line wall cavities

Receiver vanes configured to convert signals from hyperspace locations into realspace coordinates

Eradictors scramble attempts to pinpoint location of Jedi in the field by locking on to their communications with the Temple

Power conduit

Main power generator

Static discharge vanes

JEDI COUNCILS

Four councils oversee the Jedi Order's affairs. The Council of First Knowledge advises on matters requiring ancient Jedi wisdom, the Council of Reconciliation seeks peaceful resolutions of planetary disputes, the Reassignment Council organizes work for apprentices not chosen to be Padawans, and the High Council has overall decision-making powers. The central tower is the Temple Spire, the Order's most sacred place for contemplation. Although it has its own spire, the High Council also holds meetings in the other four, serving as a reminder for its members—and the Order as a whole—to maintain balance.

Reassignment Council

Main body of Temple

Temple Spire

Council of Reconciliation

Council of First Knowledge

Jedi High Council tower

THE INVASION OF NABOO

EVEN WHILE THE TRADE FEDERATION BLOCKADES NABOO with a fleet of war freighters, its leaders finalize invasion plans with their shadowy Sith mentor. The Neimoidians do not share Sidious' sinister interest in this small, relatively insignificant planet. However, they are persuaded that their victory will be easy—and ultimately profitable. On Sidious' orders, the invasion army has two primary objectives. The first is to sever Naboo's communication with the Senate. The second is to capture Queen Amidala and force her to sign a capitulation treaty. Sleek landing ships descend upon the planet, avoiding public commotion by sticking to remote areas. Under cover of darkness, the army mobilizes and takes up strategic positions. The next morning, the citizens of Theed are caught unaware by a devastating surprise attack.

LANDING SHIPS

Formations of massive C-9979 landing ships descend like vultures through Naboo's atmosphere. An elite group lands in the north of the planet, where Theed and the largest cities are found, while other groups target cities in the south and east. Each landing ship carries 11 MTTs (Multi-Troop Transports), 114 AATs (Armored Assault Tanks), and legions of droid troops. First to be deployed are droids on armed STAPs, who act as scouts for the main army, seeking out any signs of resistance—including two Jedi who have evaded capture.

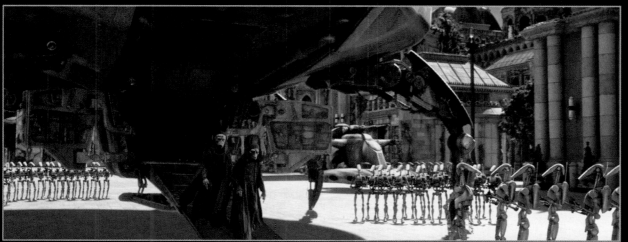

ENTER THE NEIMOIDIANS

Only once Theed is under battle droid control do the invasion's perpetrators show their faces. Nute Gunray and his attaché, Rune Haako, affect the air of conquerors as they make the short walk from their shuttle to Theed Palace to personally oversee the arrest of Queen Amidala and her government. Being naturally cautious and lazy, the Neimoidians rarely leave their ships, relying on droids to meet customers. But in this instance, they are keen to visit the palace for themselves, having been advised that its staterooms are full of priceless treasures.

THE FALL OF THEED

With its citizens rounded up into detention camps and its streets sealed, Theed becomes a ghost town, echoing only with the sounds of tanks rumbling and troops marching. The city's long era of peace and serenity has ended in a matter of hours. Queen Amidala and her staff are escorted from the palace by droid captors, to be taken to a camp. Even in her darkest hour, the Queen refuses to abandon hope, but she knows she will need some extraordinary help from somewhere if her beloved home is to be saved.

ADVANCE OF EVIL

The invasion force that advances upon Theed in the sharp light of a Naboo early morning comprises 33 large transports, each carrying 112 battle droids, and 342 battle tanks, as well as droid starfighters and infantry. Each vehicle and battle droid is pre-programmed with a ground map of the city, with specific instructions for key objectives.

DEFENSE OF NABOO

WHEN THE TRADE FEDERATION INVADES NABOO, it expects little resistance from the planet's peace-loving inhabitants. But the invaders underestimate the courage and determination of its principal species, the Naboo and the Gungans, who overcome their traditional antipathy to form an unlikely alliance in the face of the emergency. The chief advantage the natives have is knowledge of the terrain. The Gungans amass a huge army in the swamps to lure the droid forces away from Theed, while the Naboo utilize hidden passages to infiltrate the palace and hangar, enabling them to mount attacks on multiple fronts.

While the inhabitants of Naboo struggle to rescue their planet from Trade Federation control, Qui-Gon Jinn and Obi-Wan Kenobi battle for their lives against a Sith warrior who appears to have an agenda all his own.

SYMBOLIC MEETING PLACE

Naboo and Gungan leaders plan their battle strategy on the dividing line between Naboo and Gungan lands. Long considered a no-man's-land, a refuge for outcasts like Jar Jar Binks, the swamp edges will play host to regular Freedom of Naboo celebrations in years to come.

SEARCH FOR THE GUNGANS

Traversing through dense swampland along nearly impenetrable paths known only to Gungans, Jar Jar Binks guides the Naboo and Jedi to the Gungan sacred place. When they near the hidden entrance, Jar Jar is unsure of the protocol for allowing outsiders into such a restricted zone and uses a Gungan call to alert scouts to his presence. The path threads its way beneath a thick canopy of ancient trees until the party emerges in a dry clearing filled with Gungan refugees. The Gungans gather at their sacred place in times of anxiety and apparent danger. These evacuations prove to be valuable practice when the time comes for a genuine emergency.

SECRET OPERATIONS

On Captain Panaka's instructions, Theed's underground resistance movement infiltrates the hangar in advance of its liberation. Secretly, officers and guards have checked that their fighters have not been disabled by battle droids. They have also restored access to the hangar computer system in order to program battle flight-path coordinates.

GROUND WAR

Although the Naboo people are rounded up into camps en masse, the Gungans prove more difficult to reach. By the time the invading battle droids reach Otoh Gunga and the other underwater cities, they find them nearly empty and most of the Gungan populace evacuated. Convening in the swamps, the Gungans raise an army large enough to challenge Trade Federation troops on the Great Grass Plains, buying Panaka's soldiers some much-needed time.

SPACE BATTLE

Naboo's pilot squadron, Bravo Flight, led by Ric Olié, is assigned the daunting task of knocking out the transmitter aboard the Droid Control Ship orbiting Naboo. Its combined firepower barely gets through the Control Ship's deflector shields. However, a reckless spin causes a split-second breach and Anakin's craft shoots into the right-hand hangar arm toward the heart of the enemy.

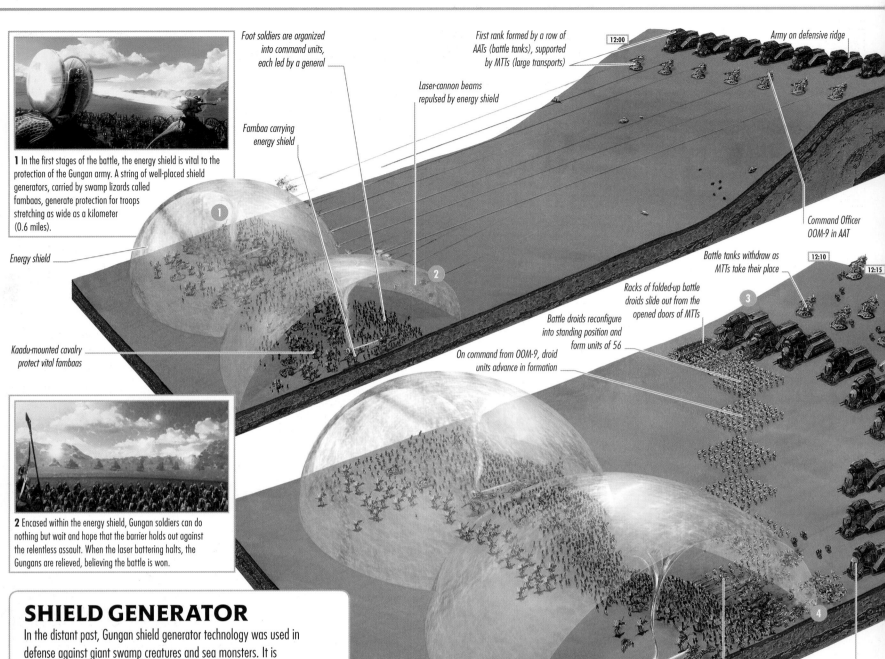

Foot soldiers are organized into command units, each led by a general

First rank formed by a row of AATs (battle tanks), supported by MTTs (large transports)

12:00

Army on defensive ridge

Laser-cannon beams repulsed by energy shield

Fambaa carrying energy shield

1 In the first stages of the battle, the energy shield is vital to the protection of the Gungan army. A string of well-placed shield generators, carried by swamp lizards called fambaas, generate protection for troops stretching as wide as a kilometer (0.6 miles).

Command Officer OOM-9 in AAT

Energy shield

Battle tanks withdraw as MTTs take their place

12:10

12:15

Racks of folded-up battle droids slide out from the opened doors of MTTs

Battle droids reconfigure into standing position and form units of 56

On command from OOM-9, droid units advance in formation

Kaadu-mounted cavalry protect vital fambaas

2 Encased within the energy shield, Gungan soldiers can do nothing but wait and hope that the barrier holds out against the relentless assault. When the laser battering halts, the Gungans are relieved, believing the battle is won.

SHIELD GENERATOR

In the distant past, Gungan shield generator technology was used in defense against giant swamp creatures and sea monsters. It is maintained today as a symbol of Gungan military pride. The energy field is produced when an emitter, carried by one fambaa, fires a stream of plasma into a projector, carried by another fambaa.

MTTs close in to trap Gungan army

Battle droids march through perimeter of energy shield and begin firing

Gungans attack a battle tank

Gungan operator controls size of dome

Pressure coils

Plasma stream from emitter enters first drum, then shoots back and forth between the two drums to build up pressure before being forced upward through release chamber

Release chamber

Shield generator apparatus destroyed by enemy laser fire

Falumpasets pull battle wagons loaded with energy balls for use in catapults

Retreating Gungan on kaadu

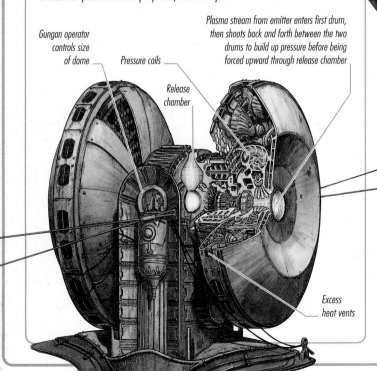

Excess heat vents

3 Deprived of an easy victory over the Gungans, Trade Federation battle tanks fall back. Agonizing moments of silence follow as MTTs (large transports) advance and begin unloading rack after rack of deadly battle droids.

GRASS PLAINS BATTLE

THE CONFRONTATION BETWEEN Gungan troops and Trade Federation droids takes place 40 kilometers (25 miles) from Theed. On the morning of the battle, Gungan troops assemble under cover of the swamps. Soon after, the Neimoidians are alerted to the military buildup by rumors spread deliberately by Captain Panaka. The Gungan strategy is to wait until the droid army emerges from Theed to meet them on their own ground—in a spot near enough to the swamps to allow a hasty retreat if necessary. The plan works: by midday, two immense armies face each other across a shallow valley between ridges of low hills...

GUNGAN BATTLE STRATEGY

Realizing that the Trade Federation's military might is far superior to their own, the Gungans plan to protect their army within a huge energy shield. The liquid energy surface repels laser bolts and large, slow-moving objects like tanks. Denied the option to wipe out the Gungans with their heavy artillery, the enemy is forced to send in individual battle droids. This gives the Gungans a fighting chance of engaging the droids long enough for the Naboo to capture the Viceroy.

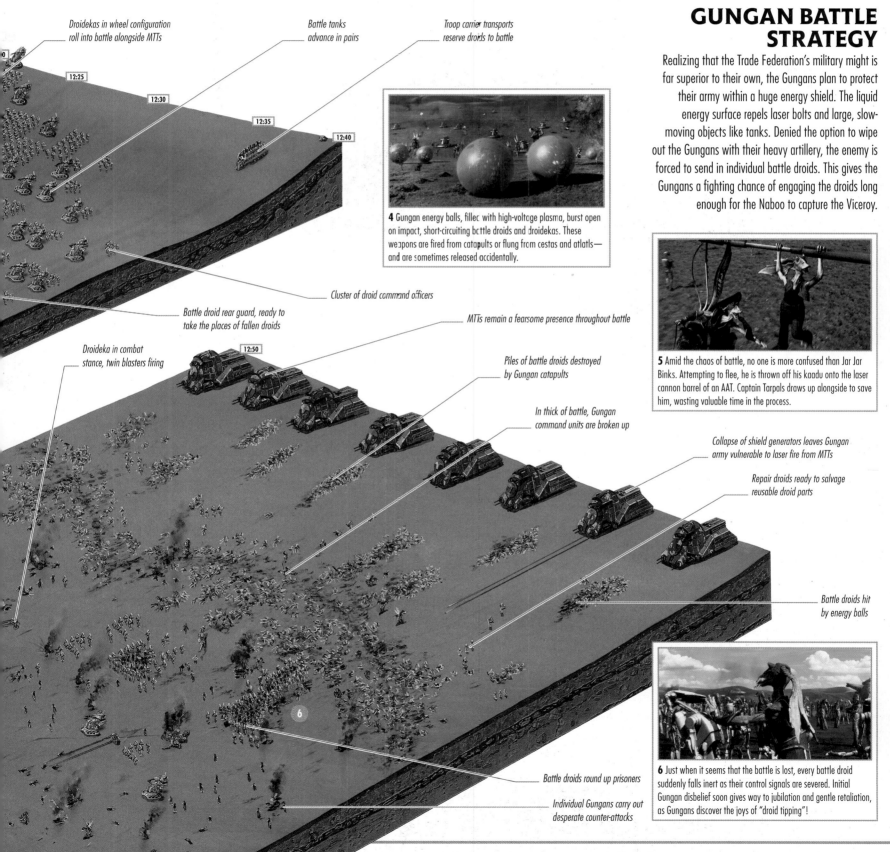

Droidekas in wheel configuration roll into battle alongside MTTs

Battle tanks advance in pairs

Troop carrier transports reserve droids to battle

12:25

12:30

12:35

12:40

4 Gungan energy balls, filled with high-voltage plasma, burst open on impact, short-circuiting battle droids and droidekas. These weapons are fired from catapults or flung from cestas and atlatls—and are sometimes released accidentally.

Cluster of droid command officers

Battle droid rear guard, ready to take the places of fallen droids

MTTs remain a fearsome presence throughout battle

5 Amid the chaos of battle, no one is more confused than Jar Jar Binks. Attempting to flee, he is thrown off his kaadu onto the laser cannon barrel of an AAT. Captain Tarpals draws up alongside to save him, wasting valuable time in the process.

Droideka in combat stance, twin blasters firing

12:50

Piles of battle droids destroyed by Gungan catapults

In thick of battle, Gungan command units are broken up

Collapse of shield generators leaves Gungan army vulnerable to laser fire from MTTs

Repair droids ready to salvage reusable droid parts

Battle droids hit by energy balls

Battle droids round up prisoners

Individual Gungans carry out desperate counter-attacks

6 Just when it seems that the battle is lost, every battle droid suddenly falls inert as their control signals are severed. Initial Gungan disbelief soon gives way to jubilation and gentle retaliation, as Gungans discover the joys of "droid tipping"!

GENERATOR BATTLE

WITH ITS SLEEK, MECHANISTIC INTERIOR LINES, Theed's immense power generator stands in stark contrast to the city's elegant, handcrafted aesthetic. Indeed, this ingenious feat of engineering is now a popular attraction in Theed. The gigantic machinery works day and night to mine and stabilize naturally occurring plasma from deep within the planet. The Naboo people rely on this plasmic energy, using it for trade and to power their own cities, spacecraft, and even the glowing bulbs on Queen Amidala's Throne-Room gown. During the Battle of Naboo, the power generator becomes the scene of a climactic battle between Darth Maul and the Jedi Qui-Gon Jinn and Obi-Wan Kenobi.

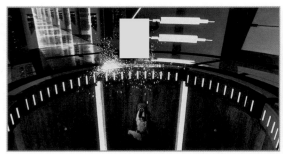

As Obi-Wan hangs on to a security beacon within the power generator's core tunnel, Darth Maul lashes out with his lightsaber.

BREAK WITH THE PAST

For centuries, Theed's energy supply was provided by small outlying mines. However, evidence of a vast plasma source below the city's cliff face led to the construction of the new generator. Its efficient machinery mines much more than the city itself needs.

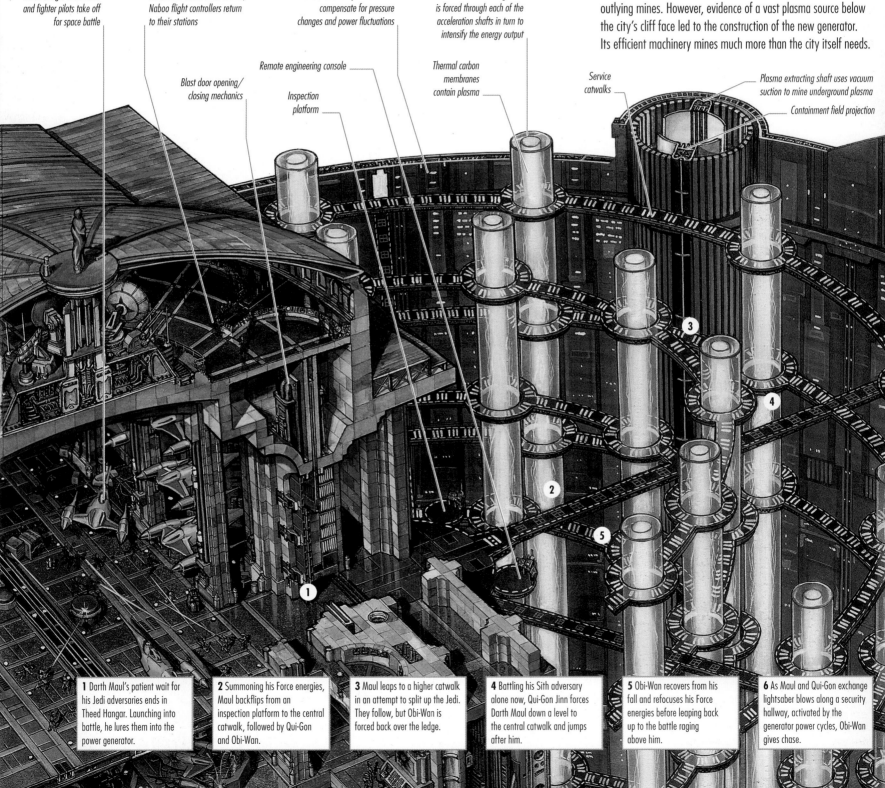

Theed Hangar is liberated and fighter pilots take off for space battle

Freed from battle droid control, Naboo flight controllers return to their stations

Panels constantly monitor and compensate for pressure changes and power fluctuations

Plasma from extracting shaft is forced through each of the acceleration shafts in turn to intensify the energy output

Remote engineering console

Blast door opening/ closing mechanics

Inspection platform

Thermal carbon membranes contain plasma

Service catwalks

Plasma extracting shaft uses vacuum suction to mine underground plasma

Containment field projection

1 Darth Maul's patient wait for his Jedi adversaries ends in Theed Hangar. Launching into battle, he lures them into the power generator.

2 Summoning his Force energies, Maul backflips from an inspection platform to the central catwalk, followed by Qui-Gon and Obi-Wan.

3 Maul leaps to a higher catwalk in an attempt to split up the Jedi. They follow, but Obi-Wan is forced back over the ledge.

4 Battling his Sith adversary alone now, Qui-Gon Jinn forces Darth Maul down a level to the central catwalk and jumps after him.

5 Obi-Wan recovers from his fall and refocuses his Force energies before leaping back up to the battle raging above him.

6 As Maul and Qui-Gon exchange lightsaber blows along a security hallway, activated by the generator power cycles, Obi-Wan gives chase.

MILITARY POWER

Strategically located in the same complex as Theed's main hangar, the power generator provides the Queen's Royal Starship and N-1 starfighter fleet with the plasma power necessary for flight and weapons usage. The generator is operated by a small staff of trained personnel from the Plasma Energy Engineering unit of the Royal Naboo Security Force.

Plasma holding tank

Power generator

Entrance to Theed Hangar

Recirculation lid periodically sweeps oxygen out of the reserve tank, preserving the fragile vacuum equilibrium

SENATORIAL PATRONAGE

The power generator's opening ceremonies were presided over by Senator Palpatine, whose interest in the deep-pit design was much noted. Soon afterward, regular tours were established to allow Theed's citizens a view of the breathtaking plasma-filled tubes.

Attesting to the Naboo respect for tradition, the number of laser doors is a deliberate reference to an ancient Naboo legend, in which Chaos is held back by six impenetrable gates

Core uses high-energy particle coils to disintegrate plasma slough

Refined plasma reserve tank

Refined and unrefined plasma conductors

Laser doors lock into position in response to potentially lethal power outputs that occur intermittently during plasma activation process

Purification chamber

Main activator

Cooling vents

Unrefined plasma is injected back into compressors

Multilayer radiation dampers

PLASMA TRADE

While reserves of plasma are maintained for emergencies and increased spacecraft use, some of the excess is now sold in off-planet trade deals. The Naboo choose not to send their own trading agents to other worlds, but sell directly through the Trade Federation.

MINING PLASMA

Deep within Naboo, plasma is constantly generated by natural ionization reactions. Theed Generator's extracting shafts draw unrefined plasma and deliver it to the processing plant. Here, a massive activator stabilizes and purifies the plasma. The refined plasma is compressed and sent to Theed's power distribution grid, while the excess is shunted to the reserve tank.

Main plasma compressor

Twin plasma compressors lead to Theed's power distribution grid

Plasma equilibrium checkpoints

Transformer drum

7 When the laser doors unlock, Obi-Wan runs through but does not count on another power surge causing the doors to close again.

8 The final stages of the battle are played out around—and over—the hazardous edge of the generator's virtually fathomless core.

55

THE CITY OF THEED

WITH SQUADRONS OF BATTLE DROIDS patrolling the streets, battle tanks guarding access routes, and Trade Federation rulers holding the palace, Theed is a city under occupation. Yet, as a result of the quick capitulation of its populace, its buildings and monuments have remained relatively unscathed—most structural damage was caused by battle tanks steering through narrow streets. With all entrances and exits blocked, the small band of Naboo defenders has no choice but to use a hazardous network of underground passages to infiltrate their own city.

1 The defenders of Naboo use droid holoprojections to locate the secret routes into the city and the palace. These highly classified maps are stored in the Royal Starship's computers. The defenders emerge from the underground tunnels near the hangar.

Pergola's Bridge has become the main crossing point over the Solleu, taking some of the strain off the more fragile Bassa Bridge further downstream

Captain Panaka's private residence

2 Under Captain Panaka's command, Naboo soldiers in a Gian speeder blast at a Trade Federation tank regiment that is guarding the entrance to Theed Hangar. This courageous action diverts the droids away from the entrance.

Secret access to subterranean tunnels

One of the tributaries of the Solleu River

Boathouse

Royal Naboo Security Forces headquarters

Theed Generator

Virdugo Plunge is the largest waterfall in Theed

Hangar entrance

Cliff edge is stabilized by hidden tension field generators

Ellié Arcadium

The Hall of Perri-Teeka, a monument to a legendary statesman

Officers' clubhouse

3 Taking advantage of the diversion caused by Panaka, the Jedi, Anakin, Amidala, and R2-D2 emerge from the corner of the hangar where they have been hiding and slip into the entrance. Panaka and his soldiers expertly dispatch the droids and join them.

UNDERGROUND TUNNELS

Like their Gungan counterparts, the Naboo have long made use of the porous qualities of their planet. The naturally forming subterranean tunnels that run underneath Theed were once made safe, extended, and carefully mapped, but have since fallen into disrepair. As head of security, Captain Panaka recently inspected these secret routes in and out of the city, but had no idea how useful they would become when their city was occupied.

4 With most droid squads needed at the Gungan battle, the hangar interior is not left well guarded. Yet warning signals from the droids that are hit alert the Command Officer to the security breach and droidekas are swiftly dispatched.

5 Pockets of battle droids guard key buildings in Theed. Nevertheless, when the Naboo defenders cross the city to reach the palace, they find they can take advantage of the city's maze of hidden passageways and connecting skywalks.

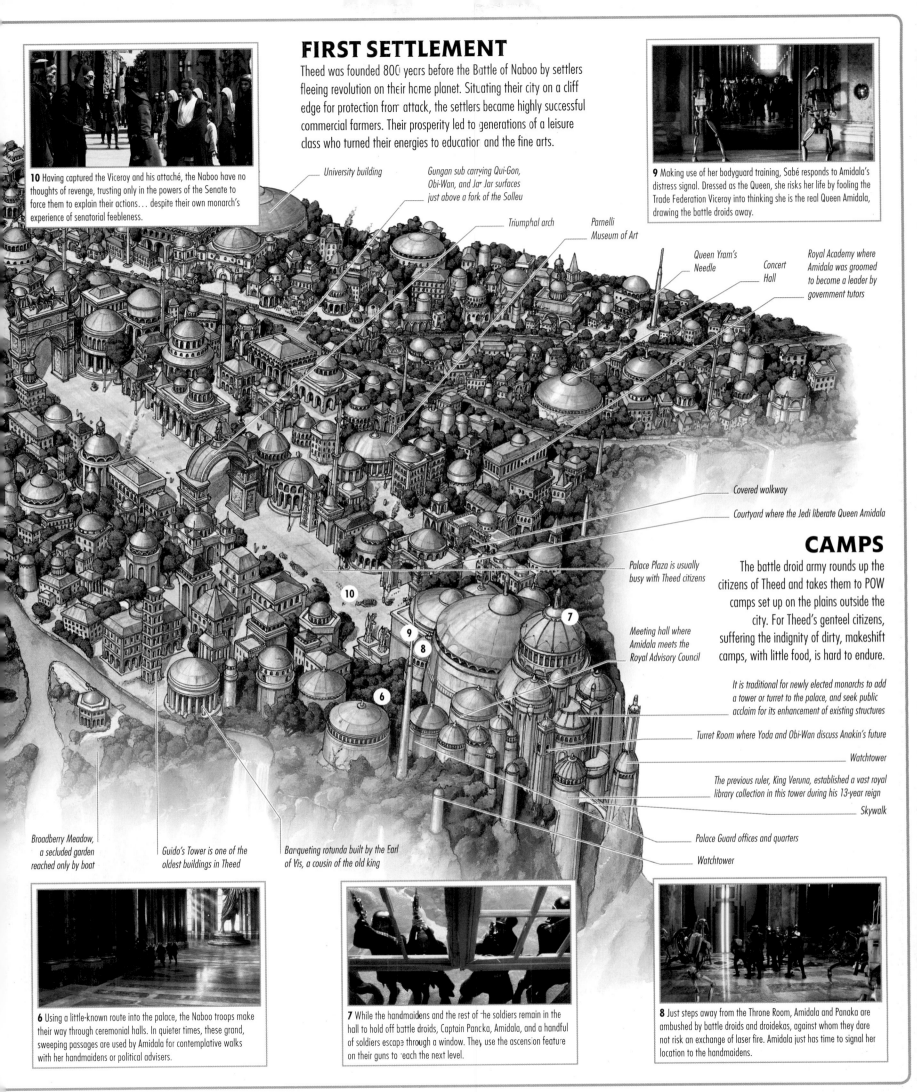

FIRST SETTLEMENT

Theed was founded 800 years before the Battle of Naboo by settlers fleeing revolution on their home planet. Situating their city on a cliff edge for protection from attack, the settlers became highly successful commercial farmers. Their prosperity led to generations of a leisure class who turned their energies to education and the fine arts.

10 Having captured the Viceroy and his attaché, the Naboo have no thoughts of revenge, trusting only in the powers of the Senate to force them to explain their actions... despite their own monarch's experience of senatorial feebleness.

9 Making use of her bodyguard training, Sabé responds to Amidala's distress signal. Dressed as the Queen, she risks her life by fooling the Trade Federation Viceroy into thinking she is the real Queen Amidala, drawing the battle droids away.

University building

Gungan sub carrying Qui-Gon, Obi-Wan, and Jar Jar surfaces just above a fork of the Solleu

Triumphal arch

Parnelli Museum of Art

Queen Yram's Needle

Concert Hall

Royal Academy where Amidala was groomed to become a leader by government tutors

Covered walkway

Courtyard where the Jedi liberate Queen Amidala

Palace Plaza is usually busy with Theed citizens

Meeting hall where Amidala meets the Royal Advisory Council

CAMPS

The battle droid army rounds up the citizens of Theed and takes them to POW camps set up on the plains outside the city. For Theed's genteel citizens, suffering the indignity of dirty, makeshift camps, with little food, is hard to endure.

It is traditional for newly elected monarchs to add a tower or turret to the palace, and seek public acclaim for its enhancement of existing structures

Turret Room where Yoda and Obi-Wan discuss Anakin's future

Watchtower

The previous ruler, King Veruna, established a vast royal library collection in this tower during his 13-year reign

Skywalk

Palace Guard offices and quarters

Watchtower

Broadberry Meadow, a secluded garden reached only by boat

Guido's Tower is one of the oldest buildings in Theed

Banqueting rotunda built by the Earl of Vis, a cousin of the old king

6 Using a little-known route into the palace, the Naboo troops make their way through ceremonial halls. In quieter times, these grand, sweeping passages are used by Amidala for contemplative walks with her handmaidens or political advisers.

7 While the handmaidens and the rest of the soldiers remain in the hall to hold off battle droids, Captain Pancka, Amidala, and a handful of soldiers escape through a window. They use the ascension feature on their guns to reach the next level.

8 Just steps away from the Throne Room, Amidala and Panaka are ambushed by battle droids and droidekas, against whom they dare not risk an exchange of laser fire. Amidala just has time to signal her location to the handmaidens.

EPISODE II
ATTACK OF THE CLONES

There is unrest in the Galactic Senate. Several thousand solar systems have declared their intentions to leave the Republic.

This separatist movement, under the leadership of the mysterious Count Dooku, has made it difficult for the limited number of Jedi Knights to maintain peace and order in the galaxy.

Senator Amidala, the former Queen of Naboo, is returning to the Galactic Senate to vote on the critical issue of creating an ARMY OF THE REPUBLIC to assist the overwhelmed Jedi....

CORUSCANT II

SEEN FROM ABOVE THE CLOUDLINE, Coruscant appears still and serene, with just the tops of the tallest buildings visible. Beneath the clouds, the galactic capital planet is a heavily populated, multilayered metropolis. Its skylanes are constantly busy with traffic, from small personal speeders to air buses and larger freighters. Most skylanes on Coruscant are autonavigated, with each vehicle traveling along a preprogrammed route to minimize the risk of collisions. The fastest traffic makes use of the highest skylanes as it travels long distances across the planet. Below the elevated skylanes, traffic moves in a more disorderly way, vying for space with garbage scows, unmarked speedervans, and small private conveyances. Vehicles may change skylanes at giant spiral interchanges, where they move up or down, or switch directions.

URBAN GROWTH

The Galactic Senate stands at the heart of the Federal District. In the 10 years since the crisis on Naboo, this area has altered almost beyond recognition. New buildings and floors house the thousands of extra departments and commissions that have been formed in the name of bolstering the stability of the Republic. In addition, corpulent senators, keen to minimize their journey to the Senate, have used every form of persuasion to ensure that their offices and suites are built as close to the chamber as possible.

ENTERTAINMENT DISTRICTS

Coruscant's sprawling entertainment districts are equally alluring and unsettling for the hordes of revelers drawn to nightclubs, gaming houses, bars, and palaces of hedonism. Such districts are generally safe if slightly seedy, awash with bright lights and gaudy partygoers. Those with more daring tastes may seek out the city's underlevels, where any vice can be indulged provided one has credits and connections. But visiting these dark and dangerous levels can be a one-way trip for naïve pleasure-seekers who get in over their heads.

THE WORKS

Coruscant's single planetwide metropolis is divided into several thousand regions, which are further subdivided into numbered sectors. Whereas official maps use this classification, most people refer to districts by colloquial names. One large sector is known as The Works. It is a manufacturing district, where, for hundreds of standard years, spacecraft parts, construction droids, and building materials of every kind were churned out at an astonishing rate. Now, much of this manufacturing is done more cheaply off-planet, and the area has fallen into disrepair. Coruscanti stay well clear of The Works, as it has gained a reputation for the most sinister kind of criminal activity—making it ideal for a clandestine meeting between two shadowy Sith leaders.

UPPER LEVEL DINERS

Exclusive stores and restaurants cater to the wealthy citizens who inhabit the highest levels of Coruscant. Small canteens serve maintenance crews and support staff working in these lofty heights. Many of the more fly-by-night canteens operate without trading licenses and are repulsor-fitted for easy getaway if officials come snooping. Located in Coco Town, Dex's Diner is one such mobile installation. In Coco Town (short for "collective commerce"), immigrants of diverse species have established mutually supportive manufacturing businesses.

SPEEDER CHASE I

AFTER A NEAR-FATAL ASSASSINATION ATTEMPT as she arrived on Coruscant, Padmé Amidala is assigned two Jedi bodyguards, who keep watch on the senator as she sleeps in her apartment. Yet a modified ASN-121 assassin/sentry droid bypasses the window shields in a further attempt on Padmé's life—only, this time, the Jedi give chase. Knowing that the droid will be programmed to return to its source, Kenobi smashes through the window and grabs onto it as it turns to flee. Meanwhile, Anakin "hotwires" an airspeeder from a nearby parking bay. In the ensuing chase, both Jedi hurtle through the skylanes in pursuit of bounty hunter Zam Wesell, who avoids the heavy circulation, high-lane interchanges, choosing instead to dip down into the lower lanes, where traffic is lighter but less orderly.

1 Anakin quickly spots the only open-top airspeeder in a parking bay—which happens to be the fastest, too. The speeder is later recovered and returned to its designated parkslot, effectively cutting short the official enquiry into the "theft" and leaving its owner, Senator Simon Greyshade, unable to press charges.

2 At the mercy of the droid's defensive stratagems, Kenobi is repeatedly scraped against the walls of buildings or dangled in the path of oncoming speeders. He narrowly escapes a collision with holodrama star Seboca from Malastare, who is entertaining a female senator from Aleen, Bogg Tyrell.

3 Kenobi struggles to hold on to the speeding assassin droid as it repeatedly sends defensive electrical shocks into his unprotected hands. Several skylanes below him, Anakin pilots his airspeeder, using the Force to seek his Master and hoping that the droid will lead him to the unknown assassin.

ROUTE KEY

Assassin droid	Obi-Wan's fall
Anakin's speeder	Zam's speeder
Zam's rifle slug	Anakin's leap

Padmé's rooms are in a high-security Senate apartment complex

Anakin takes an airspeeder from a parking balcony several floors beneath Padmé's apartment

Office occupied by regulatory body for mobile communication droids

Nicandra Counterrevolutionary Signalmen's Memorial Building

Bonadan Embassy

Only the wealthiest senators dine in the 1,000m (3,280ft)-high revolving Skysitter Restaurant

Assassin droid supporting Obi-Wan is hit by a bolt from Zam's sniper rifle

Obi-Wan freefalls for 285m (950ft) before landing in Anakin's speeder

Zam throws her speeder into a daring nose-dive

Zam waits on an upper balcony of a Trade Federation office tower

Trade Federation advertising screens

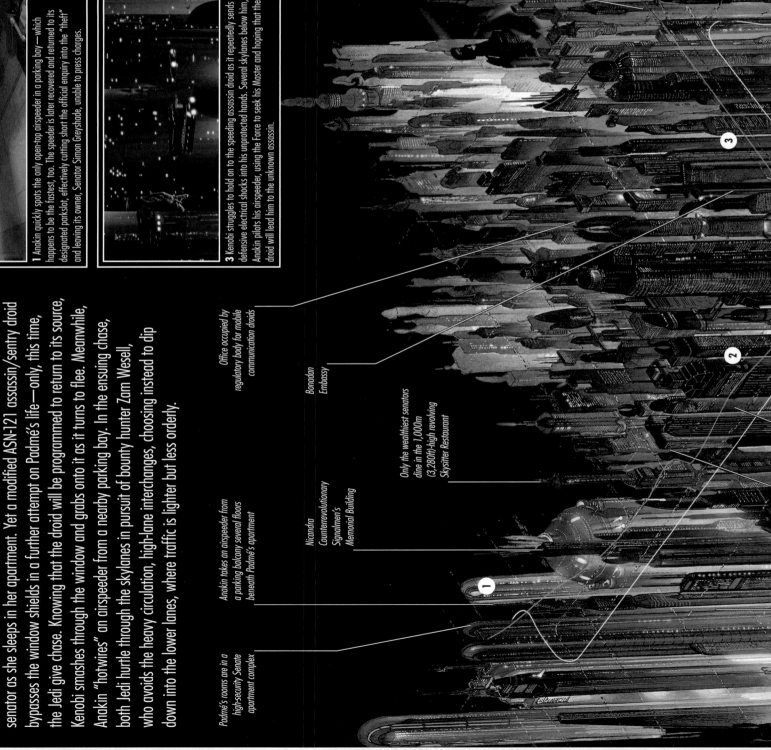

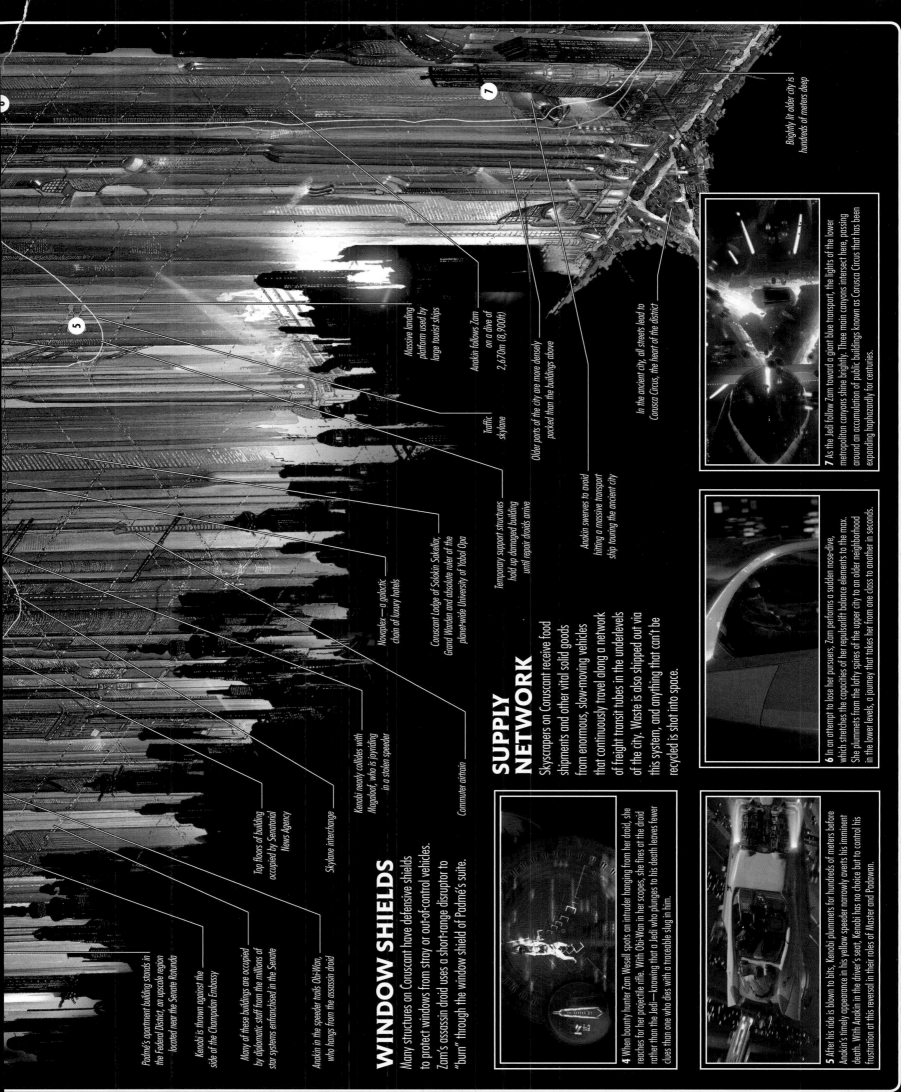

Brightly, Ir older city is
hundreds of meters deep

Massive landing
platform used by
large tourist ships

Anakin follows Zam
on a dive of
2,670m (8,900ft)

Traffic
skylane

Older parts of the city are more densely
packed than the buildings above

Anakin swerves to avoid
hitting a massive transport
ship touring the ancient city

In the ancient city, all streets lead to
Corusca Circus, the heart of the district

Temporary support structures
hold up damaged building
until repair droids arrive

Novaplex—a galactic
chain of luxury hotels

Coruscant Lodge of Solokin Sakellar,
Grand Warden and absolute ruler of the
planet-wide University of Yabol Opa

Kenobi nearly collides with
Magaloof, who is joyriding
in a stolen speeder

Commuter airtrain

Skylane interchange

Anakin in the speeder trails Obi-Wan,
who hangs from the assassin droid

Top floors of building
occupied by Senatorial
News Agency

Many of these buildings are occupied
by diplomatic staff from the millions of
star systems enfranchised in the Senate

Kenobi is thrown against the
side of the Champalan Embassy

Padmé's apartment building stands in
the Federal District, an upscale region
located near the Senate Rotunda

WINDOW SHIELDS

Many structures on Coruscant have defensive shields
to protect windows from stray or out-of-control vehicles.
Zam's assassin droid uses a short-range disruptor to
"burn" through the window shield of Padmé's suite.

4 When bounty hunter Zam Wesell spots an intruder hanging from her droid, she
reaches for her projectile rifle. With Obi-Wan in her scopes, she fires at the droid
rather than the Jedi—knowing that a Jedi who plunges to his death leaves fewer
clues than one who dies with a traceable slug in him.

SUPPLY NETWORK

Skyscrapers on Coruscant receive food
shipments and other vital solid goods
from enormous, slow-moving vehicles
that continuously travel along a network
of freight transit tubes in the underlevels
of the city. Waste is also shipped out via
this system, and anything that can't be
recycled is shot into space.

5 After his ride is blown to bits, Kenobi plummets for hundreds of meters before
Anakin's timely appearance in his yellow speeder narrowly averts his imminent
death. With Anakin in the driver's seat, Kenobi has no choice but to control his
frustration at this reversal in their roles of Master and Padawan.

6 In an attempt to lose her pursuers, Zam performs a sudden nose-dive,
which stretches the capacities of her repulsolift balance elements to the max.
She plummets from the lofty spires of the upper city to an older neighborhood
in the lower levels, a journey that takes her from one class to another in seconds.

7 As the Jedi follow Zam toward a giant blue transport, the lights of the lower
metropolitan canyons shine brightly. Three main canyons intersect here, passing
around an accumulation of public buildings known as Corusca Circus that has been
expanding haphazardly for centuries.

SPEEDER CHASE II

The pursuit continues through the lower levels of Coruscant. These are the areas the upper classes rarely see: the industrial plants that supply Coruscant with power and fuel, and the warehouse zones where essential supplies from off-world are readied for distribution around the planet. In all, the Jedi chase Zam through the skies for more than 100 kilometers (62 miles), until Anakin forces Zam to crash-land in a busy entertainment district.

8 Zam, in her sealed vehicle, deliberately leads her pursuers through the flaming exhaust vents of a recycling plant, knowing their open-top speeder will leave them dangerously exposed. These vents burn toxic waste gas into less harmful forms (atmospheric carbon dioxide and water vapor).

10 Zam flies past a HoloNet News display beacon, which provides clearly illuminated, up-to-the-minute news flashes on galactic events in a variety of common languages. On Coruscant and on many other urbanized planets, these displays can be seen wherever there are busy skylanes.

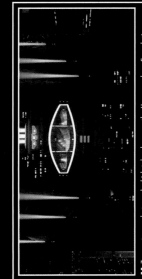

9 Bounty hunter Wesell fires a blaster bolt at the couplings of an on-surface power refinery, activating massive electrical bolts between the prongs. As the Jedi have no time to avoid them, they are enveloped in nerve-jarring lightning. The powerful shock would induce a heart attack in those not trained in the Force.

MAPPING CORUSCANT

Coruscant is divided into sectors with official coordinates, which often receive unofficial names. For example, sector H-46 is more colloquially known as Sah'c Town (named after a wealthy family that owns much of it). Sectors are further subdivided into zones: for instance, the senatorial, financial, and industrial zones through which Skywalker and Kenobi pursue Padmé's would-be assassin.

SKYTUNNELS

Certain neighborhoods of Coruscant are accessible only via skytunnels, such as the one Zam soars into. Some skytunnels serve as shortcuts through structures built by powerful but uncaring official bodies that end up blocking established skyways. Other tunnels allow civilian traffic to pass through private airspace, such as high-security banking or governmental zones.

11 Zam enters a skytunnel which takes her over the Huosnoghow Foundation—a powerful financial think tank with close links to myriad Senate budgeting offices. Zam hits 400 kph (248 mph) in a strict 200 kph (124 mph) flyzone, trusting in her superb piloting skills to win out over her pursuers.

GHOST SHIP

The *Giga*-class transport ship *Ultimo Vista* that Anakin and Obi-Wan narrowly avoid hitting is one of Coruscant's most bizarre sights. Established decades ago as a leisure cruise ship, it is now a separate, contained world in which its elderly passengers are full-time residents. Almost entirely self-sufficient, the slow-moving craft endlessly circles Coruscant on its original route to nowhere.

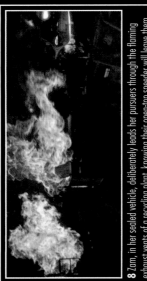

Storage

Sports fields

Apartment blocks house a population of several thousand residents

Habitation areas include forests, rivers, and seas, with a controlled climate

The largest, tallest buildings accommodate populations in the millions

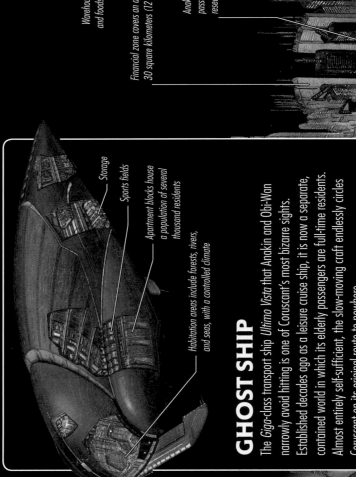

Giant conveyors continuously move goods to unloading bays in the lower levels for distribution around the planet

Half-finished buildings, supported by cranes and girders

Obi-Wan catches Anakin's lightsaber

Warehouse zone entrance portal employs massive electrostatic dampers to keep dust clouds from spreading

Steam from drying silos and heating generators

Warehouses receive imported goods and foods from all around the galaxy

Financial zone covers an area of about 30 square kilometers (12 square miles)

Anakin spots Zam's speeder passing through a droid research institute

13

12

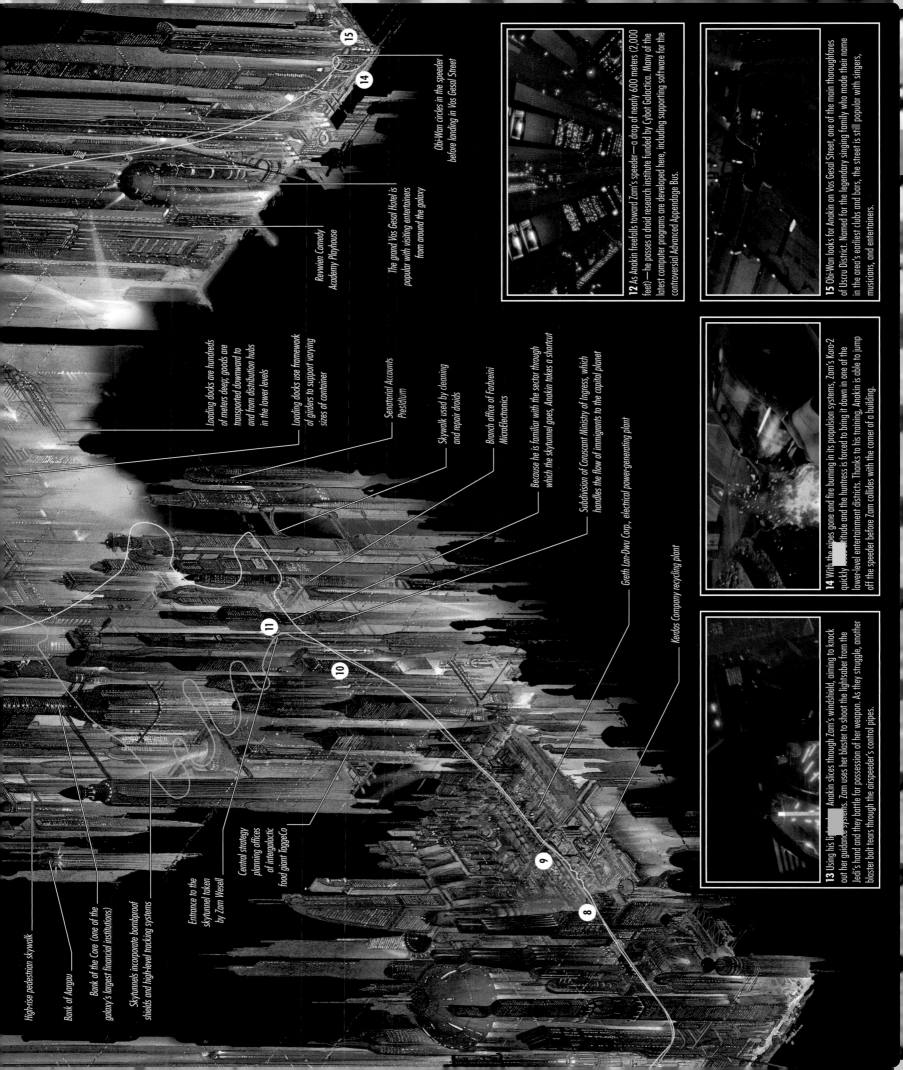

High-rise pedestrian skywalk

Bank of Aargau

Bank of the Core (one of the galaxy's largest financial institutions)

Skytunnels incorporate bombproof shields and high-level tracking systems

Entrance to the skytunnel taken by Zam Wesell

Central strategy planning offices of intergalactic food giant TaggeCo

Greth Lan-Dwu Corp., electrical power-generating plant

Kerdos Company recycling plant

Loading docks are hundreds of meters deep; goods are transported downward to and from distribution hubs in the lower levels

Loading docks use framework of girders to support varying sizes of container

Senatorial Accounts Prestilum

Skywalk used by cleaning and repair droids

Branch office of Farbreini MicroElectronics

Because he is familiar with the sector through which the skytunnel goes, Anakin takes a shortcut

Subdivision of Coruscant Ministry of Ingress, which handles the flow of immigrants to the capital planet

Rewwien Comedy Academy Playhouse

The grand Vos Gesal Hotel is popular with visiting entertainers from around the galaxy

Obi-Wan circles in the speeder before landing in Vos Gesal Street

12 As Anakin freefalls toward Zam's speeder—a drop of nearly 600 meters (2,000 feet)—he passes a droid research institute funded by Cybot Galactica. Many of the latest computer programs are developed here, including supporting software for the controversial Advanced Appendage Bus.

13 Using his lightsaber, Anakin slices through Zam's windshield, aiming to knock out her guidance systems. Zam uses her blaster to shoot the lightsaber from the Jedi's hand and they battle for possession of her weapon. As they struggle, another blaster bolt tears through the airspeeder's control pipes.

14 With the pipes gone and fire burning in its propulsion systems, Zam's Koro-2 quickly loses altitude and the huntress is forced to bring it down in one of the lower-level entertainment districts. Thanks to his training, Anakin is able to jump off the speeder before Zam collides with the corner of a building.

15 Obi-Wan looks for Anakin on Vos Gesal Street, one of the main thoroughfares of Uscru District. Named for the legendary singing family who made their name in the area's earliest clubs and bars, the street is still popular with singers, musicians, and entertainers.

OUTLANDER CLUB

THE OUTLANDER CLUB is located in Coruscant's Uscru entertainment district. The locale is a labyrinth of bars and gaming rooms, where Coruscanti revelers, underworld characters, and wide-eyed off-worlders jostle one another while staking what wealth they have on sporting events and on-site games of chance. The club stays open day and night, with some hardened gamblers spending days at a time here. When Zam slips inside, she aims to lose the pursuing Jedi in the crowded, dimly lit interior—or finish them off for good.

Some sports events shown at the Outlander are officially illegal in the Republic, such as podracing (live here from the ice-covered planet of Ando Prime). Other popular games are only barely tolerated—including nuna-ball (a violent ball-game for souped-up droids) and odupiendo-racing.

Desperate gamblers occasionally throw themselves off balcony

Highly exclusive suite in which visiting crime lords, gang bosses, and top-ranking politicians are entertained

An exotic dancer will later be eaten by visiting crime lords out of misplaced politeness

Four-armed kiughfid dealers on main gambling floor are fast and efficient at taking people's money

Visiting princess from Soun IV

The Outlander offers its own version of sabacc with house rules

Betting kiosk

Holographic gamescreens offer inexpensive but highly addictive gambling

The rodian Tyyx makes his living selling tips on podraces

Anj Rujj is one of the infamous Thugs of Thule, a gang of highly educated mercenaries

Bufon Taire's assistant bartender has been fired from most respectable bars on Coruscant

Blind molemen are escorted by a tour guide to Digisee Gaming Floor

Side entrance to alleyway

Anakin and Obi-Wan escort out wounded Zam Wesell

Chadra-Fan looking for a strong juri juice

Ayy Vida entertains clients of her owner, crime boss Hat Lo

Automixer enables users to select their species to ensure non-toxic drink

Gamblers in underlevel bet on illegal fights

ILLEGAL GAMING

Because it is tucked away in one of the less developed areas of the entertainment district, which is rarely patrolled by law enforcement crews, the club makes little secret of its policy to accept bids on just about any game in the galaxy—even the ever-popular Galactic Games, on which betting is highly illegal.

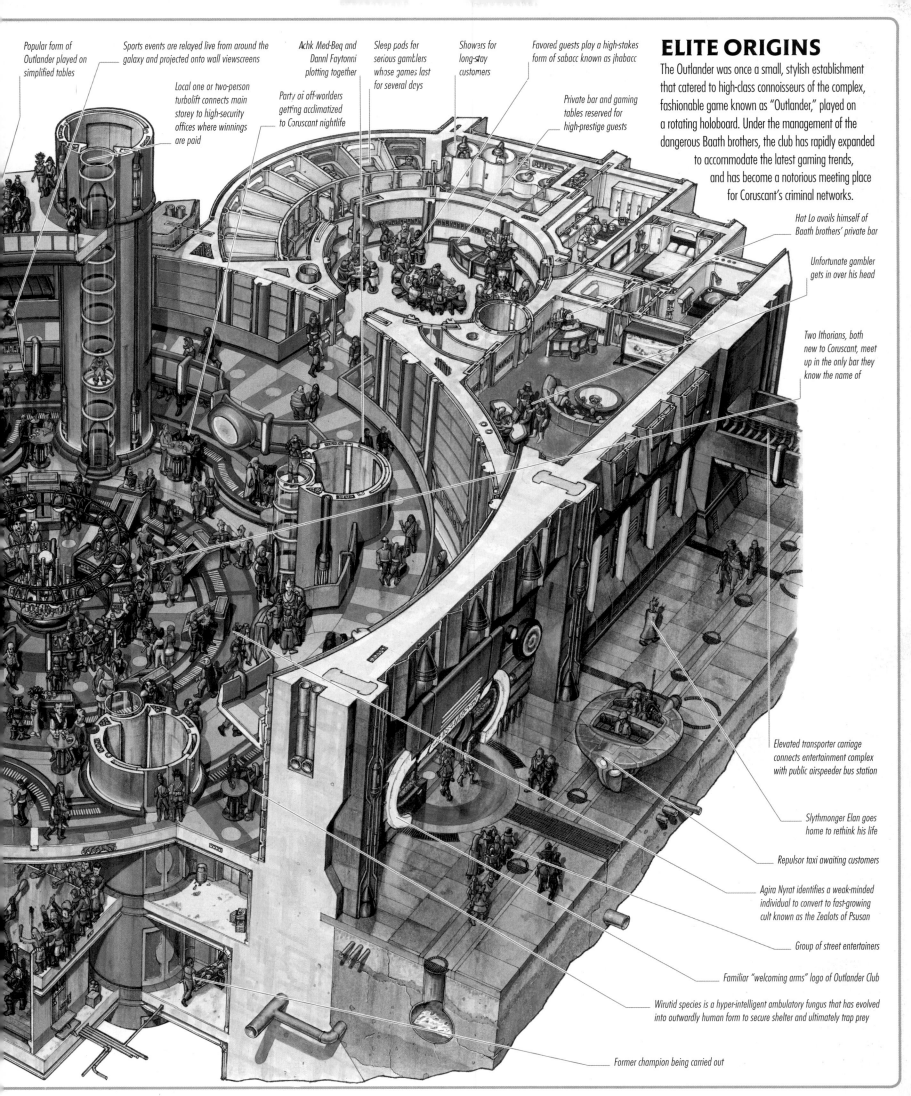

Popular form of Outlander played on simplified tables

Sports events are relayed live from around the galaxy and projected onto wall viewscreens

Local one or two-person turbolift connects main storey to high-security offices where winnings are paid

Achk Med-Beq and Dannl Faytonni plotting together

Party of off-worlders getting acclimatized to Coruscant nightlife

Sleep pods for serious gamblers whose games last for several days

Showers for long-stay customers

Favored guests play a high-stakes form of sabacc known as jhabacc

Private bar and gaming tables reserved for high-prestige guests

ELITE ORIGINS

The Outlander was once a small, stylish establishment that catered to high-class connoisseurs of the complex, fashionable game known as "Outlander," played on a rotating holoboard. Under the management of the dangerous Baath brothers, the club has rapidly expanded to accommodate the latest gaming trends, and has become a notorious meeting place for Coruscant's criminal networks.

Hat Lo avails himself of Baath brothers' private bar

Unfortunate gambler gets in over his head

Two Ithorians, both new to Coruscant, meet up in the only bar they know the name of

Elevated transporter carriage connects entertainment complex with public airspeeder bus station

Slythmonger Elan goes home to rethink his life

Repulsor taxi awaiting customers

Agira Nyrat identifies a weak-minded individual to convert to fast-growing cult known as the Zealots of Psusan

Group of street entertainers

Familiar "welcoming arms" logo of Outlander Club

Wirutid species is a hyper-intelligent ambulatory fungus that has evolved into outwardly human form to secure shelter and ultimately trap prey

Former champion being carried out

JEDI TEMPLE

FOR THE LAST 1,000 YEARS, Jedi activity in the galaxy has been centered at the Jedi Temple on Coruscant, with lesser Jedi sanctuaries, libraries, and chapter houses dotted throughout the Republic. In more ancient times, Jedi temples dominated other planets, such as Ossus, with its now-destroyed Great Library. The Temple is the home of Jedi in training for at least their first eight years, until they are accepted as Padawans to Jedi Knights. Until this time, they do not leave the Temple precinct, and have little communication with the outside world.

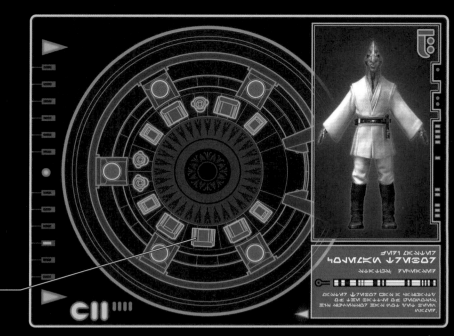

Coleman Trebor's seat

TEMPLE HANGAR

Jedi have to depart for any sector of the galaxy at a moment's notice in response to some imminent trouble or crisis. After the Naboo blockade, the Jedi Council introduced single-person Delta-7 starfighters and assigned them to all leading Jedi, with specially adapted versions for non-humanoid Knights. These ships are stored within recently constructed Temple hangars and launched from an extendible platform.

COUNCIL CHAMBER DATABANK

Temple databanks show the latest seating plan of the Jedi High Council, with information on the current location and status of its 12 members. Only Jedi with appropriate access privileges are able to view such information. Coleman Trebor, one of the latest appointees to the Council, perishes in the Battle of Geonosis, the first combat of the Clone Wars.

Temple tracking system operational

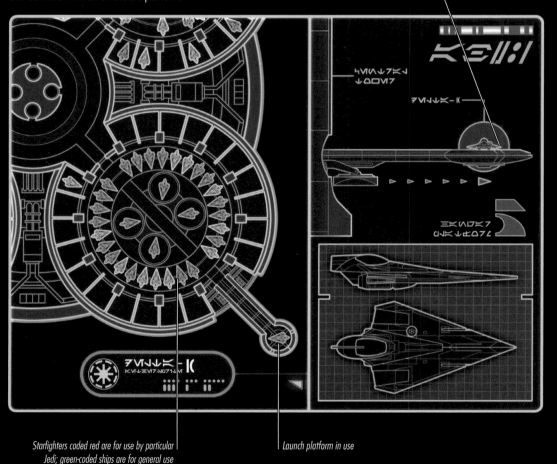

Starfighters coded red are for use by particular Jedi; green-coded ships are for general use

Launch platform in use

MEDITATION AND EDUCATION

The Jedi Temple dominates the landscape for kilometers around, its noble spires seeming almost to pierce the sky. The Temple is the heart of the ancient Jedi Order, its many serene, spacious chambers and walkways—including its room of a thousand fountains—facilitating deep contemplation of the Force. High-ranking Jedi Masters, such as lightsaber virtuoso Soara Antana, hold prestige classes for Padawans in specialized halls and instruction rooms, although much of their training takes place in the standard accommodations of the Temple Precinct.

ANALYSIS ROOMS

Analysis spaces fall under the overall jurisdiction of the Temple Archives and archivist Jocasta Nu. They are used by Jedi for many tasks, including locating the provenance of alien objects, either organic or inorganic. SP-4 and JN-66 analysis droids that staff the facility can access the computer systems of the Jedi Archives to match identification indices. Their multispectral readers and polysensitive graspers detect even the slightest odor traces. The room is therefore hermetically sealed to humans or aliens, so no contamination can occur that would cause false readings from the highly sensitive equipment.

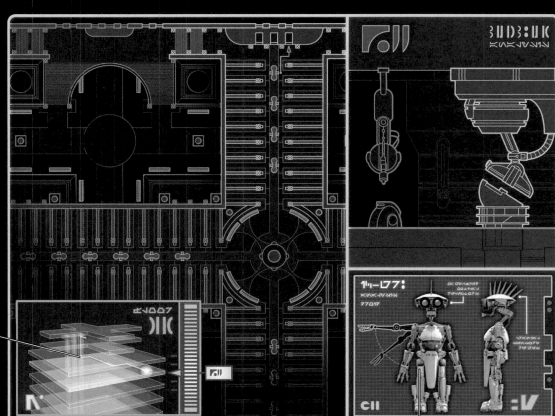

Temple data screen shows route from Archives to Analysis Rooms

Buildings added after initial construction are contained in the extensive Temple Precinct

Spaceport tower allows larger spaceships to dock in the Jedi Temple complex

Central spire of Jedi Temple

Specifications of SP-4 analysis droid

NABOO RETREATS

SINCE THE TRADE FEDERATION INVASION, Naboo has undergone a period of adjustment. New building works in the capital, Theed, have repaired the damage done by the invasion force, and Queen Jamillia has accepted the necessity of increased security for her people. A well-equipped new spaceport is a bold symbol of the people's expanded outlook. When Anakin accompanies Padmé to Naboo as her bodyguard, he visits the planet's most remote region, the Lake Country.

Like many of the rooms in the grand house, the rotunda in which Padmé and Anakin dine has associations with its former celebrated resident Omar Berenko. In this Room of Morning Mists, Berenko wrote some of his most famous works, including the disturbing and visionary epic poem, *Defense of Naboo*.

VARYKINO

The Lake Country is sealed off from Naboo's underground waterways and caverns, making the lakes safe from sea monsters. The sparse population is made up mostly of farmers and hermit-craftsworkers famed for their almost mystically bewitching glassworks. Padmé and Anakin stay at Varykino, a large villa that stands on the lake's most distant island. The house was occupied centuries earlier by the tragic Naboo poet Omar Berenko, who lived in an unconventional community of Naboo—and even Gungan—outsiders.

TRANQUIL OASIS

The Lake Country boasts some of the most idyllic water meadows on Naboo, with dramatic waterfalls and flocks of peacefully grazing shaak. The fertile land is regularly flooded by its rivers, but is pleasantly dry in summer. The communally owned meadows are maintained by the Pastoral Collective. In springtime, the festival of Glad Arrival is held here, when, for several days, the meadows are transformed by colorful pageants and music-making.

CLANDESTINE CEREMONY

Following the Battle of Geonosis, Anakin Skywalker escorts Senator Amidala back to Naboo, where they marry in secret—an act forbidden to Jedi. The simple ritual takes place on a shaded balcony at Varykino. The marriage rites are pronounced by a holy man from the region. Unknown to either bride or groom, it was on this very spot that the controversial poet Berenko was kidnapped by unknown assailants, never to be seen again.

PUBLIC SPLENDOR

Traveling by public airbus, Anakin and Padmé arrive in Theed's new Palace Courtyard. Built over a part of the city that was severely damaged by Trade Federation tanks 10 years earlier, the new enclosure is designed to foster and encourage principles of enlightened thought and practice. Theed's inhabitants wander through the courtyard's graceful walkways and sit in the shade of the circular colonnade, within which a holographic frieze depicts great philosophers and artists from the planet's history. Naboo is not entirely free from trouble, however: in recent months, migrant workers have staged protests about their work conditions, only to be forcibly removed by Theed police. Naboo's leaders are largely sheltered from these events by their security advisors in order to preserve—for the time being at least—the utopian outlook of which the planet is so proud.

KAMINO

KAMINO IS A REMOTE AND INHOSPITABLE WORLD covered in one unending ocean. Located in a dwarf satellite galaxy beyond the Outer Rim, the planet receives very little traffic and only as much trade as is necessary to supply the basic needs of its inhabitants, the amphibious Kaminoans. This highly intelligent race has specialized in the high-skill, value-added industry of human, alien, and creature cloning, supplying a select client base with workers, private security forces, and a range of unusual, one-off requests. The Kaminoans live in stilt-cities scattered across the planet's watery surface, the majority of which are devoted to cloning projects. The Kaminoans only rarely receive visitors: The remoteness of the planet and its extensive rainy season deters all but the occasional representative of a clone purchasing authority.

LANDING PLATFORMS

The bounty hunter Jango Fett makes use of one of Tipoca City's landing platforms for his spaceship, *Slave I*. Despite the severity of weather conditions on Kamino, landing platforms on the planet are generally uncovered. A shield generator array on the underside, however, can be activated to protect the ship from power overloads during electrical storms. Sensor masts provide electronic surveillance and warn of any accidental intrusions.

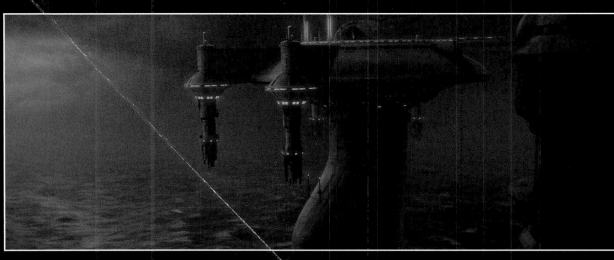

AIR–TO–SEA TRANSPORT

The amphibious Kaminoans often travel between their stilt-cities on cloned aiwhas, animals that can both fly and swim. For much of the year, severe electrical storms rage across the planet. At these times, Kaminoan aiwha-riders tend to travel underwater to escape the lashing tempests, surfacing as they near their destination. Another, more unusual imperative drives the Kaminoans under the waves—pilgrimages to the sunken cities on the seabed, relics of the ancient land-based Kaminoan civilization that existed before the entire planet was flooded. These sacred journeys are made purely to honor their ancestors, rather than for scientific or archaeological research, and seem highly inconsistent with the Kaminoans' more characteristic scientific rationalism.

CAPITAL CITY

When Obi-Wan Kenobi enters Kaminoan airspace, he is cleared to land at the planet's capital, Tipoca City, where the first shipments of the Republic's clone army are being readied. The giant domes house Kamino's largest and most prestigious military complex, although many other cloning facilities exist at other sites across the planet. The center at Tipoca extends throughout the domes, and includes hatcheries, growth pods, and learning and training facilities, as well as dormitories and dining halls. In addition to creating clones, the Kaminoans produce a range of specialized, high-tech weapons and missiles for a number of clients: for example, interrogation devices and an array of saberdarts, mainly for use by professional bounty hunters and security specialists. The cloners subcontract the manufacturing of larger weapons and vehicles to off-world suppliers such as Rothana Heavy Engineering.

TIPOCA CITY

THE KAMINOAN CAPITAL stands above the ferocious waves on massive legs anchored in the seabed, its gently sloping roof-domes shedding the driving rains that fall almost continuously. The city is actually a network of stilt structures distributed over 150 kilometers (93 miles) at the planet's equator. The central hub houses extensive cloning facilities and administrative offices occupied by the planet's Ruling Council. Because all the millions of Kaminoans who live and work in Tipoca are involved in either the cloning industry or governmental business—the two are closely interlinked—there is no public space within the central domes. Satellite cities ranged around Tipoca provide homes and recreation for the highly skilled workers.

Jango Fett's personal landing platform is an indication of the bounty hunter's importance to the cloning project. To protect *Slave I* from the elements and to facilitate repairs, a section of the platform descends into a hangar below, which is then sealed by retractable doors.

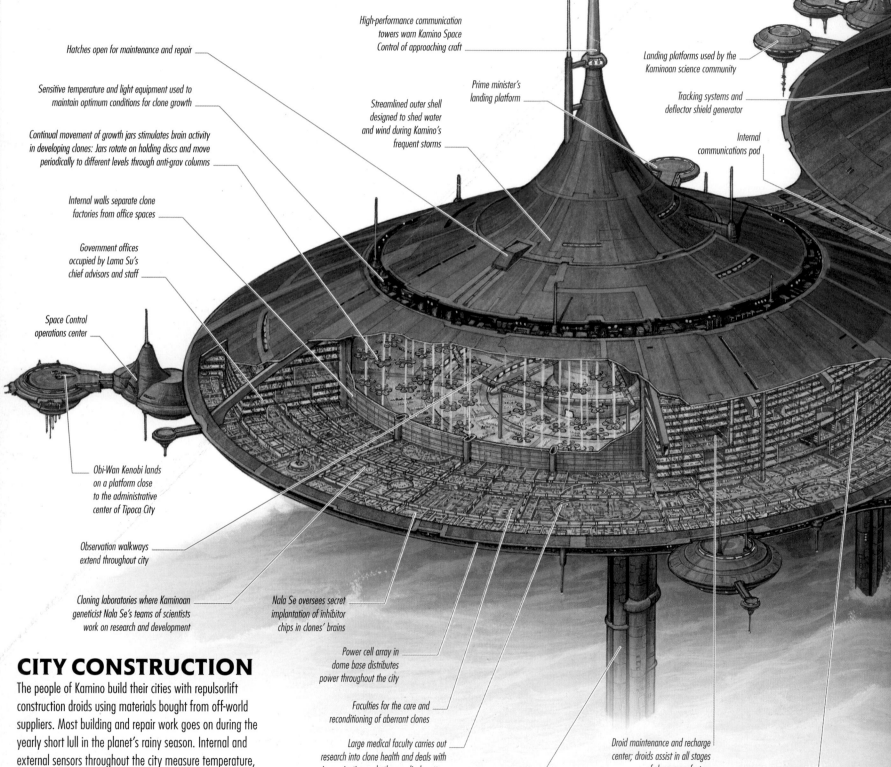

High-performance communication towers warn Kamino Space Control of approaching craft

Hatches open for maintenance and repair

Sensitive temperature and light equipment used to maintain optimum conditions for clone growth

Continual movement of growth jars stimulates brain activity in developing clones: Jars rotate on holding discs and move periodically to different levels through anti-grav columns

Internal walls separate clone factories from office spaces

Government offices occupied by Lama Su's chief advisors and staff

Space Control operations center

Prime minister's landing platform

Streamlined outer shell designed to shed water and wind during Kamino's frequent storms

Landing platforms used by the Kaminoan science community

Tracking systems and deflector shield generator

Internal communications pod

Obi-Wan Kenobi lands on a platform close to the administrative center of Tipoca City

Observation walkways extend throughout city

Cloning laboratories where Kaminoan geneticist Nala Se's teams of scientists work on research and development

Nala Se oversees secret implantation of inhibitor chips in clones' brains

Power cell array in dome base distributes power throughout the city

Faculties for the care and reconditioning of aberrant clones

Large medical faculty carries out research into clone health and deals with immunization and other medical matters

Droid maintenance and recharge center; droids assist in all stages of clone manufacture

City support pylons are secured in seabed and pump sea water to desalination chambers

Apartments for cloning scientific community, who reside for shifts of about three months before returning to their homes and families

CITY CONSTRUCTION

The people of Kamino build their cities with repulsorlift construction droids using materials bought from off-world suppliers. Most building and repair work goes on during the yearly short lull in the planet's rainy season. Internal and external sensors throughout the city measure temperature, humidity, wind speed, and lighting levels, ensuring that the domes respond to issues such as occupancy levels and the seasonal mood changes of their inhabitants.

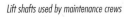

Lift shafts used by maintenance crews

Static discharge towers provide protection during electrical storms

Turbolaser turrets behind gun port doors attest to the Kaminoans' distrust of outsiders

Insulator plating

Heat exhaust vent

Kaminoan Planetary Defense substation

Power-processing networks

Fusion generator utilizes hydrogen from seawater to power city

Troop barracks

SELF-RELIANT CULTURE

Architecture on Kamino has long been characterized by domed buildings. Before the planet flooded, the Kaminoans lived in dome-shaped wattle-and-daub houses on land. As the floodwaters rose, they migrated to increasingly higher land until forced to raise their houses on stilts. Modern high-tech cities feature heavy military capabilities and high-security systems, which reflect a characteristic Kaminoan attitude of self-reliance and suspicion of others.

Ha Zurh Library and Records Office, maintained by droid librarian

Drill halls and training areas

Outdoor training grounds and extensive rainwater collection ducts

Platform where Jango Fett teaches Boba how to fish

Living areas occupied by Kaminoan military staff

Jango Fett's apartment lies in a military complex

LIVING ON KAMINO

Domestic apartments on Kamino are sparsely furnished. Certain furniture is designed to descend from the ceiling on stalks, connecting with electromagnetic floor markings. Jango Fett's apartment is typically modest, but has some concessions to human comfort in the replacement of luminous surfaces with stable furniture.

Desalination plants can turn sea water into pure distilled water for use in the city

Training areas for clone troops

Obi-Wan hangs from the edge of the landing platform

Landing platform used by Jango Fett

Untreated source water in storage tank

Compressor unit

Condenser/evaporator tanks

PATROL VEHICLES

Operating as quality-control mobile inspection labs, Observation Ships are staffed by Kaminoan scientists, who react quickly to problems and constantly look for ways to improve the cloning and training processes. Single-occupant KE-8 Enforcer Ships, equipped with powerful manipulator arms and electroshock devices, patrol the complex to identify and isolate aberrant clones. Clones who display exceptional abilities are sent to separate areas to receive specialized military education.

Observation deck

Repulsorlift array

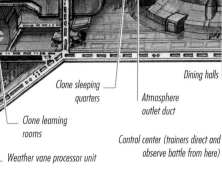

Detachable observation gondola

KE-8 Enforcer Ship

Electroshock stun device

Manipulator arms

VISITOR ACCESS

The Kaminoans are careful to keep their sterile, ultraclean cloning environments free from contamination, so visitors to the complex must stay within sealed viewing walkways. Constructed high above the main floor, walkways allow visitors an overview of the cloning process. The bulk of the clones, however, are educated beneath the main floor, in more tightly crammed facilities.

Doorway to other floors and hangars for Republic assault ships

Combat rooms where armies practice unarmed combat

Command bridge for senior Kaminoan security officials

Emergency siren

Enforcer Ship deployment and recharge stations

Computer terminals and monitoring stations track activity of Enforcer Ships and communicate with Observation Ships

Enforcer Ship ingress/egress hatch

Main processor hub for central computer system

Turbolift between main and upper floors

Kaminoan training commanders are required to update their records regularly

Viewing towers used by clone instructors to watch maneuvers

Computer terminals deliver training diagnostics

Mass troop elevator shaft

Clone army assembly floor

Atmospheric generator

Air inlet duct

Power cell storage

AT-TE loading bay

Weather vane processor unit

Weather vane monitors outside conditions to provide storm warnings and allow adjustments to building atmosphere systems

Clone learning rooms

Clone sleeping quarters

Atmosphere outlet duct

Control center (trainers direct and observe battle from here)

Clone diagnostics reprogramming laboratory

Dining halls

Energy barrier

Automated kitchens produce nutritionally balanced diet

Elite clone commando unit

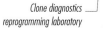

MILITARY COMPLEX

THE CLONE MILITARY EDUCATION COMPLEX, which dominates Tipoca City, is the biggest training center on Kamino. Its current production is dedicated to fulfilling the Republic contract, the largest cloning project the Kaminoan government has ever undertaken. When Obi-Wan arrives, Tipoca is already primed to deliver 200,000 clone troops, while facilities across the planet are equipped to produce millions more. As Prime Minister Lama Su walks Kenobi through Tipoca's public display floor, he has no doubt that the Jedi will be impressed with his superbly organized operation.

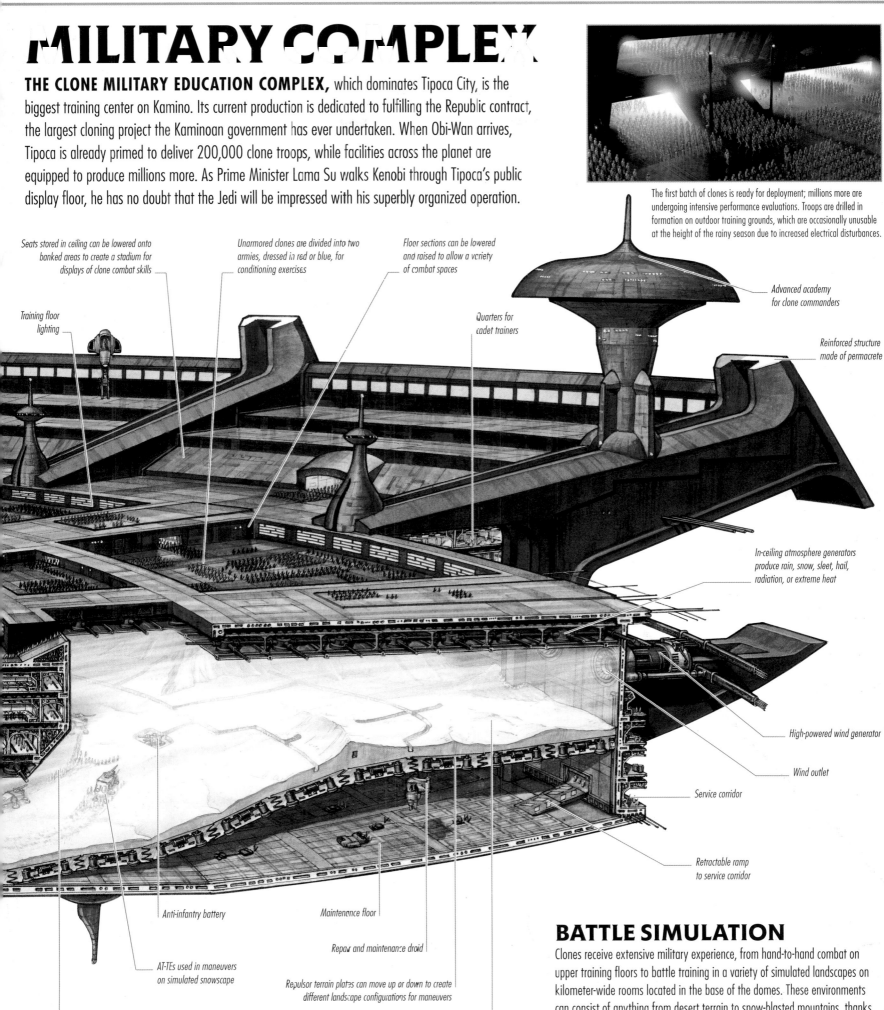

The first batch of clones is ready for deployment; millions more are undergoing intensive performance evaluations. Troops are drilled in formation on outdoor training grounds, which are occasionally unusable at the height of the rainy season due to increased electrical disturbances.

Seats stored in ceiling can be lowered onto banked areas to create a stadium for displays of clone combat skills

Unarmored clones are divided into two armies, dressed in red or blue, for conditioning exercises

Floor sections can be lowered and raised to allow a variety of combat spaces

Training floor lighting

Quarters for cadet trainers

Advanced academy for clone commanders

Reinforced structure made of permacrete

In-ceiling atmosphere generators produce rain, snow, sleet, hail, radiation, or extreme heat

High-powered wind generator

Wind outlet

Service corridor

Retractable ramp to service corridor

Anti-infantry battery

Maintenance floor

Repair and maintenance droid

AT-TEs used in maneuvers on simulated snowscape

Repulsor terrain plates can move up or down to create different landscape configurations for maneuvers

Knowing that the Jedi will be leading the troops, trainers El Les and Bric order the clones to march in double file so they can take shelter behind the commanding Jedi's lightsaber

Ice planet environment with trench system defenses

BATTLE SIMULATION

Clones receive extensive military experience, from hand-to-hand combat on upper training floors to battle training in a variety of simulated landscapes on kilometer-wide rooms located in the base of the domes. These environments can consist of anything from desert terrain to snow-blasted mountains, thanks to atmospheric systems that create climate and weather conditions, and repulsor-lifted floor plates which can shift to produce a variety of geological features.

TATOOINE II

WHEN ANAKIN SKYWALKER returns to Tatooine, he finds a world unchanged from 10 years earlier. Slavery still exists in the lawless Outer Rim, and the threat of danger hangs in the air. Yet Tatooine functions with a kind of rough order: Droid taxis navigate the spaceports, where merchants sell their wares; podraces and cantinas provide entertainment; and harsh justice is administered by Hutt crime lords. Out in the wastelands, moisture farmers eke out a living, raising their families to have a sense of community and morality. The slow turning of the galaxy's political fortunes has yet to impinge on this inward-looking world.

ANAKIN'S JOURNEY

Tusken Raiders abducted Shmi Lars as they skirted the Lars homestead on their nomadic wanderings that had lately included numerous conflicts with settlers. In search of her, Anakin sets off in the direction of the Tuskens' last sighting—the massacre of Cliegg Lars' posse of farmers. He picks up the trail from Jawas and other isolated settlers. Finally, he comes upon a camp, deep in the barren wastes.

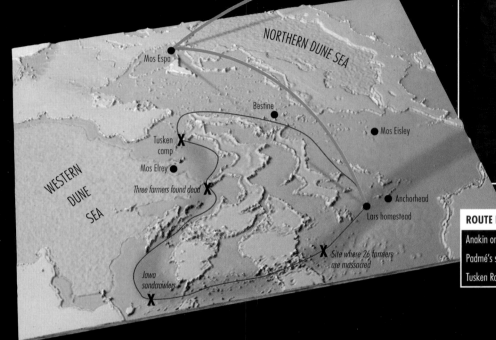

NORTHERN DUNE SEA

Mos Espa

Bestine

Mos Eisley

Tusken camp

WESTERN DUNE SEA

Mos Elrey

Three farmers found dead

Anchorhead

Lars homestead

Site where 26 farmers are massacred

Jawa sandcrawlers

ROUTE KEY

Anakin on Owen Lars' swoop bike ———
Padmé's starship ———
Tusken Raiders' route ▬▬▬

WATTO'S JUNKSHOP

In the 10 years since Anakin said farewell to his former owner, Watto has remained wedded to his used-parts dealership in a Mos Espa backstreet. Despite purchasing parts of the adjoining buildings in order to enlarge his premises, Watto's business future is uncertain thanks to numerous gambling losses. His locales are also severely understaffed, with Watto doing most of the work himself. Spoiled by his former slave's surprising skills, the Toydarian can no longer find slaves with enough technical knowledge. The hovering junk dealer now lives in constant fear of thieves and customers who default on payment.

JAWA SANDCRAWLERS

About 150 kilometers (90 miles) from the Lars homestead, on the edge of the Western Dune Sea, just beyond the giant rock canyons of the Jundland Wastes, Anakin encounters a fleet of sandcrawlers that belong to Jawas, who are working with their portable smelter beneath a tent. He questions these tiny, cloaked scrap dealers about the nomadic Tuskens. For only a few small items from his bike pannier—a multitool and a portable scanner—they point Anakin toward the east, advising him to stick to the high ground in order to gain a vantage point from which to descend on the Tusken Raiders, who travel and set up camps in the valleys.

B'THAZOSHE BRIDGE

The Jundland Wastes are dotted with unusual rock forms, many of which have significance to the Tusken tribes who have inhabited this area for thousands of years. Anakin passes under the 90 meter (300 feet)-high B'Thazoshe Bridge (which translates into basic as "bantha horn turned to stone"). Formed by ancient drainage channels, it is the largest natural bridge on Tatooine, and is considered a sacred site by the Sand People. The bridge also marks the boundary of the Tuskens' ancient hunting territory. Sand People have a tradition of letting off rounds of blaster fire before passing through—failure to do so is said to bring bad luck on the tribe.

TUSKEN RAIDER CAMP

Tusken settlements are scattered across Tatooine's deserts. Because the Tuskens are a nomadic species, they keep few possessions beyond weapons and food stores, although they set great store on the spoils of raids on Jawas or human settlers. These raids are not entirely mercenary, but are intrinsic to Tusken culture, which demands that males prove their skill in battle to maintain their standing in the tribe. Prisoners taken in such raids are usually subjected to harsh rituals.

BURIAL SITE

Cliegg buries his beloved wife, Shmi, alongside the graves of his parents, Gredda and Lef, and his brother Edern, who died aged 14 when he lost control of the family V-35 speeder. For most Tatooine farmers, the untimely death of family members and friends is a common experience that is borne stoically. Burial is a private matter for these isolated communities. Utility droids dig plots, which are marked by plain headstones. During a simple ceremony, surviving family members usually speak a few poignant last words while the body is placed beneath the hot sand.

SPACEPORTS

THE FLOW OF INTERGALACTIC TRADE makes spaceports common on most inhabited worlds. They range
from the cosmopolitan, bustling megaports on Coruscant to tiny docking bays on outworld planets such as Tatooine.
Most spaceports are noisy, polluted places populated by an entire community of pilots, mechanics, inspectors, parts dealers,
and smugglers. These professionals talk the complex language of galactic spacecraft, while spacers discuss little-known,
high-risk space routes and tell tales of encounters with pirates. Working alongside the spaceports is space traffic control,
which receives landing requests from incoming craft and assigns docking coordinates, allowing them to land safely.

TATOOINE DOCKING BAYS

Mos Espa is dotted with dozens of small to mid-size docking bays, equipped for refueling and general repairs. Many bays are rented by spacers running missions ranging from simple cargo and passenger delivery to smuggling of contraband. Arrivals are usually greeted with a flood of mechanics-for-hire, droid taxis, con-artists, beggars, and courtesans.

YT-1300 light freighter — Space traffic control — Maintenance hangar — N-1 starfighters —

THEED SPACEPORT

Dominating the land below the great cliffs, Theed Spaceport is an unprecedented development in the Naboo's tradition-bound culture. Its unadorned, functional construction is testament to the speed and urgency with which it was built. The only nod to the Naboo design aesthetic is its elegantly curved docking platform, which mimics the natural sweep of the cliffs. Built with reparation money from the Republic after the Trade Federation invasion, the spaceport accommodates the increased space traffic resulting from Senator Amidala's high-profile tenure. The spaceport also receives immigrants seeking mining work on Naboo's spice-rich moons.

CORUSCANT SPACEPORT

When Anakin Skywalker accompanies Padmé Amidala into hiding off-planet, he is advised that the least noticeable way to leave is via a freighter spaceport. The huge craft that dock here are cargo carriers, transporting luxury goods from Coruscant to every corner of the galaxy, and returning with raw materials not available on the urbanized capital planet. These craft are not passenger ships, although many impoverished emigrants obtain steerage on them. Passenger areas are made and furnished with makeshift components, with unreliable air and life-support. As well as migrants, the spaceport is busy with loading droids and overseers ensuring that each ship receives its correct load of cargo.

SPACEPORT AIRBUS

The spaceport is connected to other parts of Coruscant by civilian airbuses, which provide staff with a low-cost form of transport to and from work. The port is located some distance away from housing areas in a zone of the city dedicated to the shipping industry, so this public transportation link is essential. Crowded at certain times of day or night when work shifts begin or end, it is virtually empty when Anakin and Padmé ride it on their undercover getaway.

Cargo loading droid   Refueling droid   Auxiliary power generator   Cargo modules   Action VI bulk freighter

GEONOSIS

THE RED, OUTER RIM PLANET of Geonosis is ringed by asteroids that were created by the decimation of a local moonlet by a two kilometer-wide comet. The planet surface is scarred from falling meteors and episodic radiation storms, which have caused several mass extinctions. The semi-insectoid Geonosians—the planet's higher life-forms—were consequently driven underground, where they now inhabit hives and manufacture battle droids. The planet's barren exterior is dominated by huge insectoids called merdeths, and various other animals, including savage massiffs.

SECRET HANGAR

In his Delta-7 Jedi starfighter, Obi-Wan follows Jango and Boba Fett in their spaceship *Slave I* from Kamino to Geonosis. The bounty hunter descends toward small shutter doors located beside the docked Trade Federation core ships. Jango uses a clearance code signal to enter a hangar inside the underground droid-loading bays. These small hangars dot the perimeter of the droid loading fields, and are equipped with Geonosian fighters ready to make lightning strikes against the occasional marauding merdeth or other uninvited visitors. The Geonosians are particularly vigilant when clients are taking receipt of their droid units.

CORE SHIPS

The Geonosians have begun to fulfill their battle droid order for the Separatist Alliance, and the first fleet of battleships has arrived to take delivery of the units. Core ships detach from the orbiting Trade Federation battleships and land in docking bays that connect to the droid factory loading hangars wherever fissures in the ground make excavation possible. The ships lower in stages into the docking bays to facilitate transferral of the droids into storage holds on various levels. The core ships also undergo maintenance and are upgraded with hardware for the semi-autonomous droids.

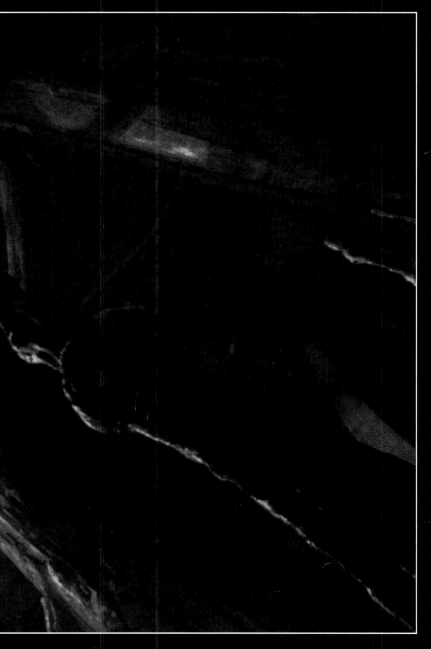

HIVE GALLERIES

The Archduke of the ruling Stalgasin hive colony, Poggle the Lesser, takes his business clients, the Neimoidians, around one of the galleries inside the hive entrance tower, toward the suite of meeting rooms provided for esteemed guests. Geonosian hives are connected to each other by kilometers of populated tunnels that extend underneath much of the planet; each hive guards its own tunnels with vigilance. Periodically, great wars are fought for control of the major hives, with battles taking place throughout the tunnel networks. Few outsiders know that Geonosian nobles like Poggle are themselves servants of ruling queens, who dwell deep below their colonies or in secret redoubts, sending emissaries to issue orders to their underlings.

ENTRANCE TOWER

The factory entrance tower that Obi-Wan encounters after he lands on Geonosis is an impressive piece of Geonosian hive architecture. Every major factory has a grand entrance like this, through which Geonosians receive visiting clients. Meeting rooms and board rooms are located along nearby corridors, which means that customers are afforded only the briefest of glimpses into the turmoil of the factory before signing the all-important contract. The Geonosis landscape is dotted with similar rock towers, constructed from solidified rock paste strengthened with a laminasteel framework. Most towers act as cooling chimneys for the heavily populated hives below, letting out hot air through side vents. The factories typically lie just beneath the surface, with living areas for the drones alongside; beneath this are the more opulent nests and public spaces occupied by the ruling caste. Deeper still are enormous caverns fed by underground streams in which an edible fungus is cultivated. The queen's egg chamber occupies the deepest level, though the Stalgasin matriarch, Karina the Great, has abandoned her chamber for more secure quarters.

DROID FACTORY

GEONOSIS' GIGANTIC FACTORIES mass-produce droids, vehicles, weapons, and military parts for a select range of shadowy clients. The underground factories are grimy, noisy, foul-smelling places cut from the rock of the planet and maintained by a slavish workforce of flightless Geonosian drones. The Geonosians tinker relentlessly with their manufacturing processes until they achieve peak efficiency, with maimed and crushed drones an unavoidable price of achieving such gains. Speed and reliability are the hives' main concerns, an attitude that appeals to the Separatist Alliance's ruthless commercial instincts. It is in this hostile environment that Anakin and Padmé find themselves battling for their lives against the machinery's inhuman might.

Droid manufacturing is virtually automated, utilizing a network of conveyor belts to turn molten metal into an army of fighting machines.

Droideka manufacturing zone

Anakin's hand is trapped inside section of super battle droid shoulder

Central hub delivers molten metal to the stamps for each part being built

Vent shaft

White mineral deposits from vaporizing gases

Retractable ledge used by winged Geonosian overseers

Geonosian drones attack Anakin and Padmé

Surplus workers in storage alcoves

Padmé's starship lands on an inspection platform

SRT (Short-Range Transport) droid picks up C-3PO

Airlock doors to small maintenance antechamber with security consoles, used by Geonosian drones to raise the alarm at Anakin and Padmé's arrival

Power-generator hub

Cooling plates extract water and usable gases from exhaust fumes for use in the factory

SLEEPING DRONES

In between shifts, workers rest in storage alcoves located in warm corridors off the factory floor. They do not actually sleep, but slow their breathing and reduce the circulation to their limbs and extremities. They remain alert despite their stillness and it takes little to rouse them. The Geonosian rulers realize the usefulness of having such a vast number of watchful (but dispensable) eyes.

Nests of spider-sponges survive on the toxic waste gases produced by the factory

Air vent

Fusion reactor unit delivers power to entire factory and regulates temperature of molten metal

Anakin jumps onto lower conveyor

Mold-stamping equipment

Worker drones build factory extensions whenever large droid orders require extra space

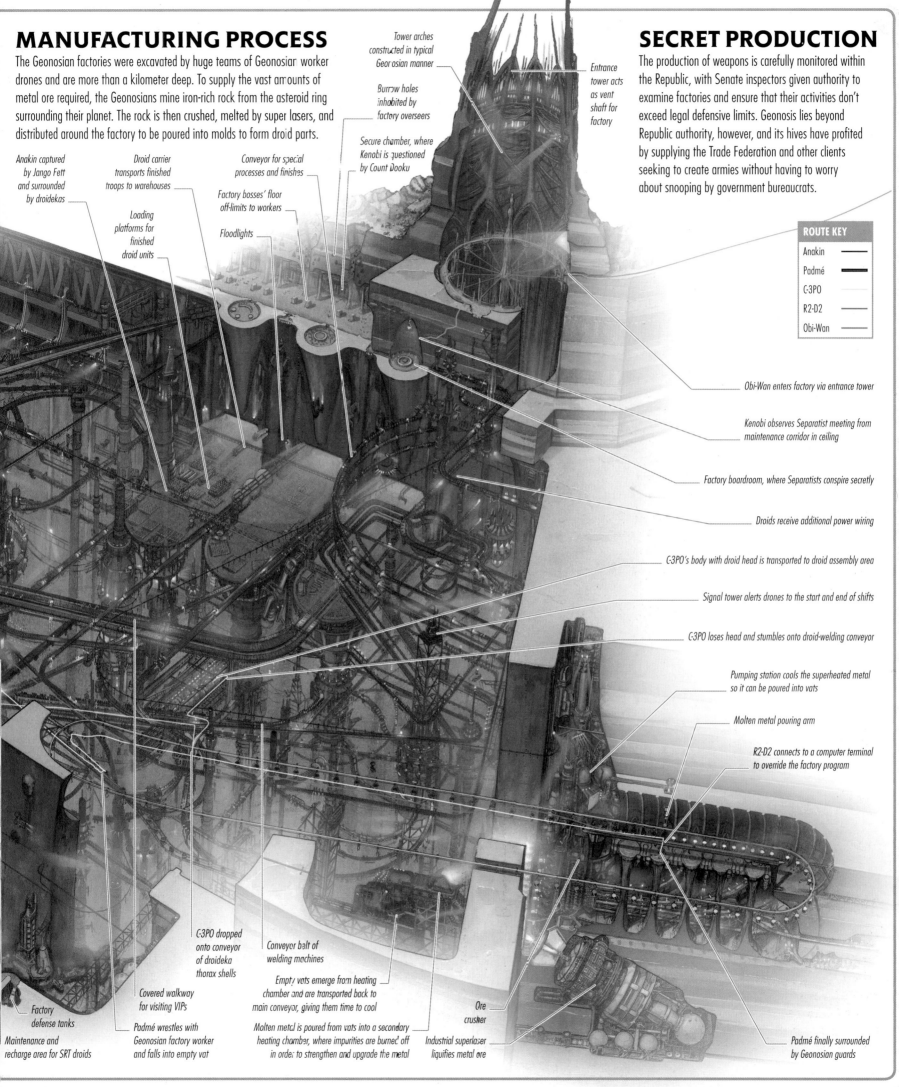

MANUFACTURING PROCESS

The Geonosian factories were excavated by huge teams of Geonosian worker drones and are more than a kilometer deep. To supply the vast amounts of metal ore required, the Geonosians mine iron-rich rock from the asteroid ring surrounding their planet. The rock is then crushed, melted by super lasers, and distributed around the factory to be poured into molds to form droid parts.

Tower arches constructed in typical Geonosian manner

Burrow holes inhabited by factory overseers

Secure chamber, where Kenobi is questioned by Count Dooku

Entrance tower acts as vent shaft for factory

Anakin captured by Jango Fett and surrounded by droidekas

Droid carrier transports finished troops to warehouses

Conveyor for special processes and finishes

Loading platforms for finished droid units

Factory bosses' floor off-limits to workers

Floodlights

SECRET PRODUCTION

The production of weapons is carefully monitored within the Republic, with Senate inspectors given authority to examine factories and ensure that their activities don't exceed legal defensive limits. Geonosis lies beyond Republic authority, however, and its hives have profited by supplying the Trade Federation and other clients seeking to create armies without having to worry about snooping by government bureaucrats.

ROUTE KEY

Anakin ————

Padmé ————

C-3PO ————

R2-D2 ————

Obi-Wan ————

Obi-Wan enters factory via entrance tower

Kenobi observes Separatist meeting from maintenance corridor in ceiling

Factory boardroom, where Separatists conspire secretly

Droids receive additional power wiring

C-3PO's body with droid head is transported to droid assembly area

Signal tower alerts drones to the start and end of shifts

C-3PO loses head and stumbles onto droid-welding conveyor

Pumping station cools the superheated metal so it can be poured into vats

Molten metal pouring arm

R2-D2 connects to a computer terminal to override the factory program

C-3PO dropped onto conveyor of droideka thorax shells

Conveyor belt of welding machines

Ore crusher

Factory defense tanks

Covered walkway for visiting VIPs

Empty vats emerge from heating chamber and are transported back to main conveyor, giving them time to cool

Maintenance and recharge area for SRT droids

Padmé wrestles with Geonosian factory worker and falls into empty vat

Molten metal is poured from vats into a secondary heating chamber, where impurities are burned off in order to strengthen and upgrade the metal

Industrial superlaser liquifies metal ore

Padmé finally surrounded by Geonosian guards

EXECUTION ARENA

FOR THE GEONOSIAN MASSES, who live most of their lives underground, a visit to the execution arena is a dramatic and festive occasion. As the surface of the planet is dominated by fierce predatory insects, the risk of the arena being attacked is an added thrill. As the ruling archduke watches imperiously, drones and aristocrats crack their forelimbs together in appreciation of staged events: public executions, unarmed prisoner combat, and choreographed battles that demonstrate the military skills of new droid prototypes or Geonosian soldier hatchlings.

The Geonosian crowds at the execution arena are at a fever pitch of excitement in anticipation of ferocious action in the ring and fear of attack by predators. Not surprisingly, they scatter en masse at the unexpected arrival of 200 lightsaber-wielding Jedi at the coliseum.

Upper ledges with bird's-eye view generally taken only by latecomers

High-ranking officials sit under membrane awnings, mainly to draw attention to their exalted position

Vertical windows in towers also serve as entrances for upper-caste, winged Geonosians

The richer Geonosian classes occupy the better-kept, lowest seats

Anakin, Padmé, and Obi-Wan on reek, surrounded by droidekas

Arena base has ancient low-relief carvings depicting famous battles and events

Soldier drones bringing out sonic cannon

Weequay Jedi Sora Bulq and apprentice Galdos Stouff defeat a dozen encircling guards

Columns of smoke given off by arch grubs being lightly grilled

Arena floor made of layers of dried silt and sand

Reek pen, with food stores to the side

Flightless Geonosians attempting to flee

BLOODY ORIGINS

The arena is a natural geological formation that has been adapted by the Geonosians with the addition of towers and excavated tunnels inside and beneath. Its blood-drenched history goes back to the first overlords of Geonosis. These legendary giants were expected to prove their fitness to rule by battling their rivals in brutal death matches for the benefit of the public.

Geonosian fighter hangars

Secure holding pen for tiny, mutant mongworsts

Acklay pen, with acklay's mate still housed inside

Growth pit for speciality fungus that interacts with chemicals in Geonosian stomachs to give off a body smell which produces euphoria

Pit of carnivorous worms being starved for future spectacle

Drainage basin

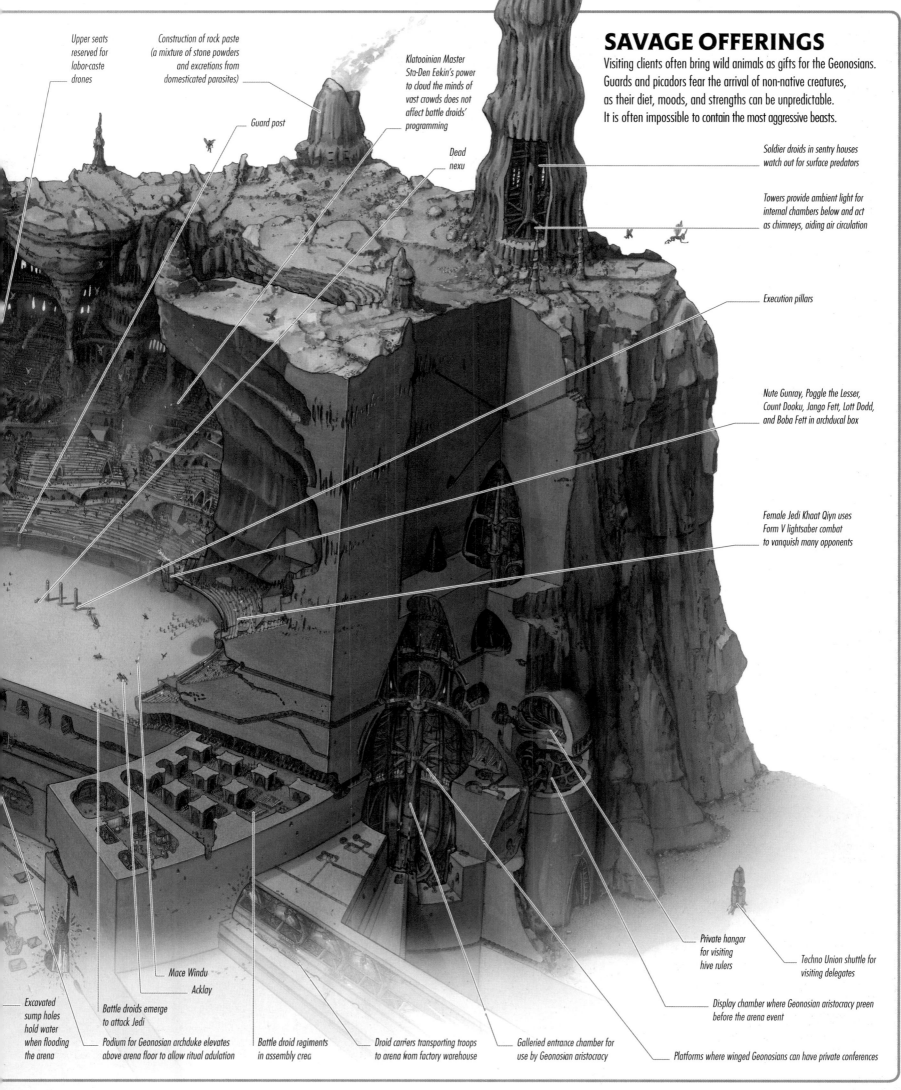

Upper seats reserved for labor-caste drones

Construction of rock paste (a mixture of stone powders and excretions from domesticated parasites)

Guard post

Klatooinian Master Sta-Den Eekin's power to cloud the minds of vast crowds does not affect battle droids' programming

Dead nexu

SAVAGE OFFERINGS

Visiting clients often bring wild animals as gifts for the Geonosians. Guards and picadors fear the arrival of non-native creatures, as their diet, moods, and strengths can be unpredictable. It is often impossible to contain the most aggressive beasts.

Soldier droids in sentry houses watch out for surface predators

Towers provide ambient light for internal chambers below and act as chimneys, aiding air circulation

Execution pillars

Nute Gunray, Poggle the Lesser, Count Dooku, Jango Fett, Lott Dodd, and Boba Fett in archducal box

Female Jedi Khaat Qiyn uses Form V lightsaber combat to vanquish many opponents

Mace Windu

Acklay

Excavated sump holes hold water when flooding the arena

Battle droids emerge to attack Jedi

Podium for Geonosian archduke elevates above arena floor to allow ritual adulation

Battle droid regiments in assembly crea

Droid carriers transporting troops to arena from factory warehouse

Galleried entrance chamber for use by Geonosian aristocracy

Private hangar for visiting hive rulers

Techno Union shuttle for visiting delegates

Display chamber where Geonosian aristocracy preen before the arena event

Platforms where winged Geonosians can have private conferences

REPUBLIC ARMY

FACING THE OMINOUS REALITY of a Separatist war machine poised for an all-out attack on the great Galactic Republic, the Senate has no choice but to respond quickly and decisively. The risks are great: The Republic must deploy an army it has neither amassed nor trained, and whose battle effectiveness is as yet unproven. The Jedi Council's skillful command, however, ensures that the Republic's bold, pre-emptive strike on the Separatist forces is effective, by utilizing a full complement of battle vehicles to achieve air and ground supremacy against formidable odds in the unfamiliar landscape of Geonosis.

With high-ranking Jedi acting as de facto generals, more than 80 regiments of clone troopers are deployed on Geonosis. The clones use imaging systems in their helmet visors to see through dense smoke on the battlefield, allowing an unbroken advance on the Trade Federation battle droids.

LAAT/C

LAAT/c (Low-Altitude Assault Transport/carrier) are used to airlift military hardware right into the thick of battle, such as AT-TEs, portable power generators and shield projectors, observation posts, field medical centers, supplies, and fixed artillery. They also ensure the heavy-strike SPHA-Ts are well defended by AT-TEs and infantry on foot to a distance of several kilometers. Magnetic clamps hold payloads in place and can be disengaged instantly, allowing the payloads to be dropped speedily. A wide wingspan allows maximum distribution of repulsorlift vanes when carrying heavy weights.

REPUBLIC TROOPERS

On Geonosis, the Republic deploys two full battle armies, with Yoda and Mace Windu commanding one each and other veteran Jedi Knights in charge of eight corps of 36,864 troops each. All other divisions are led by specially trained clones: Commanders head regiments of 2,304 men; clone captains lead companies of 144 men; lieutenants head platoons of 36 men, and sergeants command squads, each made up of nine clone troopers. Separate ranks of specialized clones operate gunships, drop ships, AT-TEs, and SPHA-Ts.

TROOPER   SERGEANT   LIEUTENANT   CAPTAIN   COMMANDER   LAAT/I GUNSHIP
192,000 DEPLOYED IN BATTLE   1600 DEPLOYED

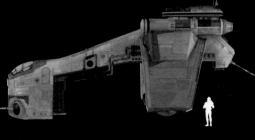

LAAT/C (AT-TE CARRIER)
400 DEPLOYED

GUNSHIPS

Fast and maneuverable LAAT/i gunships make repeated passes over the entire battlefield, responding to situations and opportunities wherever needed. They rain fire on enemy vehicles, clearing a path for the advancing clone infantry, and drop squads of clone trooper commandos at the battlefront. Commandos are specially trained for high-risk covert work and wear a higher grade armor with additional weapons capacity. Despite their strengths, gunships prove vulnerable to Separatist antiair batteries positioned in rough terrain below.

DEADLY JUGGERNAUT

Deployed in squads of four at the rear of advancing AT-TEs, SPHA-Ts combine the devastating firepower of a permanent laser-cannon emplacement with the ability to literally walk into battle on powerful articulated legs. SPHA-Ts are deployed in key positions on several battlefronts, proving particularly effective on the battlefield commanded by Yoda. They also provide an impregnable line of defense for the fleet of assault ships that land immediately outside the arena.

ASSAULT SHIPS

Acclamator-class assault ships land outside the smoking arena, unloading military vehicles and troops, and providing an assembly point for SPHA-Ts. Disembarked troops initially prevail on the flat ground of the canyon floor, where their beam weapons are most effective, while Separatist artillery persists in the rougher lands. Earlier, assault ships made preemptive strikes against Geonosian beak-wing facilities, leaving the fighters that remained unable to make headway against the Republic's orbital blockade.

AT-TE
2160 DEPLOYED

SPHA-T
100 DEPLOYED

ASSAULT SHIP
12 DEPLOYED

SEPARATIST FORCES

ALTHOUGH THE REPUBLIC FORBIDS the existence of mass armies, many private interests maintain small armies in local territories. The most powerful armies are those owned by the wealthy commerce organizations, who use a number of attack droids for purposes of debt collection and revenue enforcement. However, these trade bodies have now illegally pooled their armies to create a single, truly sinister force that threatens the hegemony of the Republic. Geonosis' barren rock landscapes are the backdrop to its clone army's first encounter with the combined ranks of the commerce organizations' droid armies.

In the Command Room behind Separatist lines, Geonosian rulers observe and direct the battle on a live-feed holomap provided by at-site camdroids. The Separatists are able to reassign battle objectives and targets to their droid forces via radio signals to their processors. In the past, the Geonosians staged large-scale training and exhibition battles from the Command Room.

SEPARATIST HARDWARE

Surprised by the Republic's assault, the Separatists mobilize all forces not already loaded onto their starships, supplementing droid contingents with battle droids direct from the factories. They have no airborne vehicles, although spider droids and hailfire droids carry ground-to-air weapons, which prove effective against Republic gunships. Techno Union starships and Trade Federation core ships carry no weapons, and rely on the defense of the droids. Droidekas were preferentially loaded into the escaping starships, and are mostly absent from the battle.

DWARF SPIDER DROIDS

Dwarf spider droids advance in front of a platoon of battle droids, closely followed by homing spider droids, and after that another infantry formation. Their low height allows the larger homing spider droids to fire over them, providing a formidable advance attack. Much of the dwarf spider droid's head space is devoted to power cells for two blasters, one mounted on the head and one underneath. Designed for use in narrow mine shafts, these droids are slow to react to fast-moving targets above or to the side because they cannot swivel their blasters independently of their heads.

BATTLE DROID	SUPER BATTLE DROID	DROIDEKA	DWARF SPIDER DROID	SONIC CANNON	HAILFIRE DROID
1,000,000 DEPLOYED	100,000 DEPLOYED	3,000 DEPLOYED	15,000 DEPLOYED	4 DEPLOYED (IN ARENA)	4,100 DEPLOYED

HOMING SPIDER DROIDS

Commerce Guild homing spider droids are effective against ground-based and airborne targets, covering wide expanses of battlefield at great speed on their all-terrain legs. Sensor equipment locks onto and keeps track of enemy targets, while their dish-shaped laser cannons supply sustained fire. Providing effective ground cover for the Trade Federation core ships, as well as their own smaller spaceships, homing spider droids manage to decimate whole contingents of Republic AT-TEs although they are eventually subdued by daring gunship assaults.

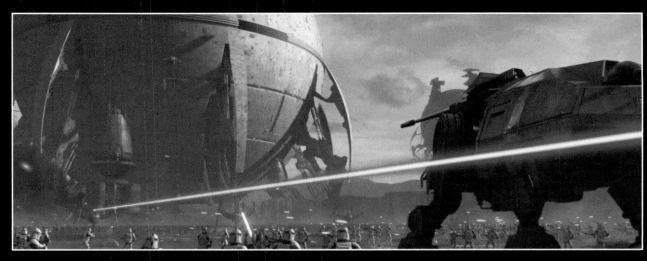

SONIC CANNON

A Geonosian soldier drone operates a sonic cannon, which fires balls of high-impact concussion energy. The Geonosians house an arsenal of these weapons at the execution arena for use in the event of outbreaks by particularly violent creatures or disturbances in the audience. Geonosians also use sonic weapons in inter-hive conflicts. Sonic cannons have an advantage in that they can be set to varying degrees of force, so they smash bones but leave rock tunnels undamaged.

HAILFIRE DROIDS

The InterGalactic Banking Clan's hailfire droids are a powerful presence on the battlefield, although their use is short-lived because they carry a limited number of missiles. They make fast, concerted charges on Republic AT-TEs, using twin chin-mounted blasters once their missiles are depleted. Missiles are effective against stationary or slow-moving targets on terrain where blaster weapons are unusable due to a lack of clear lines of sight.

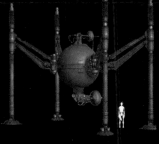

HOMING SPIDER DROID

7,500 DEPLOYED

TECHNO UNION STARSHIP

286 ON BATTLEFIELD (169 ESCAPE)

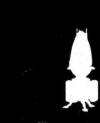

COMMERCE GUILD STARSHIP

41 IN BATTLE (36 ESCAPE)

TRADE FEDERATION CORE SHIP

60 ON BATTLEFIELD (46 ESCAPE)

6 On the battlefield that Mace Windu commands, the Separatists deploy a large number of homing spider droids and dwarf spider droids, followed by battle droid infantry formations. With clear lines of sight across the flat canyon floor, these large droids are able to make terrifyingly effective use of their blaster weapons.

7 Jedi Master Kit Fisto leads a charge of clone troopers, using his Force senses to deflect blaster bolts and protect his men. The Republic army in this part of the battle heads off an attempt by the droid forces to break through a canyon and into the clone ranks.

8 Yoda lands at the Forward Command Center beside a concentration of mighty SPHA-T guns—the Republic's heaviest artillery. Airlifted in by LAAT/c, the mobile Command Center is a fully equipped tactical communications station, receiving signal feeds from clone commanders across the battlefield.

5 Mace and Yoda's gunship lands in a large assembly area protected from rear attack by hills behind. While clone commanders oversee the unloading of clone troops and AT-TEs from assault ships, Windu takes control of clone commando units and Yoda departs for the Forward Command Center.

4 Mace Windu, Yoda, Ki-Adi-Mundi, and Kit Fisto witness a direct hit on one of the six gunships used to evacuate Jedi from the arena. These gunships carry few clone troopers in order to allow more room for Jedi passengers. Yoda silently mourns the addition of more names to the ranks of Jedi lost in the battle.

3 Separatist leaders travel by underground route from the arena to the Command Center. Already unsettled by the sudden appearance of a Republic army, they are now experiencing jammed communication signals and are unable to send in their entire droid armies, many of which are already loaded onto ships.

2 Well-armored and self-shielded Trade Federation core ships attempt to finish loading their huge cargoes rather than launching half-empty at the first sight of danger. Smaller, more vulnerable Techno Union ships attempt to escape with their payloads of droid artillery, but gunship fire prevents many from doing so.

1 Republic gunships make the first assault on Techno Union starships docked outside the arena. The Geonosians build their docking facilities and warehouses primarily in the valleys of their planet, where permanent habitation is undesirable; Geonosian cities are situated mostly on cliff faces and highlands.

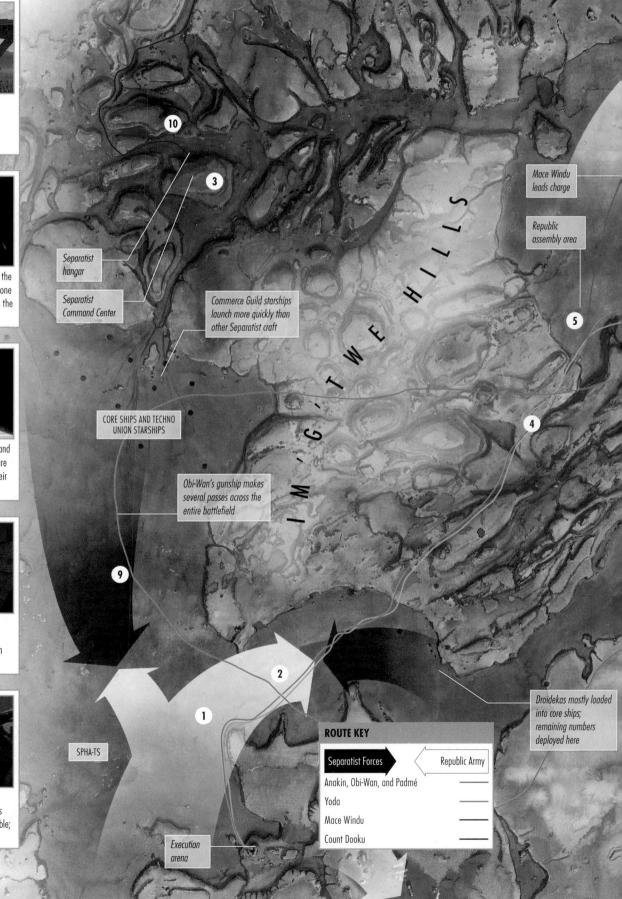

Mace Windu leads charge

Republic assembly area

IM'G'TWE HILLS

Separatist hangar

Separatist Command Center

Commerce Guild starships launch more quickly than other Separatist craft

CORE SHIPS AND TECHNO UNION STARSHIPS

Obi-Wan's gunship makes several passes across the entire battlefield

SPHA-TS

Droidekas mostly loaded into core ships; remaining numbers deployed here

Execution arena

ROUTE KEY

Separatist Forces	← Republic Army
Anakin, Obi-Wan, and Padmé	
Yoda	
Mace Windu	
Count Dooku	

9 In the battle outside the execution arena, hailfire droids roll through the ranks of spider droids, battle droids, and super battle droids toward enemy clone troopers and AT-TEs. Their missiles are most effective at ranges of less than a kilometer, and follow deliberately swerving, evasive trajectories.

10 Fearing that the battle is turning against them, Trade Federation leaders send final orders for their core ships to take off immediately. They leave the war room for a nearby hangar, beating a hasty retreat in their landing ship toward their command ship in orbit around the planet.

11 SPHA-T guns bring down a core ship with focused fire, causing antigrav repulsorlift malfunctions that produce a tractor-beam effect with the ground, greatly accelerating its fall. The SPHA-Ts can only be charged up to a certain level; after these shots, they must be replaced with charged guns from the rear lines.

12 Kenobi sees Dooku and his escort of beak-wings. The Geonosians are unable to deploy more of these fighters due to an aerial bombardment of their launch hives by assault ships commanded by Yoda, which took place simultaneously with the arena rescue; still others were neutralized by clone commando raids.

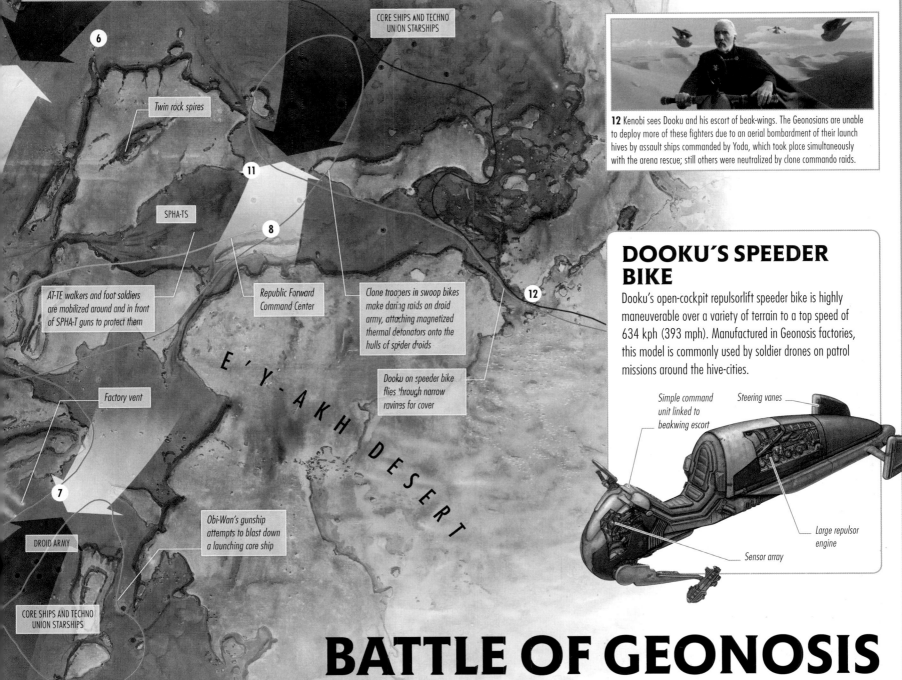

CORE SHIPS AND TECHNO UNION STARSHIPS

6

Twin rock spires

11

SPHA-TS

8

AT-TE walkers and foot soldiers are mobilized around and in front of SPHA-T guns to protect them

Factory vent

7

DROID ARMY

CORE SHIPS AND TECHNO UNION STARSHIPS

E'Y-AKH DESERT

Republic Forward Command Center

Clone troopers in swoop bikes make daring raids on droid army, attaching magnetized thermal detonators onto the hulls of spider droids

Dooku on speeder bike flies through narrow ravines for cover

12

Obi-Wan's gunship attempts to blast down a launching core ship

Obi-Wan's gunship intercepts Separatist droids making a raid through narrow canyon into Jedi ranks

0   5 KM
0   3 MILES
N

DOOKU'S SPEEDER BIKE

Dooku's open-cockpit repulsorlift speeder bike is highly maneuverable over a variety of terrain to a top speed of 634 kph (393 mph). Manufactured in Geonosis factories, this model is commonly used by soldier drones on patrol missions around the hive-cities.

Simple command unit linked to beakwing escort

Steering vanes

Large repulsor engine

Sensor array

BATTLE OF GEONOSIS

WHEN MACE WINDU'S ATTEMPT to rescue Obi-Wan, Anakin, and Padmé from the execution arena ends in failure, Master Yoda's deployment of the clone army becomes inevitable—and the launching of the Clone Wars is the outcome. While Yoda airlifts out the remaining Jedi, other sections of the Republic army focus on halting the departure of the Separatist craft filled with deadly droid troops. The rapidly escalating battle is fought on the ground between troops and battle vehicles, with a number of different fronts opening up. With powerful energy shields on their starships, neither side can overwhelm the other using their ship-mounted cannons; moreover, indiscriminate fire by Republic anti-starship weapons would endanger the droid facilities that it must capture if it hopes to uncover the secrets of the Separatist conspiracy.

HANGAR DUELS

IN HIS DEALINGS WITH THE GEONOSIANS, Count Dooku avails himself of a dedicated hangar removed from the war room and those hangars used by financial and industrial cartel officials. Dooku's hangar lies northward of the main battlefield, in an abandoned factory outpost, where his getaway vessel is manned by an FA-4 pilot droid and stands ready for takeoff. The remoteness of the building suits Dooku's hidden agenda, but the long journey to his ship is almost his undoing: Carrying the Geonosians' secret plans for their ultimate weapon, he is soon sighted by Master Kenobi. . .

DOOKU'S FLIGHT

Leaving the Separatist Command Center, Dooku flies to his hangar by speeder bike, located many miles away across the E'Y-Akh Desert. He skirts around the edge of the battlefield behind Separatist lines, passing close by the gunship in which Obi-Wan travels with Anakin and Padmé.

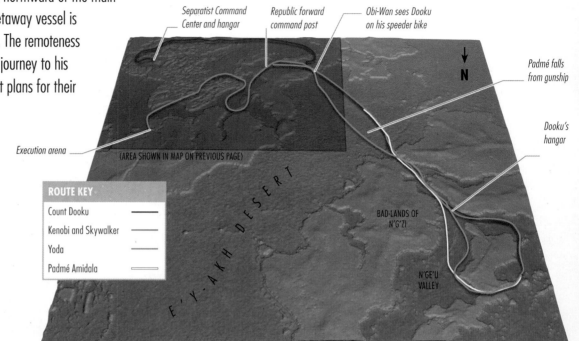

Separatist Command Center and hangar

Republic forward command post

Obi-Wan sees Dooku on his speeder bike

Padmé falls from gunship

Dooku's hangar

Execution arena

(AREA SHOWN IN MAP ON PREVIOUS PAGE)

E'Y-AKH DESERT

ROUTE KEY

Count Dooku	————
Kenobi and Skywalker	————
Yoda	————
Padmé Amidala	————

BAD-LANDS OF N'G'ZI

N'GE'U VALLEY

BATTLE OF WILLS

Alerted by his Force sensitivity, Yoda comes to the aid of Kenobi and Skywalker. Dooku projects ceiling chunks toward Yoda, which risks bringing the entire structure down on both of them. Yoda intercepts and redirects each piece with ease.

LIGHTSABER COMBAT

Yoda knows only too well that if Count Dooku is not stopped from leaving Geonosis, he will rally more planets to his cause. In the half-light of the renegade leader's secret hangar, Yoda wields the lightsaber he so reluctantly uses in combat, attempting to block Dooku's path to his ship.

SEALING THE HANGAR

On Padmé's arrival, contingents of clone troopers seal all the entrances from potential intervention by Separatist troops. Once the battle is over, Republic technicians and intelligence analysts will inspect the building for clues to Dooku's whereabouts.

ABANDONED FACTORY

Dooku's hangar is situated in the pinnacle of a tower above an abandoned factory that once supplied highly specialized, aquatic sonic weapons to both sides during a short-lived civil war on the swamp planet of Derenzil. The risk of the project made a security hangar for Geonosian fighters necessary. The Geonosians build or expand their factories when they receive big orders; afterward, once the project is completed, they relocate the surplus workers or consign them to dormancy.

Vent

Docking clamp for beak-wing fighters

Flight entrance

Geonosian wall construction absorbs shocks from docking spaceships

Maintenance floor used by Dooku's Geonosian fighter escort

Yoda uses the Force to prevent gas-release trunking from crushing Obi-Wan and Anakin

Obi-Wan and Anakin, lying wounded

Inspection walkway

Power feeds and systems diagnostics

Yoda

Dooku escapes into his spaceship

Launch chute designed for Geonosian fighter-class ships

Padmé's gunship

Southwest entrance

Stylized floor mosaic recalls Geonosian egg-nest pattern

Dooku's speeder bike

GEONOSIAN CANYON

Padmé fires at Dooku's solar sailer in a forlorn attempt to stop the dastardly ex-Jedi from leaving the planet. Nevertheless, his ship shoots safely across the wide canyon expanse outside the hangar. This canyon is a former industrial region now totally uninhabited by Geonosians. Like many of the planet's valleys, the flat plain is occasionally flooded by sudden storms or vast groundwater eruptions.

Fuel stores

Reactor powers hangar machinery

Walkway to north entrance (where Kenobi and Skywalker arrive)

EPISODE III
REVENGE OF THE SITH

War! The Republic is crumbling under attacks by the ruthless Sith Lord, Count Dooku. There are heroes on both sides. Evil is everywhere.

In a stunning move, the fiendish droid leader, General Grievous, has swept into the Republic capital and kidnapped Chancellor Palpatine, leader of the Galactic Senate.

As the Separatist Droid Army attempts to flee the besieged capital with their valuable hostage, two Jedi Knights lead a desperate mission to rescue the captive Chancellor....

1 Newly returned from the Outer Rim Sieges, Obi-Wan and Anakin are dispatched to rescue Supreme Chancellor Palpatine. They must recover him alive, as his death from any cause would be a severe blow to the Republic.

2 In their agile Eta-2 *Actis* Interceptors, the Jedi weave between the larger craft slugging out a set-piece engagement. They make their passage through the fighting fleets count, striking at Separatist targets as they go.

JEDI TO THE RESCUE

To rescue the Chancellor before the Separatist Alliance holds the Republic to ransom, the Jedi prepare a special assault squadron led by Anakin Skywalker and Obi-Wan Kenobi with clone force backup. Anakin's boldness and audacity drive the mission to success, and he is lauded as a hero for saving Palpatine. But his cold execution of Count Dooku aboard *Invisible Hand* pushes him closer to the dark side of the Force.

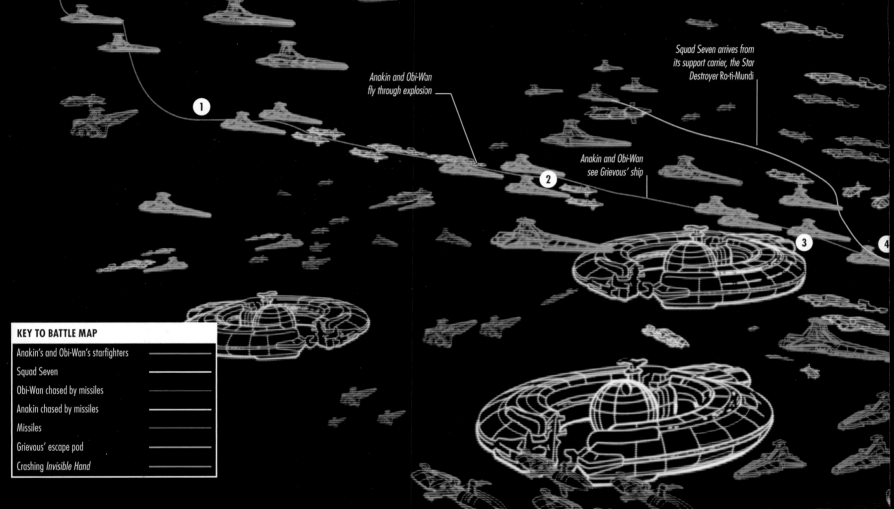

Squad Seven arrives from its support carrier, the Star Destroyer Ro-ti-Mundi

Anakin and Obi-Wan fly through explosion

Anakin and Obi-Wan see Grievous' ship

KEY TO BATTLE MAP

Anakin's and Obi-Wan's starfighters	
Squad Seven	
Obi-Wan chased by missiles	
Anakin chased by missiles	
Missiles	
Grievous' escape pod	
Crashing *Invisible Hand*	

CORUSCANT BATTLE

IN A CUNNING AND AUDACIOUS MOVE, the Separatist Alliance brings the Clone Wars to Coruscant, raining death and destruction upon the helpless citizens of the galactic capital. The fierce attack on the planet is a cover for General Grievous' daring foray to kidnap Supreme Chancellor Palpatine, aiming to bring a swift end to the conflict. While the main battle between Separatist and Republic forces rages on the fringe of space, the Jedi High Council determines that the best way to rescue the Chancellor is to make a lightning raid on the Separatist command ship, *Invisible Hand*, where Palpatine is being held.

SPACE ARMADAS

Both the Separatist Alliance and the Republic have invested heavily in new ships for their space navies, though the former keeps most of its fleet in the Outer Rim. During the battle of Coruscant, the Republic fields a far greater number of heavy craft, such as the *Venator*-class Star Destroyers. The Separatists counter by deploying tens of thousands of vulture droids to supplement their adversary's crewed starfighters.

10 As his ship begins to break up, Grievous escapes, leaving Palpatine and the Jedi to their fate. They will survive a fiery re-entry thanks only to Anakin's piloting skills and the efforts of Coruscant's emergency teams.

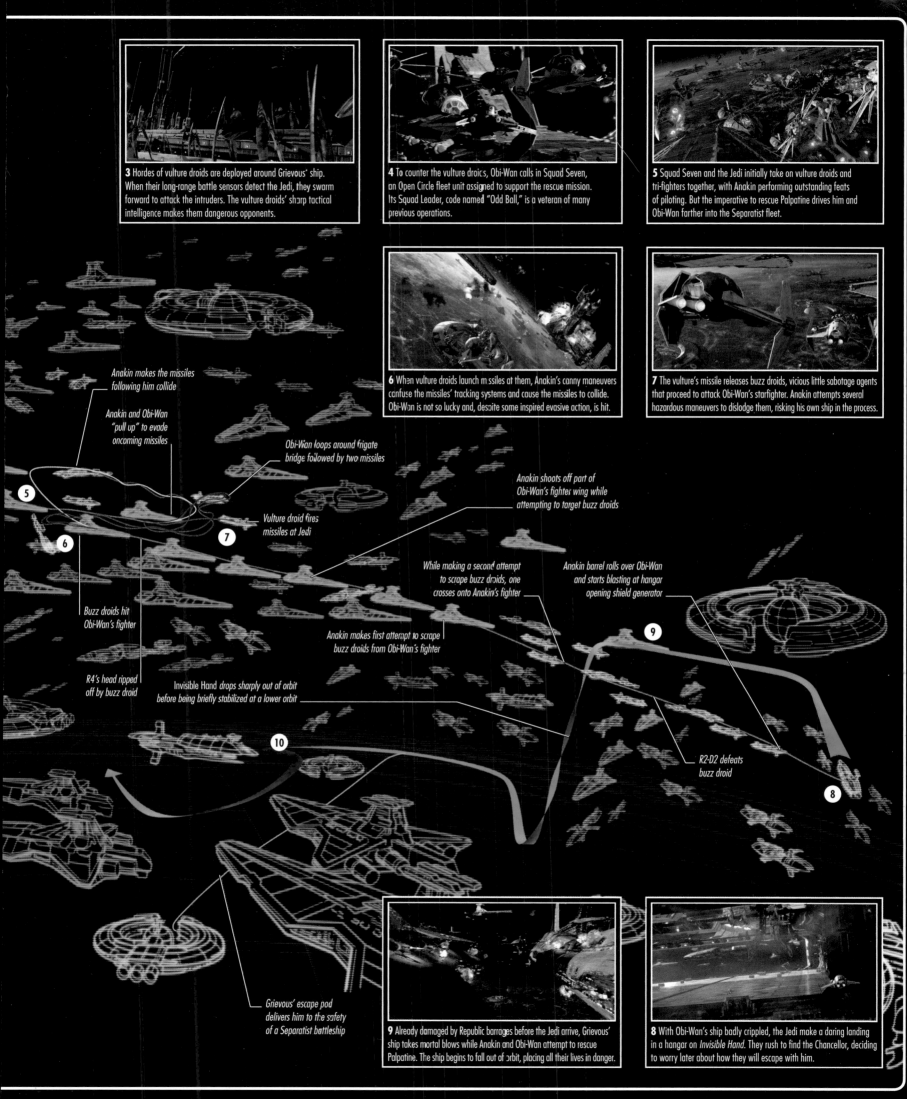

3 Hordes of vulture droids are deployed around Grievous' ship. When their long-range battle sensors detect the Jedi, they swarm forward to attack the intruders. The vulture droids' sharp tactical intelligence makes them dangerous opponents.

4 To counter the vulture droids, Obi-Wan calls in Squad Seven, an Open Circle fleet unit assigned to support the rescue mission. Its Squad Leader, code named "Odd Ball," is a veteran of many previous operations.

5 Squad Seven and the Jedi initially take on vulture droids and tri-fighters together, with Anakin performing outstanding feats of piloting. But the imperative to rescue Palpatine drives him and Obi-Wan farther into the Separatist fleet.

6 When vulture droids launch missiles at them, Anakin's canny maneuvers confuse the missiles' tracking systems and cause the missiles to collide. Obi-Wan is not so lucky and, despite some inspired evasive action, is hit.

7 The vulture's missile releases buzz droids, vicious little sabotage agents that proceed to attack Obi-Wan's starfighter. Anakin attempts several hazardous maneuvers to dislodge them, risking his own ship in the process.

Anakin makes the missiles following him collide

Anakin and Obi-Wan "pull up" to evade oncoming missiles

Obi-Wan loops around frigate bridge followed by two missiles

Anakin shoots off part of Obi-Wan's fighter wing while attempting to target buzz droids

Vulture droid fires missiles at Jedi

While making a second attempt to scrape buzz droids, one crosses onto Anakin's fighter

Anakin barrel rolls over Obi-Wan and starts blasting at hangar opening shield generator

Buzz droids hit Obi-Wan's fighter

Anakin makes first attempt to scrape buzz droids from Obi-Wan's fighter

R4's head ripped off by buzz droid

Invisible Hand drops sharply out of orbit before being briefly stabilized at a lower orbit

R2-D2 defeats buzz droid

Grievous' escape pod delivers him to the safety of a Separatist battleship

9 Already damaged by Republic barrages before the Jedi arrive, Grievous' ship takes mortal blows while Anakin and Obi-Wan attempt to rescue Palpatine. The ship begins to fall out of orbit, placing all their lives in danger.

8 With Obi-Wan's ship badly crippled, the Jedi make a daring landing in a hangar on *Invisible Hand*. They rush to find the Chancellor, deciding to worry later about how they will escape with him.

JEDI TEMPLE COMPLEX

A REPOSITORY OF THE FORCE

Jedi scholars disagree on the location of the Order's first temple, making cases for Coruscant, Jedha, and Ossus as well as worlds shrouded in myth, such as Tython and Ahch-To. But all agree Coruscant's temple was built around and within a natural spire considered sacred by local Coruscanti as a locus of power, which drew Force-wielders of numerous traditions. The roots of this now-hidden mountain conceal forgotten grottos and lost shrines that remain rich wellsprings of the Force.

THE HEART AND HOME

of the Jedi Order, the Jedi Temple was reclaimed from Sith usurpers some 1,000 years ago—seemingly ending a cycle of victories and defeats that stretched back for millennia. The ancient edifice, built and rebuilt over the centuries, fulfills several roles. It is a place of spiritual growth—a center for contemplation, meditation, and the study of the Force. It serves as a martial-arts academy, training potential Jedi and honing their physical skills to perfection. It is the Order's administrative center and headquarters for Jedi operations during the Clone Wars. And it is a repository of knowledge—open and forbidden, light and dark—that has been safeguarded and studied by generations of Jedi Masters.

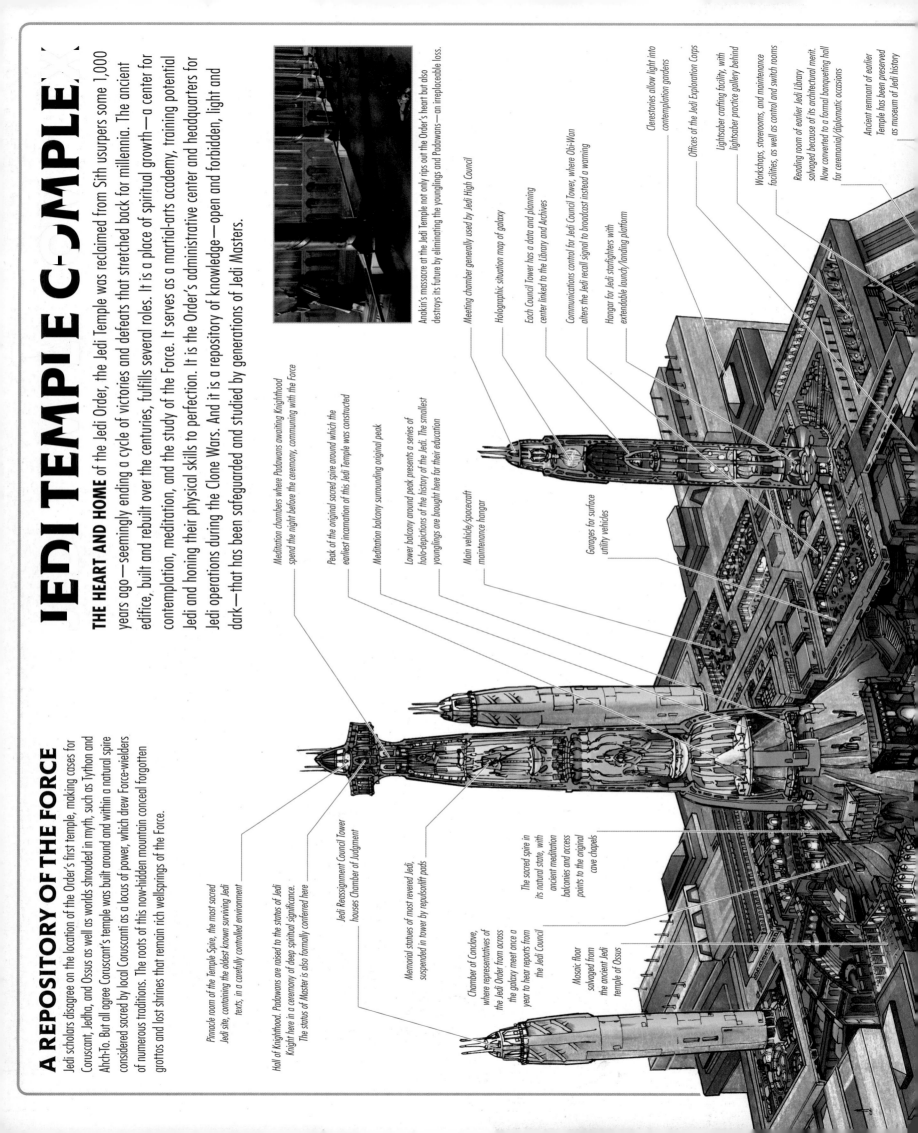

Pinnacle room of the Temple Spire, the most sacred Jedi site, containing the oldest known surviving Jedi texts, in a carefully controlled environment

Hall of Knighthood. Padawans are raised to the status of Jedi Knight here in a ceremony of deep spiritual significance. The status of Master is also formally conferred here

Jedi Reassignment Council Tower houses Chamber of Judgment

Memorial statues of most revered Jedi, suspended in tower by repulsorlift pads

Chamber of Conclave, where representatives of the Jedi Order from across the galaxy meet once a year to hear reports from the Jedi Council

Mosaic floor salvaged from the ancient Jedi Temple of Ossus

The sacred spire in its natural state, with ancient meditation balconies and access points to the original cave chapels

Meditation chambers where Padawans awaiting Knighthood spend the night before the ceremony, communing with the Force

Peak of the original sacred spire around which the earliest incarnation of this Jedi Temple was constructed

Meditation balcony surrounding original peak

Lower balcony around peak presents a series of holo-depictions of the history of the Jedi. The smallest younglings are brought here for their education

Main vehicle/spacecraft maintenance hangar

Garages for surface utility vehicles

Anakin's massacre at the Jedi Temple not only rips out the Order's heart but also destroys its future by eliminating the younglings and Padawans—an irreplaceable loss.

Meeting chamber generally used by Jedi High Council

Holographic situation map of galaxy

Each Council Tower has a data and planning center linked to the library and Archives

Communications control for Jedi Council Tower, where Obi-Wan alters the Jedi recall signal to broadcast instead a warning

Hangar for Jedi starfighters with extendable launch/landing platform

Clerestories allow light into contemplation gardens

Offices of the Jedi Exploration Corps

Lightsaber crafting facility, with lightsaber practice gallery behind

Workshops, storerooms, and maintenance facilities, as well as control and switch rooms

Reading room of earlier Jedi library salvaged because of its architectural merit. Now converted to a formal banqueting hall for ceremonial/diplomatic occasions

Ancient remnant of earlier Temple has been preserved as museum of Jedi history

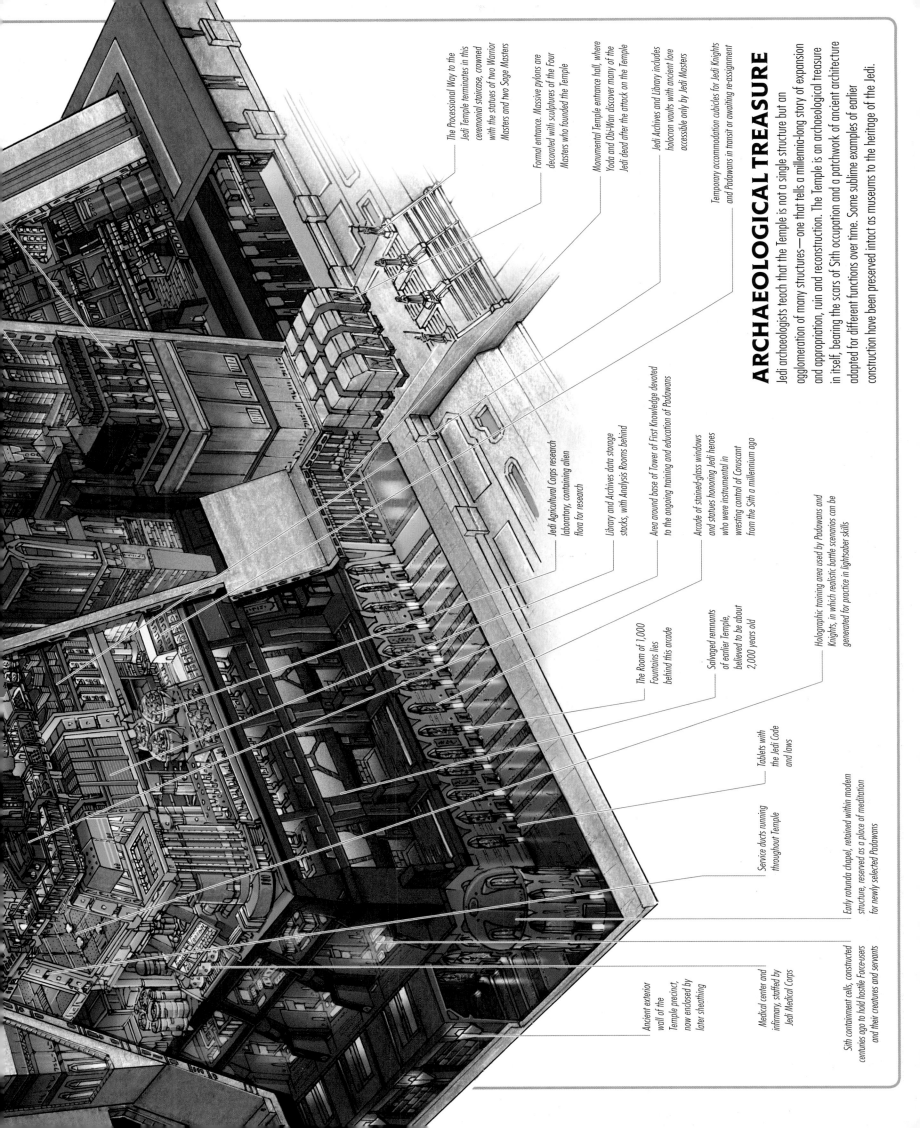

ARCHAEOLOGICAL TREASURE

Jedi archaeologists teach that the Temple is not a single structure but an agglomeration of many structures—one that tells a millennia-long story of expansion and appropriation, ruin and reconstruction. The Temple is an archaeological treasure in itself, bearing the scars of Sith occupation and a patchwork of ancient architecture adapted for different functions over time. Some sublime examples of earlier construction have been preserved intact as museums to the heritage of the Jedi.

The Processional Way to the Jedi Temple terminates in this ceremonial staircase, crowned with the statues of two Warrior Masters and two Sage Masters

Formal entrance. Massive pylons are decorated with sculptures of the Four Masters who founded the Temple

Monumental Temple entrance hall, where Yoda and Obi-Wan discover many of the Jedi dead after the attack on the Temple

Jedi Archives and Library includes holocron vaults with ancient lore accessible only by Jedi Masters

Temporary accommodation cubicles for Jedi Knights and Padawans in transit or awaiting re-assignment

Jedi Agricultural Corps research laboratory, containing alien flora for research

Library and Archives data storage stacks, with Analysis Rooms behind

Area around base of Tower of First Knowledge devoted to the ongoing training and education of Padawans

Arcade of stained-glass windows and statues honoring Jedi heroes who were instrumental in wresting control of Coruscant from the Sith a millennium ago

The Room of 1,000 Fountains lies behind this arcade

Salvaged remnants of earlier Temple, believed to be about 2,000 years old

Holographic training area used by Padawans and Knights, in which realistic battle scenarios can be generated for practice in lightsaber skills

Tablets with the Jedi Code and laws

Service ducts running throughout Temple

Early rotunda chapel, retained within modern structure, reserved as a place of meditation for newly selected Padawans

Ancient exterior wall of the Temple precinct, now enclosed by later sheathing

Medical center and infirmary, staffed by Jedi Medical Corps

Sith containment cells, constructed centuries ago to hold hostile Force-users and their creatures and servants

HOME AWAY FROM HOME

Although Chancellor Palpatine maintains private apartments in the exclusive *500 Republica* residential tower, his office complex also includes a small accommodation suite. Here, the Chancellor can rest during periods of crisis that may require round-the-clock attention or freshen up before a formal function. The suite is reached via a concealed entrance from the Chancellor's office. A hidden passage also allows the Chancellor's aides to discreetly access this area.

Bas-relief found in an archaeological excavation of an unknown world depicts struggle between Jedi and Sith minions on an ancient battlefield

The Chancellor's Archive. Files and correspondence of former Chancellors, stored on holodiscs

Statue of Sistros, concealing Palpatine's lightsaber, has a lining of neuranium under its bronzium exterior

Duranium reinforced, blast-hardened ferrocrete exterior walls

Chancellor's private 'fresher

Access to hidden passage and Archive

Lanthanide alloy sheath isolating suite from rest of building. Provides added protection against fire and impact

Double-glazed transparisteel panoramic window

Covert datalinks allow Palpatine to access Sith databanks concealed elsewhere, monitor private Holonet transmissions, and maintain contact with his secret minions

Palpatine's private office, used when dealing with Republic and Sith matters

Decorative grilles over faux windows conceal building service exhaust vents

Multipurpose anteroom annexes for meetings, waiting, and serving refreshments

Sith Chalice — a form of incense burner used in ancient meditation rituals, recovered during expedition to Malachor

The Chancellor's working office, part of his Secretariat suite, is located directly below the Galactic Senate. It is here that the Chancellor's Podium rests when not elevated into the Senate chamber itself.

Chancellor's offic[e] desk, equipped w[ith] data feeds from [...] private office and [...] working office in [...] Galactic Sena[te]

PALPATINE'S OFFICE

AS THE ELECTED LEADER of the Galactic Senate, the Supreme Chancellor is the most powerful being in the Republic, making the Chancellor's office a hub of power in the galaxy. Chancellor Palpatine has a "working office" in the Chancellery Secretariat, below the Galactic Senate chamber, but his formal, ceremonial office (where he is, in fact, more often to be found) is in the nearby Senate Office Building. Here, the Chancellor's Suite contains both public and private offices for the Supreme Executive of the galaxy, together with meeting areas, space for diplomatic receptions, and administrative offices for the Chancellor's aides. It also contains personal quarters for the Chancellor.

Chancellor's Chair of Office with ultra-dense lanthanide alloy armor. Equipped with a defensive shield, it also provides direct, secure communication with Palpatine's aides and includes a Red Guard summoner

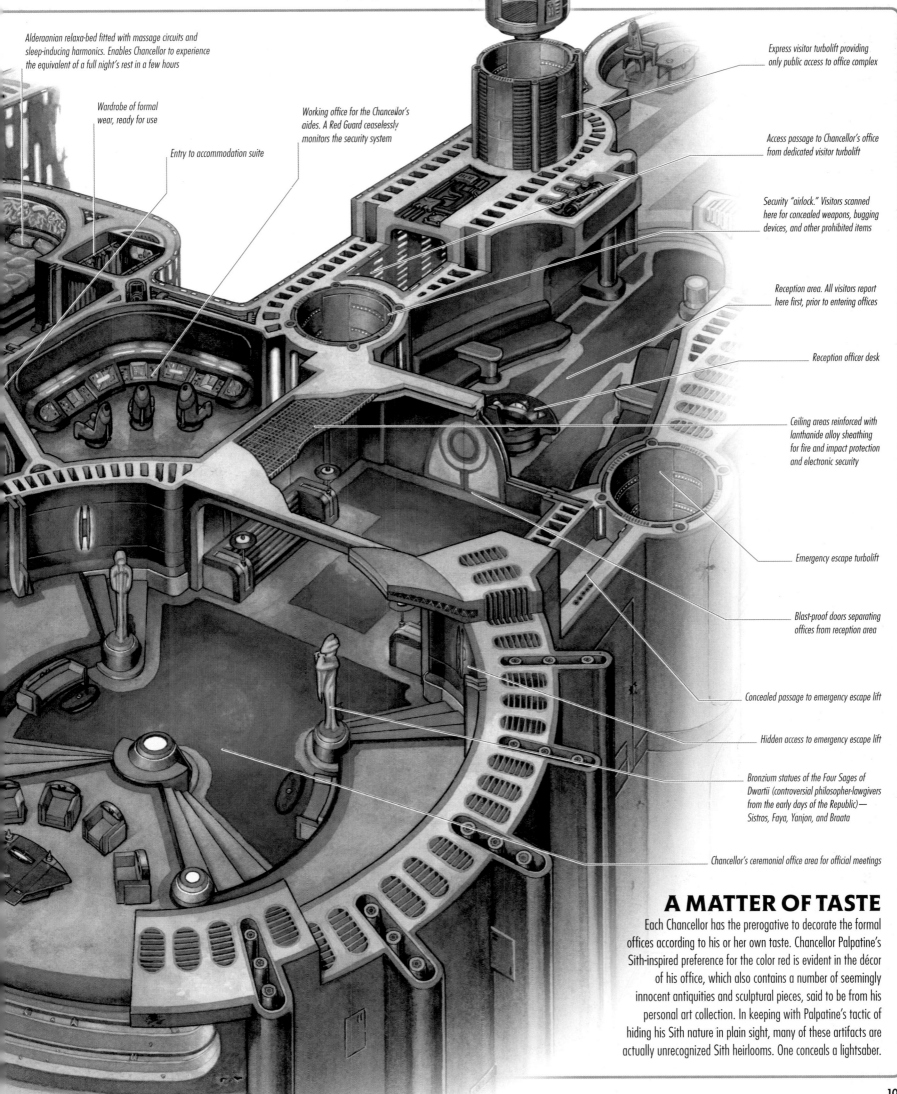

Alderaanian relaxa-bed fitted with massage circuits and sleep-inducing harmonics. Enables Chancellor to experience the equivalent of a full night's rest in a few hours

Wardrobe of formal wear, ready for use

Entry to accommodation suite

Working office for the Chancellor's aides. A Red Guard ceaselessly monitors the security system

Express visitor turbolift providing only public access to office complex

Access passage to Chancellor's office from dedicated visitor turbolift

Security "airlock." Visitors scanned here for concealed weapons, bugging devices, and other prohibited items

Reception area. All visitors report here first, prior to entering offices

Reception officer desk

Ceiling areas reinforced with lanthanide alloy sheathing for fire and impact protection and electronic security

Emergency escape turbolift

Blast-proof doors separating offices from reception area

Concealed passage to emergency escape lift

Hidden access to emergency escape lift

Bronzium statues of the Four Sages of Dwartii (controversial philosopher-lawgivers from the early days of the Republic)— Sistros, Faya, Yanjon, and Braata

Chancellor's ceremonial office area for official meetings

A MATTER OF TASTE

Each Chancellor has the prerogative to decorate the formal offices according to his or her own taste. Chancellor Palpatine's Sith-inspired preference for the color red is evident in the décor of his office, which also contains a number of seemingly innocent antiquities and sculptural pieces, said to be from his personal art collection. In keeping with Palpatine's tactic of hiding his Sith nature in plain sight, many of these artifacts are actually unrecognized Sith heirlooms. One conceals a lightsaber.

UTAPAU

A REMOTE PLANET in the Outer Rim's Tarabba sector, many-mooned Utapau is a quiet, neutral backwater largely ignored by the rest of the galaxy. Its windswept surface, riven with chasms and ridged by fossilized dunes, gives little hint that its sinkholes house vertical cities that harvest minerals from the waters of the planet's subterranean world-ocean. Utapau was settled eons ago, with the original colonists evolving into two separate species: the tall, long-lived Pau'ans and the diminutive Utai. In a bond forged by the necessities of taming Utapau's harsh environment, these two peoples have established a symbiotic relationship, filling complementary niches.

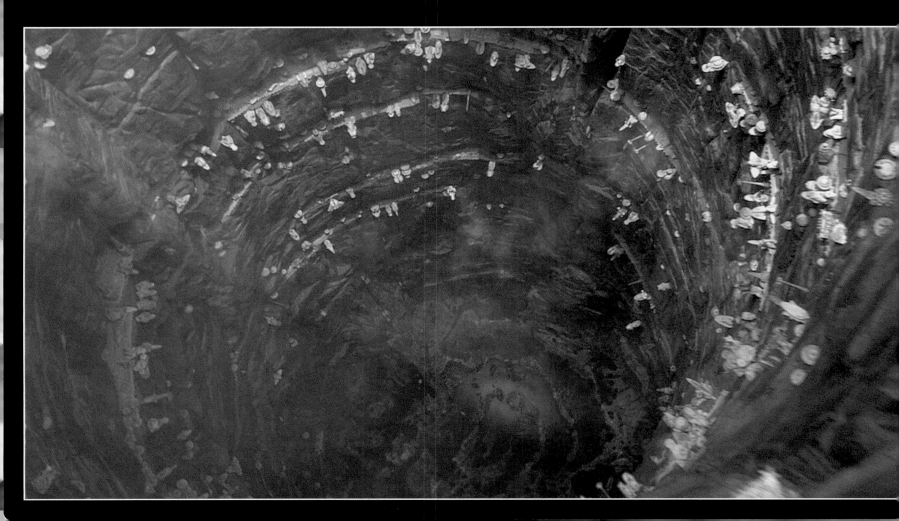

STOLEN NEUTRALITY

Due to its remote location, Utapau is initially able to maintain its neutrality as turmoil engulfs the galaxy, joining neither the Republic nor any other faction. That changes when General Grievous selects Utapau as a hiding place for the Separatist Council in the final days of the war. Republic forces led by Obi-Wan Kenobi subsequently invade the planet, killing Grievous. After the Clone Wars, a steady stream of refugees leaves Utapau, seeking sanctuary on new worlds.

OSSIC ARCHITECTURE

In a world with few trees, bone has replaced timber as a structural material on Utapau. Used raw, seasoned, processed or fossilized, the bones of almost all Utapau's animals are used in construction, creating a unique form of architecture known as "Ossic." The skeletons of the great creatures that roam the lower caves and world-ocean provide bones massive enough to become load-bearing beams, while heavy fossil bone is mined in the sinkholes and caves.

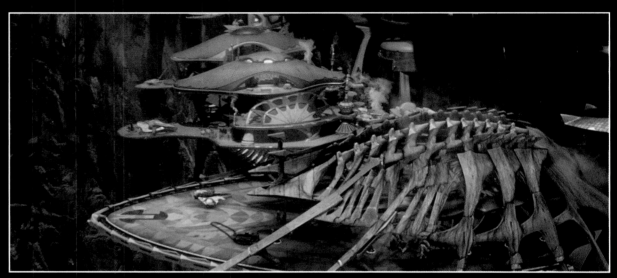

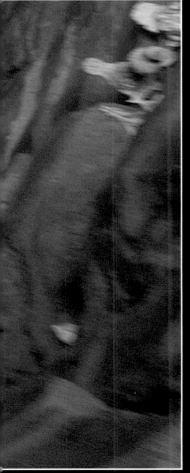

SINKHOLE SANCTUARIES

Pau'ans and Utai are rare sights on Utapau's stormy surface, though recent Amanin colonists have moved out across its plains. Complex tidal forces created by Utapau's nine moons cause massive currents in the world-ocean that erode the underside of its outer crust. These currents also generate groundquakes that cause sections to collapse, creating sinkholes and yawning stress-fracture chasms. Inside these sanctuaries, the Pau'ans and Utai have built underground communities. Most Utapaucn settlements are clustered on a lone "continent," the most stable of its surface plates.

TRADING PORT

Utapau's thinly populated surface and general lack of natural resources meant that the planet had little to offer off-world trade until the value of the minerals, salts, and chemicals derived from the enriched waters of the world-ocean were discovered. To connect Utapau to the interstellar economy, Pau City has developed as the main port for off-world trade, with massive docking bays lining its upper levels, capable of handling ships up to the size of a Trade Federation core ship.

PAU CITY

CAPITAL OF UTAPAU, Pau City boasts almost a million inhabitants, making it by far the largest of Utapau's sinkhole communities. Built underground, in mostly natural caves, Pau City's external access points and spacecraft docking facilities are constructed within the Pau Sinkhole, sheltered from the winds of the planet's surface. The city has 11 levels, which extend around the entire circumference of the sinkhole. To facilitate movement between its levels and to support its role as a tradeport, the city's cliff-face exterior is dotted with large and small landing platforms for craft ranging from bulk carriers to tiny inter-level flitters and dactillions. Subterranean passageways link Pau City with nearby secondary access sinkholes and settlements.

KEY TO MAIN CITY LEVELS

A
B
C
D

Pau City's Grand Hall of the Traders' Guild, now converted by the Techno Union to a factory building Mankvim-814 interceptors

Vent holes providing natural light

Elite residential towers for the wealthy and powerful

Many tall buildings in Pau City act as cavern roof supports, with flat-topped, shock-absorbing "pads" on top of the structure helping to stabilize the rock ceiling in case of groundquakes

Pahum Cultural Center, Pau City's main performance and exhibition venue

The Promenade of Seven Guilds, the main thoroughfare and ceremonial avenue

Wind turbine. Pau City harnesses energy from the surface windstorms to help power the city

Timon Medon Plaza, named after the Unifier of Utapau. To left of plaza is the Utapau Council Chambers

Utapau Off-world Trade Commission, which regulates and controls the off-world mineral trade

Passenger reception facilities and port control buildings

Obi-Wan's landing stage on arrival at Utapau

Port facilities, including main commercial and diplomatic landing stages for off-world craft

Examples of Ossic architecture. Landing platform structures made from the bones of ruhau-whales

Despite his ability to wield multiple lightsabers, General Grievous' planned ambush for Obi-Wan Kenobi is unsuccessful. The resourceful Jedi Master ultimately defeats the Separatist General using a conventional weapon.

Dactillion roost, where they rest and sleep between flights while "on duty"

Varactyl stables and dactillion landing point

Sinkhole air traffic control

A. CIVIC LEVEL

Pau City's highest level is occupied by the government and bureaucracy, including the Port Administration. The city's major civic and ceremonial buildings are located on this level, together with cultural and recreational facilities and the residences of the Pau'an elite, who manage the planet's civic affairs and trade. In the twilight world of Pau City, being close to natural light from the surface is a status symbol.

General Grievous' ship at Level 10 docking bay

Factories manufacturing domestic appliances and light technology

Seawater extraction and mineral processing plant

High-speed turbolift connecting to lower levels

Pumping station bringing water from the world-ocean to processing plants for mineral extraction

Ossic architecture warehouses

Landing stages for bulk carriers shipping extracted minerals and other manufactured goods

Freight elevator for transporting heavy goods and materials between levels

B. WEALTH LEVEL

Pau'ans place great importance on those industries and trade interests that drive the planet's economy. Consequently, the seawater processing plants from which trace elements and minerals are derived and other important industries are located high up in the city, with easy access to the landing stages and port facilities for cargo loading. Middle-class Pau'ans and the few wealthy Utai also live on this level.

Freight elevator

Utai workers' accommodation

Hydroponic food facilities cultivating ocean-kelps and cave-molds, as well as small food plants high in nutrition

Pens where small livestock are raised

D. MINING LEVEL

Pau's City's lowest level is where waste disposal and mining takes place. Bone mines provide fossilized bone for use in city construction, while building stone and some other ores are also mined here. Although miners may encounter giant resputi and other ferocious creatures in the darkness of the deep caves, the beautiful grottoes and settling ponds of the sinkhole floor are popular places to relax.

C. PRODUCE LEVEL

Functional facilities, city services, and some heavy industries are located toward the bottom of the sinkhole. The Produce Level is where Pau City's main food supplies are produced. Plants, such as ocean-kelps, are grown hydroponically in vast "greenhouse" buildings, and small animals are raised for food. Utapauns prefer their meat uncooked, and freshly butchered meat is delivered every day throughout the city. The dactillions and varactyls are also bred and trained on this level. The city's lower levels are where the Utai mostly make their homes.

Landing stage for meat and other produce to be transported

Bone mine. Source of fossilized bone for building construction

Caverns where the fierce resputi-seals make their lairs. Mine workers are often attacked by breeding resputi if they enter their territory

Grottoes and pools of Coranth. The water is colored blue-green due to calcium minerals absorbed through the crustal rocks

KASHYYYK

THE PLANET KASHYYYK is home to the Wookiees, fierce warriors and clever craftspeople, who share the Kashyyyk system with the reptilian Trandoshans. Located in the Mid Rim's Mytaranor sector, this verdant world sits at the intersection of four well-traveled hyperspace routes and houses an important HoloNet relay station—which makes it a crucial prize during the Clone Wars. Much of the planet is covered with lush forests, dominated by the mighty wroshyr trees in which the Wookiees make their homes. Kashyyyk's trees reach vertiginous heights, the apex of a complex ecosystem that becomes more dangerous the deeper one goes, reaching lightless levels prowled by katarns, wyrm-weavers, and strange, savage creatures spoken of in fireside tales delivered by grizzled Wookiee elders.

DEFENDER OF THE HOME TREE

Yoda modestly claims to have good relations with the Wookiees. He has, in fact, been honored with the ancient title "Defender of the Home Tree" for his role as a Jedi negotiator in several previous incidents involving the Wookiees and their system neighbors, the Trandoshans. For this, and other assistance to the Wookiees, Yoda is also considered a member of the honor families of many Wookiee leaders, as well as all the inhabitants of Kachirho.

ISLAND ASSAULT

Corporate Alliance tank droids and droid gunships launch a massive attack on Kachirho, intending to overrun the settlement and capture the Claatuvac archives before securing the nearby relay station complex. Wookiee warriors flock to Kachirho to help defend the region. Oevvaor catamarans and fluttercraft are thrown into the battle alongside Republic forces in an attempt to repel the invaders and prevent the capture of the town.

SECRETS OF THE GUILD

Besides a strategic location, Kashyyyk offers another valuable prize of war: the lagoons and fjords of the tropical Wawaatt Archipelago shelter the settlements of the ancient Claatuvac Guild, Wookiee cartographers and navigators legendary for their knowledge of secret hyperspace routes crisscrossing the galaxy. The Guild's chief settlement at Kachirho houses its data, which could help the Separatists reverse their declining fortunes in the Clone Wars.

TREACHEROUS ALLIES

Without warning, the clone troopers of the Republic attack the Jedi and Wookiees in response to Chancellor Palpatine's Order 66 command. In the midst of the pitched battle at Kachirho, former allies become foes, creating confusion and sowing death and destruction. Kashyyyk will become an enslaved world, stripped even of its name and designated Imperial territory G5-623. This dark period sees many Wookiees worked to death as slave laborers, but years later the world will be liberated by the forces of the New Republic.

WOOKIEE TREE

THE GIANT WROSHYR TREES OF KASHYYYK dominate the landscape and environment of the planet, with over 1,000 different varieties that have adapted to growing everywhere except at its poles. Living up to 50,000 years, wroshyr trees grow to massive size, reaching several kilometers in height in the deep forests. They form the backbone of a complex multilayered vertical ecosystem, extending from the roots to the crown of the tree. Wroshyr trees are an integral part of the lives of the Wookiees, who inhabit them and refer to themselves as "The People of the Trees." They form the foundation of the material, social, and spiritual culture of the Wookiees.

Kachirho settlement takes its name from Tarfful's home tree and includes several inhabited wroshyrs. Yoda's command post is in the Tree Kachirho, while the headquarters of the Claatuvac Guild is the Tree Vikkilynn.

HOME AND PROTECTOR

Wroshyr trees are so huge that entire communities can live within their hollowed out trunks, which, like caves, provide both shelter from the elements and defense against the many predators that roam the lower levels of Kashyyyk's forests. In the deep forest, Wookiee towns and cities expand outside the tree trunks by constructing platforms resting upon the interlocked branches of close-growing wroshyrs. In coastal environments, such as that of the lagoon-side town of Kachirho, where wroshyrs do not grow so thickly together, settlements are composed of individual tree communities. The tropical wroshyrs of Wowaatt Archipelago are much smaller than the deep forest giants, averaging 300–400 meters (1,000–1,300 feet).

School and crèche, located high in tree for safety

Public walkway around tree interior

Communication antenna complex, including HoloNet and local microwave links

Sap distillery for water supply. Wookiees prefer the slightly sweet taste of distilled sapwater to rainwater

Entertainment complex with bars and restaurants

Theater for performance of traditional Wookiee entertainment

Family dwelling area

Ornately decorated balconies have ceremonial or official functions

Power generator for communication system and electronic equipment

Area for light manufacturing and craftwork

Tree Carers gather seeds from the wroshyr cones when they form every 100 years and save them for planting new trees

Dwelling of the family of Tree Carers, who have quasi-religious status. Members often act as community shamans

Religious shrine, presided over by the Tree Carers

Central markets

Balcony and platform designs derived from shapes of giant fungi

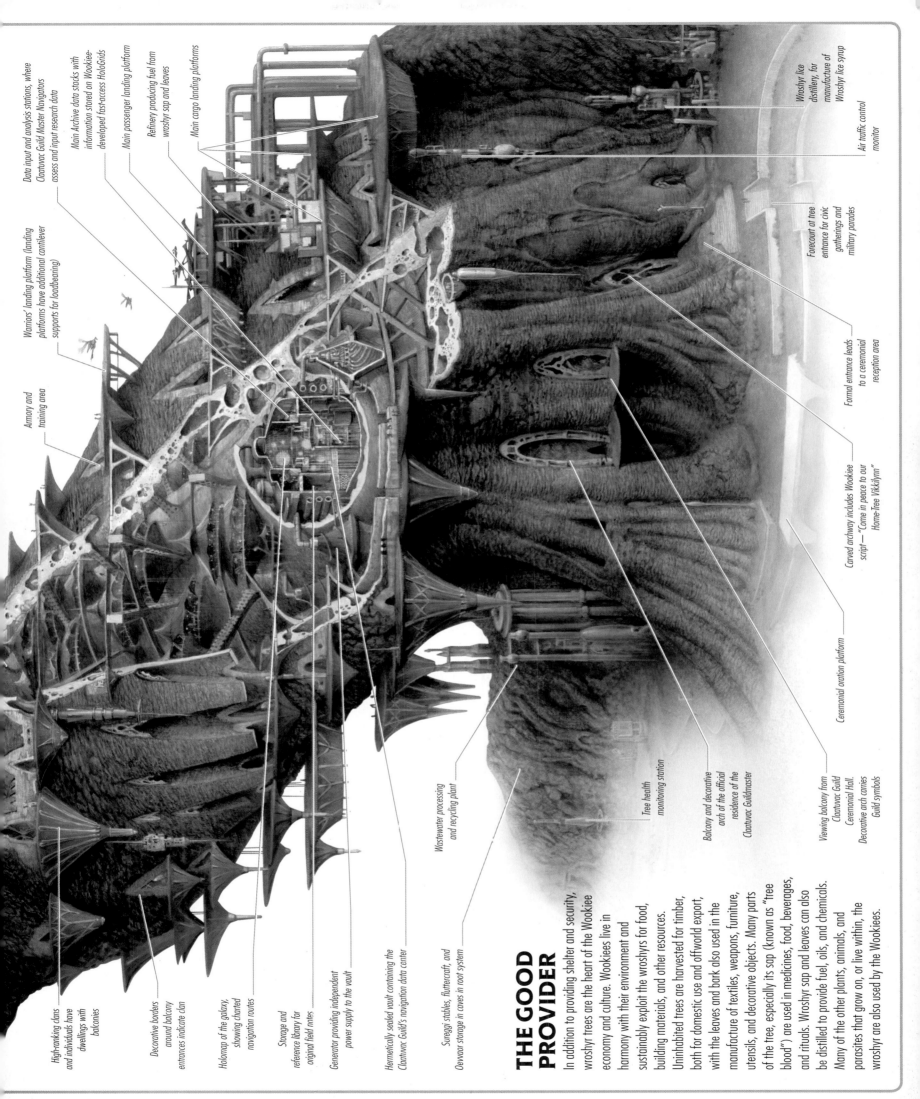

Data input and analysis stations, where Claatuvac Guild Master Navigators assess and input research data

Main Archive data stacks with information stored on Wookiee-developed fast-access HoloGrids

Main passenger landing platform

Refinery producing fuel from wroshyr sap and leaves

Main cargo landing platforms

Warriors' landing platform (landing platforms have additional cantilever supports for loadbearing)

Armory and training area

Wroshyr lice distillery, for manufacture of wroshyr lice syrup

Air traffic control monitor

Forecourt at tree entrance for civic gatherings and military parades

Formal entrance leads to a ceremonial reception area

Carved archway includes Wookiee script — "Come in peace to our Home-Tree Vikkilynn"

Ceremonial oration platform

Balcony and decorative arch of the official residence of the Claatuvac Guildmaster

Tree health monitoring station

Viewing balcony from Claatuvac Guild Ceremonial Hall. Decorative arch carries Guild symbols

Wastewater processing and recycling plant

High-ranking clans and individuals have dwellings with balconies

Decorative borders around balcony entrances indicate clan

Holomap of the galaxy, showing charted navigation routes

Storage and reference library for original field notes

Generator providing independent power supply to the vault

Hermetically sealed vault containing the Claatuvac Guild's navigation data center

Sureggi stables, fluttercraft, and Oevvaor storage in caves in root system

THE GOOD PROVIDER

In addition to providing shelter and security, wroshyr trees are the heart of the Wookiee economy and culture. Wookiees live in harmony with their environment and sustainably exploit the wroshyrs for food, building materials, and other resources. Uninhabited trees are harvested for timber, both for domestic use and offworld export, with the leaves and bark also used in the manufacture of textiles, weapons, furniture, utensils, and decorative objects. Many parts of the tree, especially its sap (known as "tree blood") are used in medicines, food, beverages, and rituals. Wroshyr sap and leaves can also be distilled to provide fuel, oils, and chemicals. Many of the other plants, animals, and parasites that grow on, or live within, the wroshyr are also used by the Wookiees.

BATTLEFRONTS

AFTER THREE YEARS OF CONFLICT, the Republic seems to be winning the Clone Wars. The Jedi are spread thinly throughout the galaxy, acting as generals in command of clone troops. Separatist leaders such as Wat Tambor and Shu Mai have already seen their homeworlds captured by Republic forces, while other Council members' homeworlds are also under siege. Victory for the Republic is in sight when Palpatine's treacherous Order 66 turns the clone troops against their Jedi commanders.

While on patrol for signs of Separatist activity on recaptured Saleucami, Stass Allie is murdered by her wingmen, who fire on her Aratech 74-Z speeder bike.

FUNGUS-WORLD TREACHERY

Strategically located near the Perlemian Trade Route, Felucia is the site of many hard-fought battles during the Clone Wars. The planet is dominated by forests of fungi in hallucinatory colors, and is a valuable source of medicinal spice. Native Felucians share the world with Gossam colonists, among them Shu Mai, Presidente of the Separatist-allied Commerce Guild. Jedi Master Aayla Secura leads an assault on Felucia during the Outer Rim Sieges, where she is assassinated as part of Order 66.

BATTLEFRONT KASHYYYK

The Jedi are determined to assist the Wookiees in defending the planet against a major Separatist assault, and Yoda commits his battalion to the strategically important tree-city of Kachirho. Republic and Wookiee forces prepare to repel the invaders along Kachirho's relatively narrow lagoon frontage, the only viable approach for a seaborne assault on the settlement due to the rugged terrain of the Wawaatt islands.

STRATEGIC TARGET

Kashyyyk's strategic importance is such that, although Jedi Luminara Unduli is already on the planet, additional clone troops under generals Yoda and Vos are dispatched to reinforce Kashyyyk's defenses. While Separatist Alliance forces are repulsed at several landing points on the planet, a massive attack is mounted against the lagoon-city of Kachirho. When the Jedi's clone forces turn against them, Luminara is captured and later executed, though Yoda escapes with the help of Chewbacca and Tarfful.

HAVw A6 Juggernauts are the Republic's answer to the tank droids

This designation indicates an active Republic/Wookiee attack craft

AT-AP "pod walkers" are also deployed in force to support the Republic ground troops and counter the Separatist Alliance spider droids

BRIDGES OF NEIMOIDIA

Homeworld of Separatist Council member Nute Gunray, Cato Neimoidia is famous for its "aerial cities" constructed on vast bridges across the planet's abyssal canyons. A Neimoidian colonial purse-world, Cato Neimoidia's capitulation is a prime strategic goal that would help to end the war. Its bridge cities are under aerial attack from a force led by Jedi Master Plo Koon when he is shot down by his own squadron.

CRYSTAL TRAP

Mygeeto's natural crystal towers, home to the Lurmen species before they were reduced to slave status, are a stronghold of the InterGalactic Banking Clan. On a mission to wipe out entrenched Clan forces on the planet, Jedi Master Ki-Adi-Mundi meets his fate at the hands of the Galactic Marines under the command of Commander Bacara.

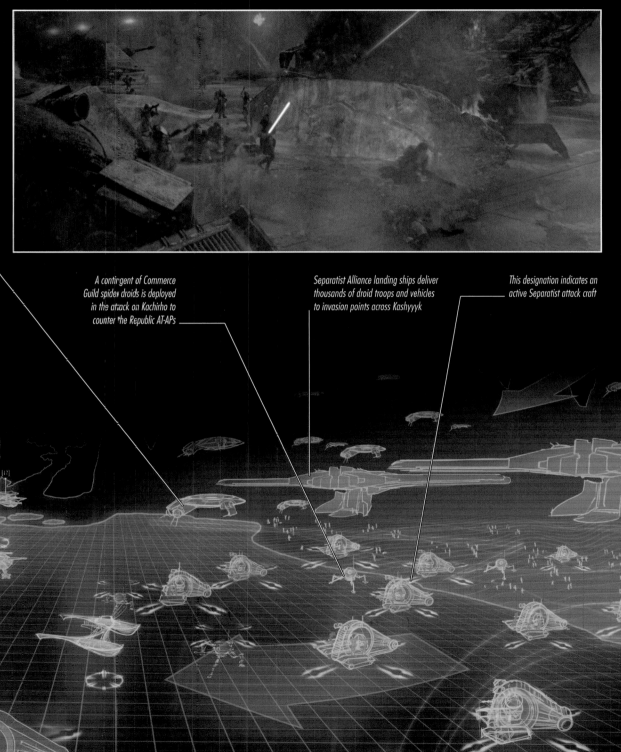

Separatist droid gunships rule the skies at the Battle of Kachirho, while Republic air support concentrates on attacking ground forces

Corporate Alliance tank droids, best suited to frontal assaults, form the backbone of the Separatist ground force at Kachirho

A contingent of Commerce Guild spider droids is deployed in the attack on Kachirho to counter the Republic AT-APs

Separatist Alliance landing ships deliver thousands of droid troops and vehicles to invasion points across Kashyyyk

This designation indicates an active Separatist attack craft

Wookiee Oevvaor catamarans join the heavier Republic units to help repulse the attack. Their agile maneuverability makes them extremely effective against Separatist droid forces

MUSTAFAR

VIOLENTLY VOLCANIC MUSTAFAR is a remote Outer Rim planet that plays a pivotal role in the rise of the Galactic Empire. Though a world in its own right, Mustafar is dwarfed by the great gas giant Jestefad, with which it is twinned. A hellish world of intense heat, savage obsidian mountain ranges, lava rivers, and continuously erupting volcanoes, Mustafar is owned by the Techno Union, which mines the molten precious metals found in the planet's incessant lava flows. Used by the Separatist Council as a hideout during the Clone Wars, Mustafar becomes infamous as the site of the Council's massacre, which clears the way for the rise of the Galactic Empire.

RISE TO POWER

Mustafar was once the site of a Sith temple, a fact well-known to Darth Sidious. During the Clone Wars Sidious maintains a secret outpost here in a former mining complex—which attracts little attention on a planet dotted with Techno Union operations, mining towns, and bolt-holes belonging to the Black Sun crime syndicate. Sidious later chooses Mustafar as the site of the Separatists' final redoubt and Darth Vader's massacre of their leaders, with the planet's dark heritage amplifying the power of this key moment in the rise of the Sith.

HELLHOLE PLANET

Mustafar is a terrifying planet where surface temperatures scorch any unshielded structure or being. Buildings, mining platforms, and robots are all protected by repulsor screens that deflect the heat and suppress the constant eruptions within the lava flows. The Mustafarians swathe themselves in insulating fabrics to survive. Yet, at 800°C (1500°F), Mustafar's lava is "cooler" than normal lava due to unusual mineral allotropes that are molten at lower temperatures.

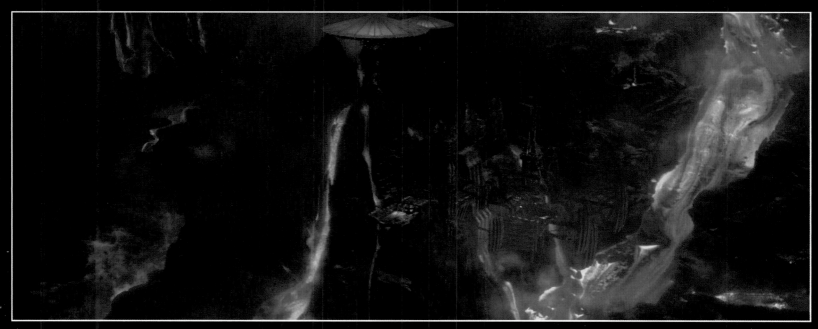

INTELLIGENT ARTHROPODS

Though Mustafar's environment is harsh, hardy life-forms still make the planet their home. Two species now occupy the planet, evolved from extremophile arthropods that developed in insulated caves deep in the mountains. With their chitinous exoskeletons and low-water biology, Mustafarians are able to withstand their world's unforgiving elements but still require insulating clothes and breathing apparatus to work on its surface.

A FIERY RELATIONSHIP

Twin planets Mustafar and Jestefad orbit so close that the massive gravitational field of the gas giant subjects its tiny neighbor to immense tidal forces. These heat Mustafar's interior, melting it and producing its constant volcanic activity. Jestefad's huge electromagnetic field also swamps Mustafar, generating wild electrical storms. Only the counter-balancing gravitational pull from another, more distant gas giant neighbor, Lefrani, prevents Mustafar from being permanently captured as Jestefad's moon.

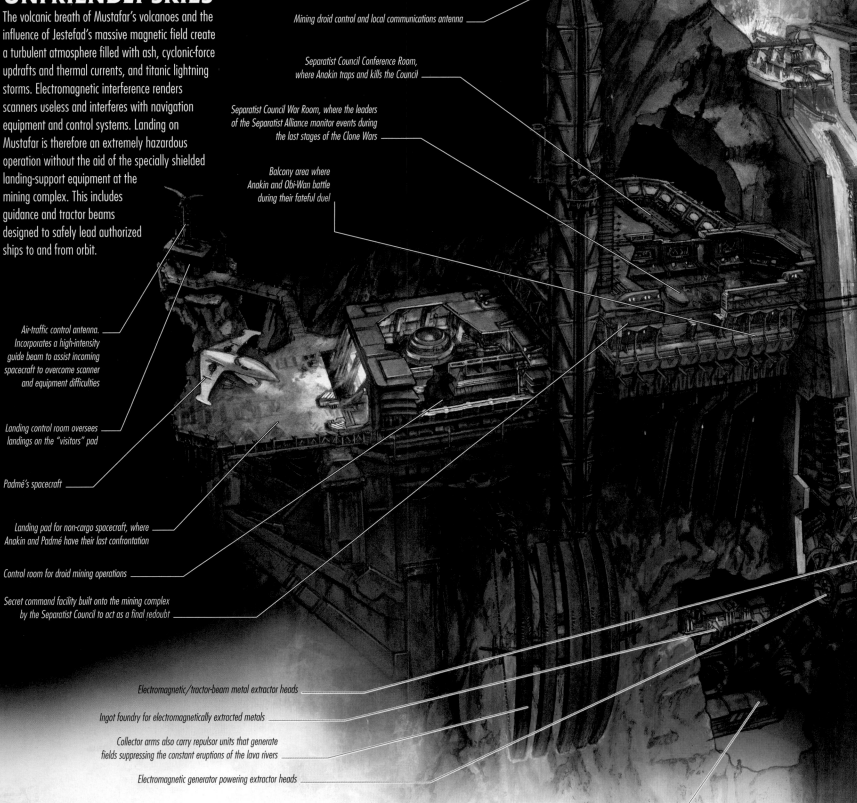

UNFRIENDLY SKIES

The volcanic breath of Mustafar's volcanoes and the influence of Jestefad's massive magnetic field create a turbulent atmosphere filled with ash, cyclonic-force updrafts and thermal currents, and titanic lightning storms. Electromagnetic interference renders scanners useless and interferes with navigation equipment and control systems. Landing on Mustafar is therefore an extremely hazardous operation without the aid of the specially shielded landing-support equipment at the mining complex. This includes guidance and tractor beams designed to safely lead authorized ships to and from orbit.

Mining droid control and local communications antenna

Separatist Council Conference Room, where Anakin traps and kills the Council

Separatist Council War Room, where the leaders of the Separatist Alliance monitor events during the last stages of the Clone Wars

Balcony area where Anakin and Obi-Wan battle during their fateful duel

Air-traffic control antenna. Incorporates a high-intensity guide beam to assist incoming spacecraft to overcome scanner and equipment difficulties

Landing control room oversees landings on the "visitors" pad

Padmé's spacecraft

Landing pad for non-cargo spacecraft, where Anakin and Padmé have their last confrontation

Control room for droid mining operations

Secret command facility built onto the mining complex by the Separatist Council to act as a final redoubt

Electromagnetic/tractor-beam metal extractor heads

Ingot foundry for electromagnetically extracted metals

Collector arms also carry repulsor units that generate fields suppressing the constant eruptions of the lava rivers

Electromagnetic generator powering extractor heads

Geothermal power generators providing main power supply for mining complex

Lava run-off is channeled back into lava river for further mining by droids and Mustafarians

MUSTAFAR MINES

IF NOT FOR THE VALUABLE METALS dissolved in its lava flows, Mustafar would be ignored by galactic civilization. But the planet's tortured interior continually spews forth lava rich in rare heavy elements and precious ores. This molten wealth prompted the Techno Union to establish a lava mining operation, using electromagnetic extraction technologies, as well as manual mining by the Mustafarians, to remove the valuable materials from the molten rock matrix of the lava. Mustafar has been a literal gold mine for the Techno Union for almost 300 standard-years.

In addition to the secret Separatist hideout, Mustafar's mining complex conceals the Techno Union's droid production operation, located inside the mountain on which the mine sits.

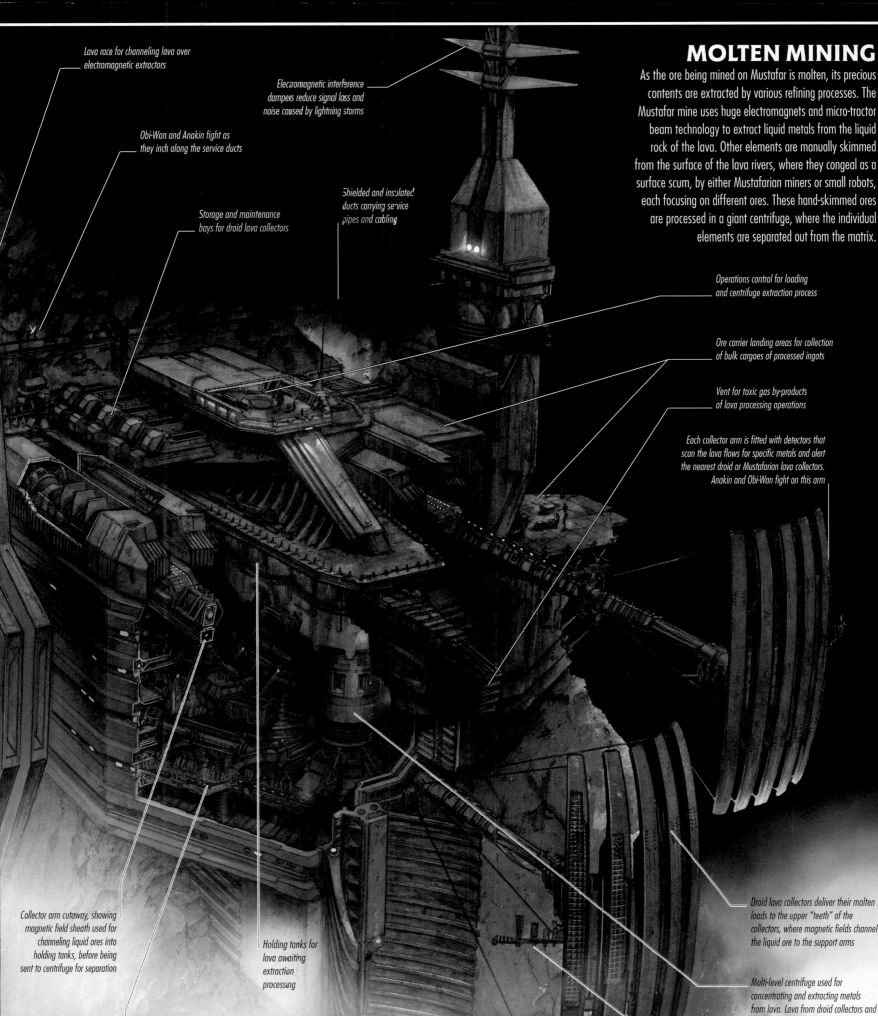

MOLTEN MINING

As the ore being mined on Mustafar is molten, its precious contents are extracted by various refining processes. The Mustafar mine uses huge electromagnets and micro-tractor beam technology to extract liquid metals from the liquid rock of the lava. Other elements are manually skimmed from the surface of the lava rivers, where they congeal as a surface scum, by either Mustafarian miners or small robots, each focusing on different ores. These hand-skimmed ores are processed in a giant centrifuge, where the individual elements are separated out from the matrix.

Lava race for channeling lava over electromagnetic extractors

Electromagnetic interference dampers reduce signal loss and noise caused by lightning storms

Obi-Wan and Anakin fight as they inch along the service ducts

Storage and maintenance bays for droid lava collectors

Shielded and insulated ducts carrying service pipes and cabling

Operations control for loading and centrifuge extraction process

Ore carrier landing areas for collection of bulk cargoes of processed ingots

Vent for toxic gas by-products of lava processing operations

Each collector arm is fitted with detectors that scan the lava flows for specific metals and alert the nearest droid or Mustafarian lava collectors. Anakin and Obi-Wan fight on this arm

Collector arm cutaway, showing magnetic field sheath used for channeling liquid ores into holding tanks, before being sent to centrifuge for separation

Holding tanks for lava awaiting extraction processing

Droid lava collectors deliver their molten loads to the upper "teeth" of the collectors, where magnetic fields channel the liquid ore to the support arms

Ingot foundry, where pure metals recovered by the centrifuge are molded into ingots for transport

Waste heat radiator from factory operations

Multi-level centrifuge used for concentrating and extracting metals from lava. Lava from droid collectors and Mustafarians is processed separately

Droid "dock" assemblies. Collector droids can attach themselves to these points for short-term recharging

MIRROR OF THE SOUL

As Anakin's soul surrenders fully to the dark side, violent Mustafar seems to mirror his turmoil. Lefrani eclipses Mustafar's sun, just as Anakin's massacre of the Separatist Council eclipses the light of the Force within him. The violent eruptions of the lava rivers, when the repulsor fields are shut down during his duel with Obi-Wan, seem almost driven by Anakin's own pulsing hatred of everyone that he believes has conspired against him and thwarted his desires. Only in the deepest core of his being does he still treasure his love for Padmé.

2 Anakin forces Obi-Wan back into the mining complex, and their battle rages through the Separatist headquarters, where the evidence of Anakin's treacherous massacre of the Council is all around them.

3 The flailing lightsabers of the Jedi and Sith smash fittings and equipment in the mining complex. This wanton damage deactivates the repulsor fields protecting the mining complex, allowing the lava rivers to erupt.

Fralideja is one of the few remaining Mustafarian settlements. The local population was almost destroyed by a cataclysmic eruption centuries ago

Residence for Techno Union mine management staff and technicians. The building's dome conceals a small landing pad. Palpatine lands here when he comes to rescue Anakin

A Mustafarian rite of passage requires youths to leap across the lavafall on a lava flea without wearing any protective clothing

1 Obi-Wan's appearance in the door of Padmé's ship drives Anakin into a fury. Believing himself betrayed by both the woman he loves and his friend, he attacks, leaving Padmé critically injured and forcing Obi-Wan into a duel.

8

9 10

MUSTAFAR DUEL

MUSTAFAR BECOMES THE LOCATION of the fateful duel between Anakin and Obi-Wan after the Jedi Master follows his friend to the remote outpost. Corrupted by Palpatine, Skywalker is sinking more deeply into his Sith persona, massacring the Separatist Council and choking Padmé when he believes she has betrayed him to his Master. In his rage and self-doubt, Anakin gives himself over to Sith fury and focuses all his hatred on Obi-Wan, attempting to murder his mentor in a lightsaber battle.

10 After easily defeating Anakin's ill-judged attack, leaving him maimed, burned, and helpless, Obi-Wan is unable to kill the friend he has loved as a brother. He turns away from Anakin's torment, leaving him to his fate.

4 As Anakin and Obi-Wan clash along the length of the War Room's observation balcony, lava eruptions from the rivers reflect Anakin's own savage battle-lust and hint at an unforseen threat to the complex.

Lava geysers erupt at points all along the river, but they are repressed around the mining complex by its repulsor fields

Secret battle droid factory concealed inside mountain, with the mining complex used as cover

Concealed weapons emplacement, with heavy defensive blaster-batteries. There is a ring of these emplacements around the mining complex

Deep within the mountain is a massive cavern, with a simmering lava lake. The secret Separatist conference room projects into this cavern

Mustafarian architecture is based on the shape of the kahel cave fungus, a highly symbolic plant in their culture

① ② ③ ④ ⑤ ⑥ ⑦

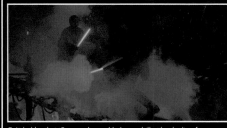

5 Aided by their Force-enhanced balance skills, the dueling former friends inch along the mining complex's service ducts. A mining droid, lacking instructions from its abandoned control room after delivering a load, hovers nearby.

7 Even while searching for a way to escape the fallen collector arm floating in the lava river, Anakin's fury drives him to continue his attack on Obi-Wan, who is forced to keep defending himself.

6 Lava bombs from the erupting river fall around the duelists as they fight on one of the collectors. Even a "cool lava" ball is hot enough to weaken the support arm and lead to its collapse.

9 Driven by the dark side to greed and overweening arrogance, Anakin refuses to accept that Obi-Wan has the advantage when his Master occupies the high ground on the bank of the lava river.

8 Abandoning the collector arm by leaping onto mining equipment, the duelists continue their fight. Anakin pursues Obi-Wan, who has commandeered a mining platform. He boards the platform, and the two clash again.

SITH SANCTUARY

With its repulsor fields offline, the mining complex where Anakin and Obi-Wan duel soon falls into ruin. But the Sith will return to Mustafar, with both Darth Sidious and Darth Vader using the planet as a focus for meditation on the power of the dark side. Mustafar also gains an evil reputation among fugitive Jedi as a place where exiles from the all-but-extinct Order are brought for interrogation, torment, and death.

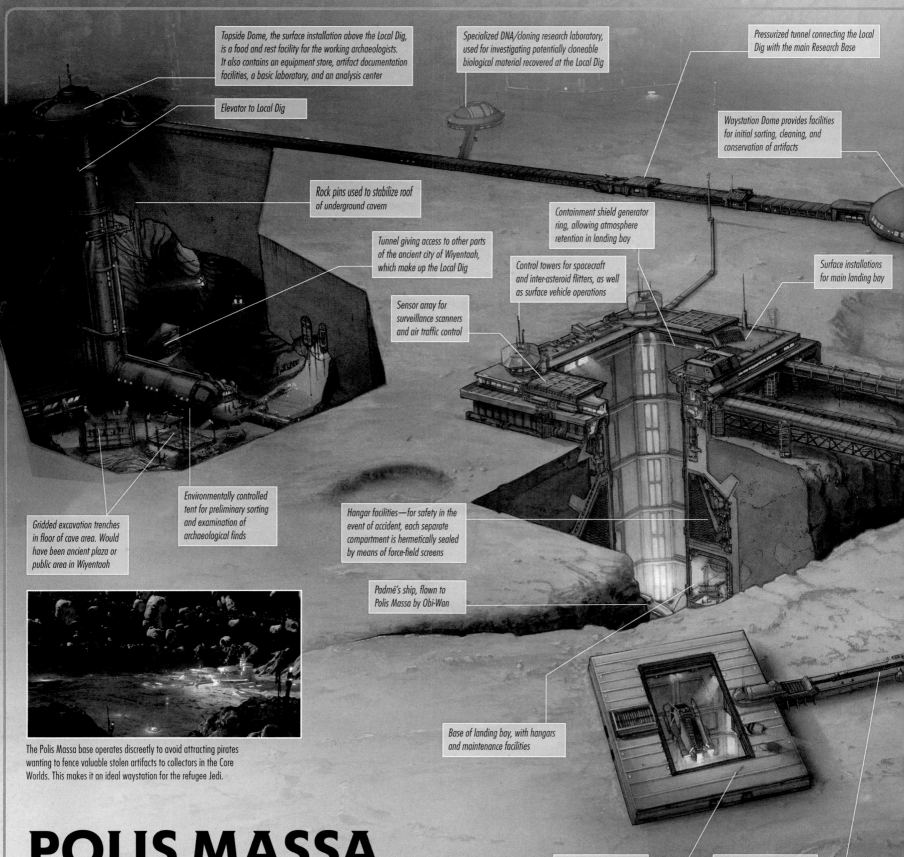

Topside Dome, the surface installation above the Local Dig, is a food and rest facility for the working archaeologists. It also contains an equipment store, artifact documentation facilities, a basic laboratory, and an analysis center

Specialized DNA/cloning research laboratory, used for investigating potentially cloneable biological material recovered at the Local Dig

Pressurized tunnel connecting the Local Dig with the main Research Base

Elevator to Local Dig

Waystation Dome provides facilities for initial sorting, cleaning, and conservation of artifacts

Rock pins used to stabilize roof of underground cavern

Containment shield generator ring, allowing atmosphere retention in landing bay

Tunnel giving access to other parts of the ancient city of Wiyentaah, which make up the Local Dig

Control towers for spacecraft and inter-asteroid flitters, as well as surface vehicle operations

Surface installations for main landing bay

Sensor array for surveillance scanners and air traffic control

Environmentally controlled tent for preliminary sorting and examination of archaeological finds

Hangar facilities—for safety in the event of accident, each separate compartment is hermetically sealed by means of force-field screens

Gridded excavation trenches in floor of cave area. Would have been ancient plaza or public area in Wiyentaah

Padmé's ship, flown to Polis Massa by Obi-Wan

The Polis Massa base operates discreetly to avoid attracting pirates wanting to fence valuable stolen artifacts to collectors in the Core Worlds. This makes it an ideal waystation for the refugee Jedi.

Base of landing bay, with hangars and maintenance facilities

POLIS MASSA

A REMOTE OUTER RIM asteroid system, on the fringes of the Subterrel sector, Polis Massa was originally an arid but inhabited planet that was fragmented in an ancient cataclysm. Once home to the now-vanished Eellayin people, the rocky fragments of Polis Massa hold relics of their originally subterranean civilization. Almost 500 years before the demise of the Galactic Republic, the Archaeological Research Council of Kallidah established a Research Base on one of the largest asteroid remnants of ancient Polis Massa because the Kallidahin believed themselves to be descendants of the Eellayin.

Small landing bay for inter-asteroid flitters used by archaeological team

Pressurized accessway from landing bay to biomedical building. Also provides access to underground storage area

ARCHAEOLOGICAL TREASURE TROVE

For 500 years, the archaeologists of Polis Massa Base have surveyed and excavated throughout the asteroid belt, seeking traces of their legendary forebears. Remnants of the Eellayin civilization have been scant. However, 50 standard-years ago, on their very doorstep, researchers uncovered the ruins of Wiyentaah, an underground city of the ancient Polis Massans. Since that time, the Local Dig, as it is called, has been progressively excavated and its finds cataloged.

RESURRECTING THE PAST

Polis Massa's archaeological team includes xenobiologists, who are constantly seeking to learn more about all alien species, not just their ancestors. They search for examples of ancient biological materials from which they may be able to resurrect extinct organisms into living species, using cloning skills learned from the Kaminoans. Their research requires Polis Massa to be equipped with a sophisticated biomedical facility, making it an ideal place to take the injured Padmé.

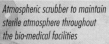

Tantive III—the ship is too large to land in the main landing hangar

Mooring masts, where large ships that cannot berth in the hangars must be tethered, as there is not enough gravitational force to hold them to the asteroid's surface

Library and recreation area for archaeologist residents

Main habitation area, which is also designed to be an emergency shelter in the event of damage to the base

Atmospheric scrubber to maintain sterile atmosphere throughout the bio-medical facilities

Surgical suites—this is where Padmé is treated and Luke and Leia are born

Main archaeological research facility, with laboratories and analysis equipment, conservation facilities, data archive, and packing facilities

Main food production area, where food plants, genetically engineered for high crop yield, are grown hydroponically

Main bio-medical research area, where experiments to resurrect lost species by cloning are carried out

Palaeobotany/palaeobiology laboratories for investigating plant and other biological remains

Medical center for treatment of minor injuries and illnesses among personnel and visitors

Maintenance hangar for surface vehicles

Main communication center, providing communication across the Polis Massa asteroid belt, as well as interstellar contact and Holonet access

Backup power generator

Loading bay, used to transfer archaeological cargo into surface vehicles for transfer to tethered spacecraft

Main power generator, using fusion reactor system

Elevator to underground artifact storage area

Artificial gravity generator. Provides gravity to all parts of the Research Base, hangars, and Local Dig

Dating laboratories, using radiometric techniques to establish the age of material recovered from the excavation

Parking apron for asteroid surface vehicles

Environmental control unit for underground artifact storage area

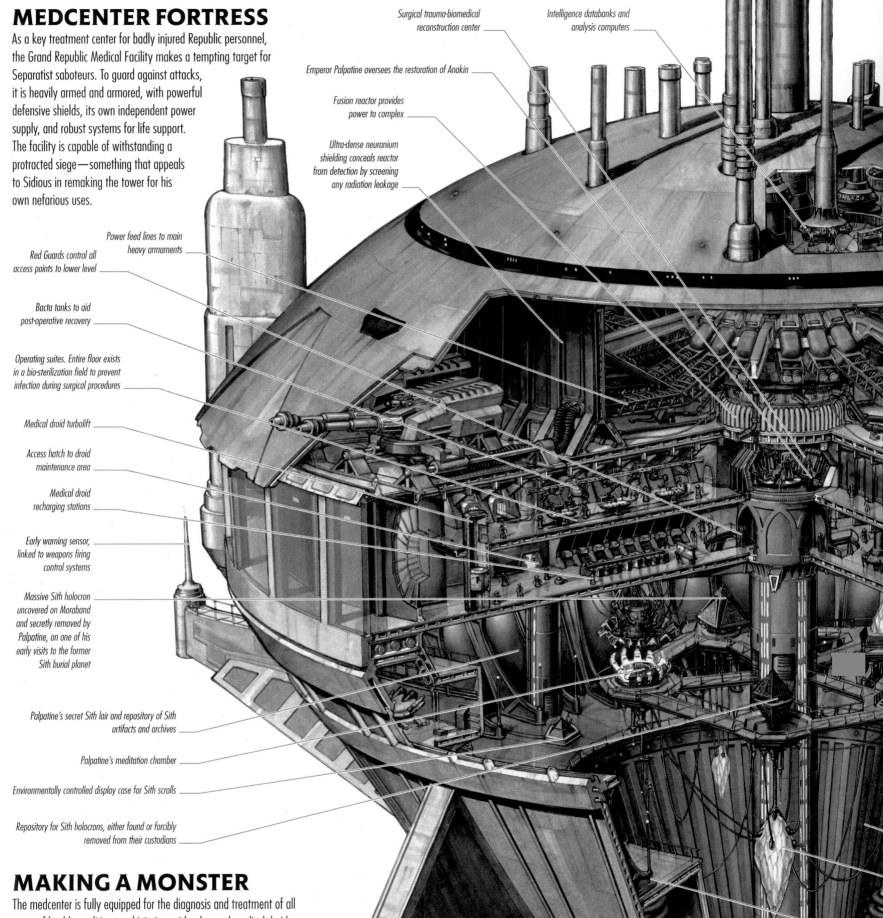

MEDCENTER FORTRESS

As a key treatment center for badly injured Republic personnel, the Grand Republic Medical Facility makes a tempting target for Separatist saboteurs. To guard against attacks, it is heavily armed and armored, with powerful defensive shields, its own independent power supply, and robust systems for life support. The facility is capable of withstanding a protracted siege—something that appeals to Sidious in remaking the tower for his own nefarious uses.

Surgical trauma-biomedical reconstruction center

Intelligence databanks and analysis computers

Emperor Palpatine oversees the restoration of Anakin

Fusion reactor provides power to complex

Ultra-dense neuranium shielding conceals reactor from detection by screening any radiation leakage

Power feed lines to main heavy armaments

Red Guards control all access points to lower level

Bacta tanks to aid post-operative recovery

Operating suites. Entire floor exists in a bio-sterilization field to prevent infection during surgical procedures

Medical droid turbolift

Access hatch to droid maintenance area

Medical droid recharging stations

Early warning sensor, linked to weapons firing control systems

Massive Sith holocron uncovered on Moraband and secretly removed by Palpatine, on one of his early visits to the former Sith burial planet

Palpatine's secret Sith lair and repository of Sith artifacts and archives

Palpatine's meditation chamber

Environmentally controlled display case for Sith scrolls

Repository for Sith holocrons, either found or forcibly removed from their custodians

MAKING A MONSTER

The medcenter is fully equipped for the diagnosis and treatment of all types of health conditions and injuries, with advanced medical droids and extensive databanks. Its droid doctors' life-saving surgical techniques restore Darth Vader's mobility with biomechanical limbs and life-support systems concealed inside fearsome body armor. Vader then benefits from the power of the Sith artifacts concealed on the lower levels, which are isolated from the main facility by bio-key access and Red Guards.

MEDCENTER

THE CITIZENS OF CORUSCANT know the Grand Republic Medical Facility as a specialist hospital that treats cases from all over the galaxy requiring leading-edge surgical techniques and biomechanical reconstruction. And for much of the Clone Wars, the medcenter is exactly that. But late in the conflict, the facility gains a new, secret purpose, with its benevolent face concealing a dark heart. The lower levels of the medcenter become Sidious' Sith retreat, a focus for meditation and a repository for his collection of secret Sith artifacts and lore. It is within these walls that the fallen Anakin Skywalker is treated and transformed after his battle with Obi-Wan Kenobi.

Topmost level of facility, housing communication and intelligence-gathering equipment

VLD2261 long-range heavy blaster defense battery, controlled from Red Guard security station on level below

Early warning and perimeter-scanning consoles

Exterior durasteel shell conceals building armor of ianthanide/duralium alloy

Ancient Sith ritual altar originally found on Ziost

Windowed gallery provides breathtaking view of Coruscant's endless cityscape

Medical diagnostic station for minor illness or injury

Sacred Sith artifact, the Great Crystal of Acntonaii

KDD2055 short-range turbolaser rapid-fire defense battery

Targeting and fire control station for turbolaser

Dark-side reservoir, emanating from the many Sith crystals and artifacts. Darth Vader's recovery will be aided by an "immersion" in this wellspring of evil

Massive Sith-imbued kyber crystal, slivers from which will be used in Sith lightsabers

Sith weapons stored around walls of gallery

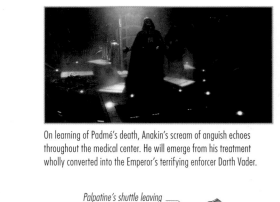

On learning of Padmé's death, Anakin's scream of anguish echoes throughout the medical center. He will emerge from his treatment wholly converted into the Emperor's terrifying enforcer Darth Vader.

Palpatine's shuttle leaving

Landing stage

HIDING IN PLAIN SIGHT

After Chancellor Palpatine's life is threatened by the rogue clone CT-5555, the medcenter is temporarily shuttered to bolster security. During this time, Sidious moves his collection of Sith artifacts from a dilapidated tower in The Works district, which he fears might be discovered by the Jedi. After declaring himself Emperor, Sidious will move his retreat again—to the Jedi Temple itself, remade as the forbidding Imperial Palace to symbolize the Sith's long-awaited revenge.

EPISODE IV
A NEW HOPE

It is a period of civil war. Rebel spaceships, striking from a hidden base, have won their first victory against the evil Galactic Empire.

During the battle, Rebel spies managed to steal secret plans to the Empire's ultimate weapon, the DEATH STAR, an armored space station with enough power to destroy an entire planet.

Pursued by the Empire's sinister agents, Princess Leia races home aboard her starship, custodian of the stolen plans that can save her people and restore freedom to the galaxy….

TATOOINE III

INHABITABLE ONLY in one small area of its northern hemisphere, Tatooine is as rugged and desolate a planet as exists anywhere in the galaxy's Outer Rim. Baked by day, near frozen at night, the desert world might never have been colonized by humans had its ancient seabeds not dangled the promise of mineral wealth to a few desperate settlers from the Core willing to bet their lives on a lucky strike. With massacres and swindling, Tatooine's indigenous Sand People and Jawas were the first to warn the newcomers not to get their hopes up. But still they came. Pilfering from the parched air what little moisture there was, the farmers grew more hardened and embittered with each passing generation; accepting of the smugglers, slave traders, and outlaws who followed in their wake, they finally became resigned to lives of adversity.

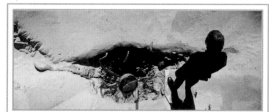

8 Returning to Tatooine to save Han Solo from Jabba the Hutt, Luke Skywalker, now a Jedi Knight, is captured and forced to walk the plank over the Pit of Carkoon, lair of the insatiable sarlacc. Luke prepares to catch the lightsaber R2-D2 will propel to him from the deck of Jabba's sail barge.

"Flaming Ragerunner" insignia

ROUTE KEY

C-3PO's route from escape pod	
R2-D2's route from escape pod	
Jawa sandcrawler circuit	
Interrupted portion of Jawa sandcrawler circuit	
R2-D2's escape route from Lars homestead	
Luke and C-3PO follow R2-D2's tracks in landspeeder	
Ben, Luke, and the droids travel to Ben's house	
Luke, Obi-Wan, and the droids set out to Anchorhead	
Luke races home (and back)	
Luke takes Obi-Wan and the droids to Mos Eisley	
Jabba's sail barge	

Map labels: BEGGAR'S CANYON, MOS TAIKE, MOS ESPA, MOS ENTHA, MOSPIC HIGH RANGE, JAWA MOUNTAIN FORTRESS, XELRIC DRAW, WRECK OF THE REPUBLIC FREIGHTER *SPICE SIREN*, HUBBA HEIGHTS, BEN'S HOUSE, PIKA OASIS, JUNDLAND, REMAINS OF OLD TUSKEN CAMP, WESTERN DUNE SEA, MOS ELREY, C-3PO picked up by Jawa sandcrawler, ESCAPE POD LANDING SITE

Luke and C-3PO spot R2-D2 as he enters the craggy canyons of the Jundlund Wastes

Central airfoil provides stability for daredevil maneuvers

Airspeed sensor

Pneumatic cannon (laser cannon removed for repairs)

Lightweight lattice construction

Pilot relies on computer displays and holographic terrain-following maps

Ion engine can attain supersonic speeds

Inertia damper coils of matched DCJ-45 repulsorlifts

T-16 SKYHOPPER

Many Tatooine youths with nothing better to do race battered skyhoppers for kicks. Levitated by repulsorlifts, propelled by an ion engine, and outfitted with a pneumatic cannon package, Luke's modified skyhopper is the perfect craft for making quick hops to Bestine or bulls-eyeing womp rats in the Jawa Heights. Luke is so fond of his skyhopper that when he damages its airfoil, he resorts to toying with a scale model he has had since his early adolescence.

1 Having bickered with R2-D2 about the best route to take, C-3PO sets out alone. Joints almost frozen, he staggers toward the summit of a towering sand dune. Typical of those that crawl slowly across Tatooine's Jundland Wastes, the dune is necklaced with the bleached bones of a greater krayt dragon.

7 Rejoining Obi-Wan and the droids, Luke speeds to Mos Eisley, stopping only briefly to gaze on the spaceport from a steep-sided bluff. While Mos Eisley is the group's best chance of finding safe transport off Tatooine, they will have to be cautious, Obi-Wan warns, because the city teems with thieves and villains.

SOROSUUB X–34 LANDSPEEDER

Landspeeders are a standard personal transport on Tatooine. Although superseded by the XP-38, SoroSuub's "Thirty-four" is still considered a classic because of its no-frills design and powerful engine. Even without modifications, the X-34 can attain top speeds of 250 kph (155 mph), and is highly maneuverable in tight quarters.

Top engine fuel lines

Combustion chamber

Power generator

Antigrav generator

Duraplex windscreen

Service access panel

Fuel filler cap

Fuel tank

Forward scanner

Repulsor antigrav conduit

Port engine fuel lines

Repulsor elements

NORTHERN DUNE SEA

EANTHA PLAINS

Stormtroopers charged with finding the missing droids intercept the Jawa sandcrawler as it leaves Bestine

JABBA'S PALACE

SITE OF TUSKEN SLAUGHTER BY BANDIT ALKHARA

B'OMARR FLATS

PIT OF CARKOON

8

On the journey to Mos Eisley, Ben, Luke, and the droids shelter overnight in Bestine

GREAT MESRA PLATEAU

BESTINE

BIGUR'S CANYON

WASTES

ARNTHOUT

MOS EISLEY

1

WRECK OF THE PIRATE VESSEL *HYDIAN MARAUDER*

RUMORED LOCATION OF KITONAK COLONY

Sluuce Canyon is well-used route to Mos Eisley valley from high ground

WRECK OF THE HUTT TRANSPORT *RIMRUNNER*

MOTESTA OASIS

JAWA HEIGHTS

DARKLIGHTER HOMESTEAD

TOSCHE STATION

ANCHORHEAD

LARS HOMESTEAD

6

GREAT CHOTT SALT FLAT COMMUNITY

6 Hurrying home, Luke discovers that the Lars farm has been burned, along with the bodies of his foster parents, Uncle Owen and Aunt Beru. His own life suddenly reduced to ashes, a grief-stricken Luke resolves to learn the ways of the Force and to become a Jedi—like his father.

5 Revived by Obi-Wan from the blows of a Tusken gaffi stick, Luke offers Ben a landspeeder ride to the settlement of Anchorhead. Along the way, they chance upon a crippled sandcrawler and its Jawa crew, who have been massacred by Imperial troops, possibly in search of the droids.

4 The two droids wind up as possessions of the moisture-farming Lars family. Under cover of darkness, however, R2-D2 escapes the compound, setting out in search of Obi-Wan Kenobi. The next morning, Luke pursues with C-3PO— only to be waylaid by a band of vicious Tusken Raiders.

DESERT DANGERS

With its vast unpopulated stretches of rock and sand, its primitive surface roads, and the unlighted alleyways of its principal settlements, Tatooine offers ample opportunities for personal misfortune. For sentients and droids alike, safety is as scarce as water, and banditry, abduction, and hijacking have been raised to art forms. Casual travelers risk being shot at by Tusken Raiders. Moisture farmers are frequently robbed of their profits by gangs of outlaws. And a lone droid need always be fearful of being abducted by Jawas. Tatooine's local authorities are too overwhelmed to deal with petty crime, and the troops of the Imperial garrison couldn't care less.

2 With suns-set, Tatooine's temperatures plunge, the darkened rocky canyons fill with unsettling sounds, and even R2-D2 is forced to reconsider his route. Stunned to immobility by an ionization blaster fired by a Jawa, the astromech is carried off by a group entrepreneurial beings, led by Dathcha.

3 On the hazy horizon, reflected sunlight glints off the thick bow-plating of a massive sandcrawler. Once used by ore-prospecting colonists, then abandoned to the wastes, the steam-powered transports are now piloted by clans of tech-scavenging Jawas, ever on the alert for abandoned or disoriented droids.

LARS HOMESTEAD

SHADOWS SHORTEN as Tatooine's twin suns climb high above the Jundland Wastes, whose southern extreme is home to the several dozen moisture farms that make up the Great Chott salt flat community. Founded in the waning days of the Galactic Republic by Cliegg Lars and bequeathed to his son, Owen, the underground homestead is a warren of interconnected rooms, with vast storage areas and a marginally profitable hydroponic garden. Baked by the midday heat and scoured by gritty winds, the farm's pourstone entry dome and scattered moisture vaporators are the only exceptions to the glaring monotony of the desiccated seabed.

Luke brings up the difficult question of when he can join the Academy—unaware that his life is soon to change forever.

TYPICAL FARMSTEAD

Ringed by rudimentary weather monitors and motion-detection sensors, the farm sprawls across a bleached expanse of low ridges and hard-packed ground. Many of the homestead's sand-pitted moisture vaporators are decades old and in need of almost constant maintenance. Desperate to conserve power from solar radiation and small fusion-cell generators, the compound is shut down at nightfall—except for perimeter security sensors, which warn of roaming Tuskens and desert monsters.

Storage room for emergency rations and medical supplies is frequent haunt for womp rats

Dining room furniture originally supplied by mining company

Cup of nutrient-enhanced blue milk

Beru Whitesun Lars sets the dining room table for lunch

Coolth unit

Blue milk dispenser

Humidity sensor controls air-moisture levels in hydroponics chamber

Owen Lars emerges from storage area with replacement parts for power converters

Electrostatic repeller keeps courtyard and room entrances free of blowing sand

Air intake/exhaust vanes control temperature in hydroponics chamber

Fusion-generator supply tanks

Training datapad for Imperial Academy

Galley kitchen

Shape-memory, self-sealing containers and quick-prep devices prevent food from losing moisture to dry air

Combination water and sonic shower

Compost-capable refresher unit

Refresher station

Low-yield, flow-regulated wash basin

EG-6 power droid is several hundred years old

Pipes deliver water throughout homestead

Vaporator moisture condenser, or chilling bar

Patch-in droid unit can converse with vaporator in binary language code

Binary brain unit

Water-filled cistern adjusts PH levels

Wed 15 "Septoid 2" Treadwell toolkit droid sometimes chases sandflies, mistaking their whine for malfunctioning vaporators

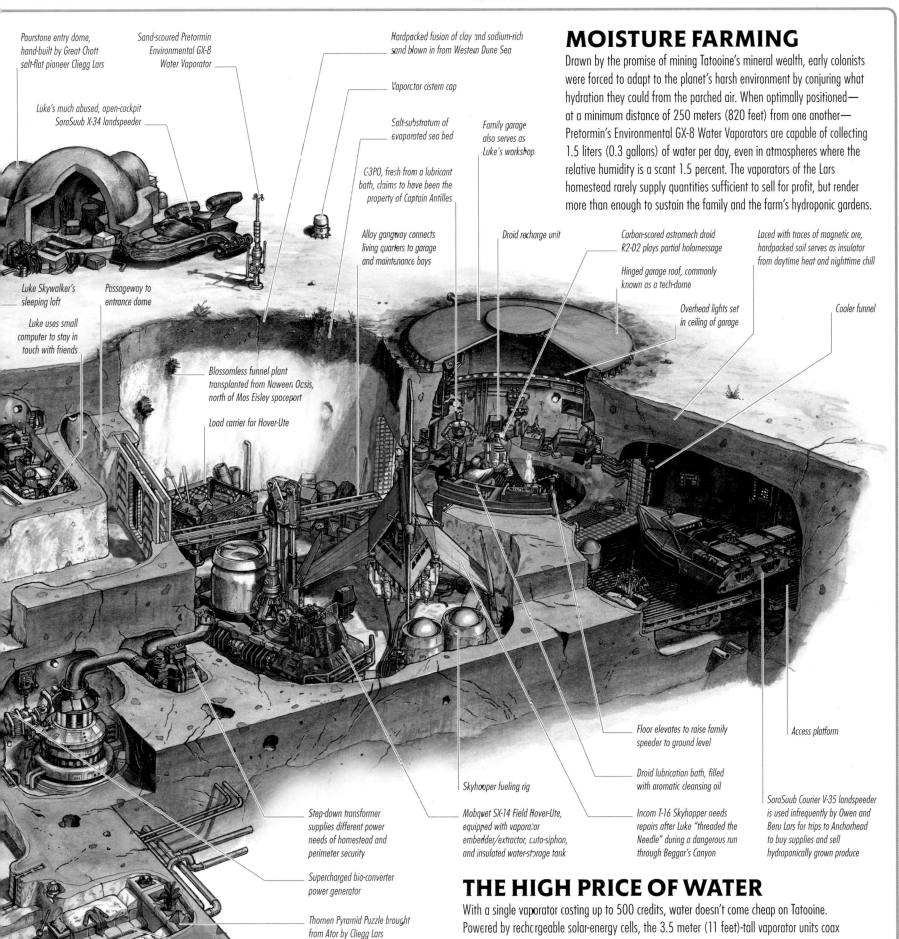

Pourstone entry dome, hand-built by Great Chott salt-flat pioneer Cliegg Lars

Sand-scoured Pretormin Environmental GX-8 Water Vaporator

Hardpacked fusion of clay and sodium-rich sand blown in from Western Dune Sea

Luke's much abused, open-cockpit SoroSuub X-34 landspeeder

Vaporctor cistern cap

Salt-substratum of evaporated sea bed

Family garage also serves as Luke's workshop

C-3PO, fresh from a lubricant bath, claims to have been the property of Captain Antilles

Droid recharge unit

Carbon-scored astromech droid R2-D2 plays partial holomessage

Laced with traces of magnetic ore, hardpacked soil serves as insulator from daytime heat and nighttime chill

Alloy gangway connects living quarters to garage and maintenance bays

Hinged garage roof, commonly known as a tech-dome

Luke Skywalker's sleeping loft

Passageway to entrance dome

Overhead lights set in ceiling of garage

Cooler funnel

Luke uses small computer to stay in touch with friends

Blossomless funnel plant transplanted from Naween Ocsis, north of Mos Eisley spaceport

Load carrier for Hover-Ute

Floor elevates to raise family speeder to ground level

Access platform

Droid lubrication bath, filled with aromatic cleansing oil

Skyhooper fueling rig

Step-down transformer supplies different power needs of homestead and perimeter security

Mobquet SX-14 Field Hover-Ute, equipped with vaporator embedder/extractor, auto-siphon, and insulated water-storage tank

Incom T-16 Skyhopper needs repairs after Luke "threaded the Needle" during a dangerous run through Beggar's Canyon

SoroSuub Courier V-35 landspeeder is used infrequently by Owen and Beru Lars for trips to Anchorhead to buy supplies and sell hydroponically grown produce

Supercharged bio-converter power generator

Thornen Pyramid Puzzle brought from Ator by Cliegg Lars

Owen and Beru's bedroom

Clothes storage bins make use of sand-trap technology

Woven rug patterned after Tatooine rock and cave paintings belonged to Cliegg's second wife, Shmi Skywalker

MOISTURE FARMING

Drawn by the promise of mining Tatooine's mineral wealth, early colonists were forced to adapt to the planet's harsh environment by conjuring what hydration they could from the parched air. When optimally positioned— at a minimum distance of 250 meters (820 feet) from one another— Pretormin's Environmental GX-8 Water Vaporators are capable of collecting 1.5 liters (0.3 gallons) of water per day, even in atmospheres where the relative humidity is a scant 1.5 percent. The vaporators of the Lars homestead rarely supply quantities sufficient to sell for profit, but render more than enough to sustain the family and the farm's hydroponic gardens.

THE HIGH PRICE OF WATER

With a single vaporator costing up to 500 credits, water doesn't come cheap on Tatooine. Powered by rechargeable solar-energy cells, the 3.5 meter (11 feet)-tall vaporator units coax moisture from the air by means of refrigerated condensers, or chilling bars, which generate low-energy ionization fields. Captured water accumulates on the condensers and is pumped or gravity-directed into storage cisterns. Higher-end Pretormin models come equipped with computers, which tweak the strength of the ionization and refrigeration fields to compensate for alterations in wind speed and temperature. The computers also allow for communication between the units via binary programming language, in conjunction with a droid interface— a mainstay trading item supplied to the farms by roving groups of Jawa tech-scavengers.

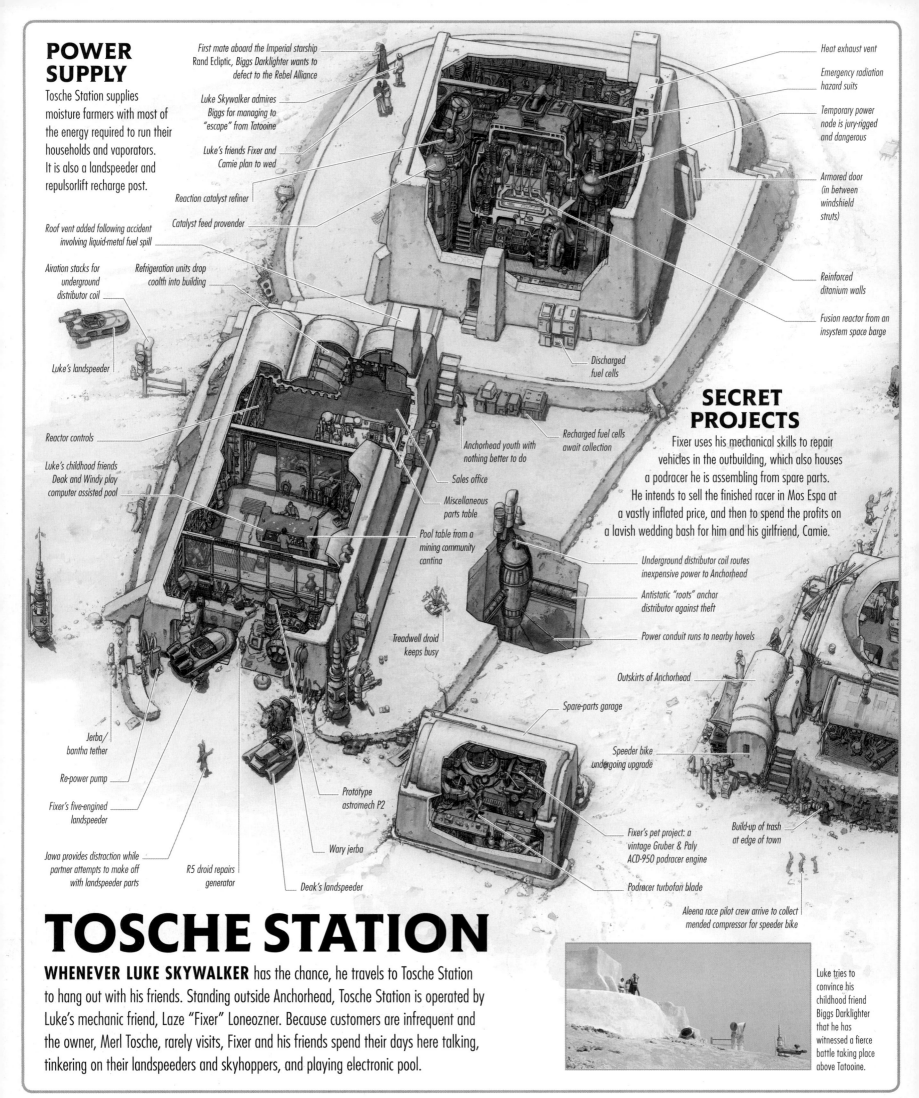

POWER SUPPLY

Tosche Station supplies moisture farmers with most of the energy required to run their households and vaporators. It is also a landspeeder and repulsorlift recharge post.

First mate aboard the Imperial starship *Rand Ecliptic, Biggs Darklighter* wants to defect to the Rebel Alliance

Luke Skywalker admires Biggs for managing to "escape" from Tatooine

Luke's friends Fixer and Camie plan to wed

Reaction catalyst refiner

Catalyst feed provender

Roof vent added following accident involving liquid-metal fuel spill

Airation stacks for underground distributor coil

Refrigeration units drop coolth into building

Luke's landspeeder

Reactor controls

Luke's childhood friends Deak and Windy play computer assisted pool

Jerba/ bantha tether

Re-power pump

Fixer's five-engined landspeeder

Jawa provides distraction while partner attempts to make off with landspeeder parts

R5 droid repairs generator

Prototype astromech P2

Wary jerba

Deak's landspeeder

Anchorhead youth with nothing better to do

Sales office

Miscellaneous parts table

Pool table from a mining community cantina

Treadwell droid keeps busy

Discharged fuel cells

Recharged fuel cells await collection

Heat exhaust vent

Emergency radiation hazard suits

Temporary power node is jury-rigged and dangerous

Armored door (in between windshield struts)

Reinforced ditanium walls

Fusion reactor from an insystem space barge

SECRET PROJECTS

Fixer uses his mechanical skills to repair vehicles in the outbuilding, which also houses a podracer he is assembling from spare parts. He intends to sell the finished racer in Mos Espa at a vastly inflated price, and then to spend the profits on a lavish wedding bash for him and his girlfriend, Camie.

Underground distributor coil routes inexpensive power to Anchorhead

Antistatic "roots" anchor distributor against theft

Power conduit runs to nearby hovels

Outskirts of Anchorhead

Spare-parts garage

Speeder bike undergoing upgrade

Fixer's pet project: a vintage Gruber & Paly ACD-950 podracer engine

Podracer turbofan blade

Build-up of trash at edge of town

Aleena race pilot crew arrive to collect mended compressor for speeder bike

TOSCHE STATION

WHENEVER LUKE SKYWALKER has the chance, he travels to Tosche Station to hang out with his friends. Standing outside Anchorhead, Tosche Station is operated by Luke's mechanic friend, Laze "Fixer" Loneozner. Because customers are infrequent and the owner, Merl Tosche, rarely visits, Fixer and his friends spend their days here talking, tinkering on their landspeeders and skyhoppers, and playing electronic pool.

Luke tries to convince his childhood friend Biggs Darklighter that he has witnessed a fierce battle taking place above Tatooine.

BEN'S HOUSE

TATOOINE IS DOTTED with remote dwellings built by those in search of profitable areas with higher-than-average nighttime condensation. Typically, these frontier moisture farmers return to safer and more populous areas after a single harsh season. One such abandoned dwelling, constructed over a well-sheltered cave, became the home of a Jedi Knight in hiding—Obi-Wan "Ben" Kenobi.

Ben's home is located on a remote bluff in the Jundlund Wastes, surrounded on all sides by the Western Dune Sea. The nearest settlement is Bestine.

BASIC HOME

Ben Kenobi's simple house consists of one main room in which he lives and sleeps. He uses the natural cellar for food and water storage, and constructs mechanical items, for trading with Jawas, on a workbench.

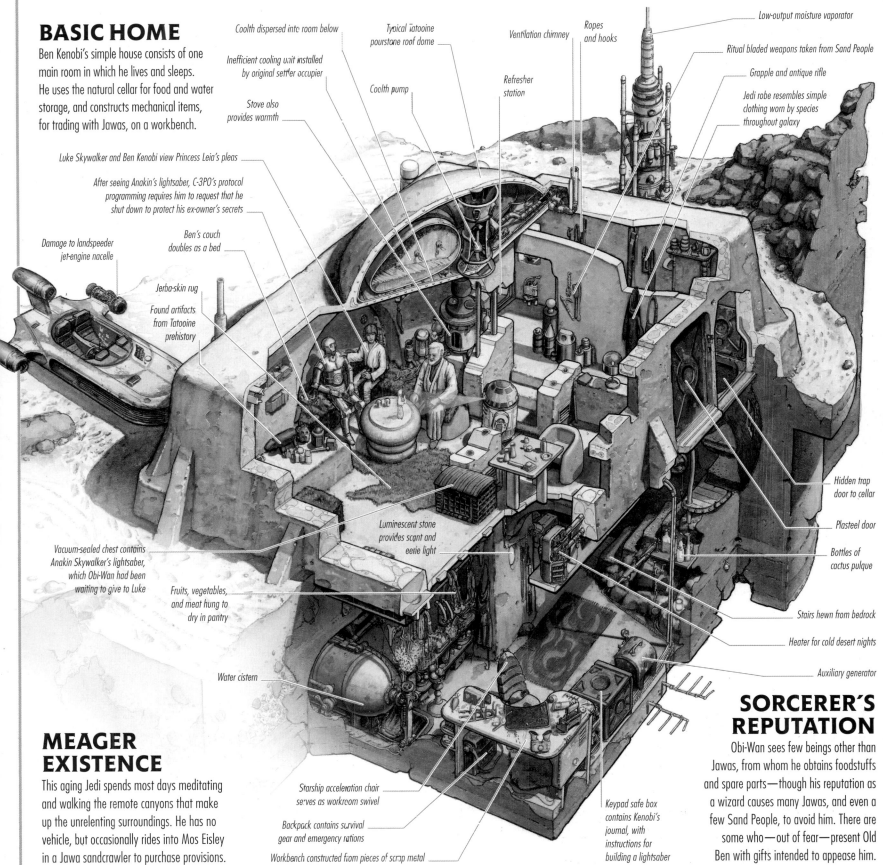

Coolth dispersed into room below

Typical Tatooine pourstone roof dome

Ventilation chimney

Ropes and hooks

Low-output moisture vaporator

Ritual bladed weapons taken from Sand People

Inefficient cooling unit installed by original settler occupier

Coolth pump

Refresher station

Grapple and antique rifle

Jedi robe resembles simple clothing worn by species throughout galaxy

Stove also provides warmth

Luke Skywalker and Ben Kenobi view Princess Leia's pleas

After seeing Anakin's lightsaber, C-3PO's protocol programming requires him to request that he shut down to protect his ex-owner's secrets

Damage to landspeeder jet-engine nacelle

Ben's couch doubles as a bed

Jerba-skin rug

Found artifacts from Tatooine prehistory

Hidden trap door to cellar

Plasteel door

Bottles of cactus pulque

Vacuum-sealed chest contains Anakin Skywalker's lightsaber, which Obi-Wan had been waiting to give to Luke

Luminescent stone provides scant and eerie light

Fruits, vegetables, and meat hung to dry in pantry

Stairs hewn from bedrock

Heater for cold desert nights

Auxiliary generator

Water cistern

MEAGER EXISTENCE

This aging Jedi spends most days meditating and walking the remote canyons that make up the unrelenting surroundings. He has no vehicle, but occasionally rides into Mos Eisley in a Jawa sandcrawler to purchase provisions.

Starship acceleration chair serves as workroom swivel

Backpack contains survival gear and emergency rations

Workbench constructed from pieces of scrap metal

Keypad safe box contains Kenobi's journal, with instructions for building a lightsaber

SORCERER'S REPUTATION

Obi-Wan sees few beings other than Jawas, from whom he obtains foodstuffs and spare parts—though his reputation as a wizard causes many Jawas, and even a few Sand People, to avoid him. There are some who—out of fear—present Old Ben with gifts intended to appease him.

MOS EISLEY

THE UNRULY SPACEPORT of Mos Eisley sprawls in a broad valley south-east of Tatooine's Jundland Wastes. The old quarter was originally laid out like a wheel, with a teeming market place located adjacent to water and power distribution centers. Now, bargains on vaporators, cooling units, and hydroponic produce can be found in the bazaars and junkyards of the newer quarter, the hub of which is Chalmun's Spaceport Cantina.

11 Having struck a sweet deal with Obi-Wan and Luke for passage to Alderaan, Han Solo finds Jabba the Hutt and his gang of mercenaries and bounty hunters waiting for him in Docking Bay 94. Han bargains with the Hutt for one final chance to pay for a load of spice he was forced to jettison.

CITY–WIDE TRAFFIC

With no central landing area, the whole of Mos Eisley is cratered with 362 docking bays, many of which are large enough to accommodate space freighters. All the bays are under the ostensible control of the city prefect and a handful of overworked customs agents.

1 Luke Skywalker races toward Mos Eisley with Ben Kenobi, C-3PO, and R2-D2 crammed into his landspeeder. A slum of ramshackle pourstone buildings, the area is populated by squatters, failed moisture farmers, scavengers, and those outlaws who have come to Tatooine to lose or reinvent themselves.

2 Teams of ASP-7 droids assist in the loading of a Gallofree Yards, civilian-use GR-45 medium transport. Easily programmed and equipped with magnetized feet, clawed hands, and voice synthesizers, the agile droids will have the vessel's cargo loaded by suns-set.

3 Familiar with the layout of the city from previous visits, Obi-Wan directs Luke toward Chalmun's Cantina, on the far side of the city. Where Outer Curved Street and Straight Street intersect at the new city center, the skyline is dominated by hotels, casinos, and tall complexes built by off-world corporations.

ONE CITY'S MISFORTUNE

Long a haven for spacers, thieves, smugglers, and rogues of all species and variety, Mos Eisley prides itself on being a wretched hive of scum and villainy. The spaceport's status swelled when podracing fell out of favor, and slave traders and criminals like Jabba the Hutt abandoned that sport's epicenter to the north, Mos Espa. Jabba's increased presence attracted the notice of starship design corporations Ubrikkian and Queblux, both of which constructed high-rise buildings in the gentrified heart of the old city.

Millennium Falcon makes a hasty exit

Former podracer spare parts dealership

Passenger ship belonging to Roon Tours, which offers short vacations in Tatooine for wealthy, jaded tourists seeking unusual thrills

Hutt-owned exotic restaurant, Court of the Fountain

Overcrowded city jail

Illegally parked GR-45 medium transport

OUTER CURVED STREET

Spaceport Speeders, where Luke and Ben sell the family speeder

Docking Bay 94

Headquarters of Quebe-Luxfause Systems, manufacturers of queblux power technology

Water distribution plant

Spaceport Express

SPACERS ROW

PARADISE ROAD

Masse Goskey's famous Arms Emporium

Entrance dome to Jabba the Hutt's townhouse, known as the Desilijic Complex, much of which is constructed over extensive system of caves and grottos

Jabba's private box

Felvath Kurs Arena (named in honor of the legendary Loovrian pit-fighter) features all types of combat spectacles

Many of Mos Eisley's citizens ride rontos, jerbas, dewbacks, and other beasts

The sight of an insectile Neimoidian shuttle is an indication that shady dealings are afoot somewhere in Mos Eisley's criminal dens

4 Luke maneuvers the landspeeder into Straight Street toward what was once the heart of the Old City. As varied as the city's vehicles and droids, Mos Eisley's residents and transients have come to Tatooine from worlds as near as Ryloth and Piroket, and as distant as Nar Shaddaa and Ord Mantell.

5 Startled by a recklessly-piloted S-swoop, a ronto pack-beast rears up to avoid a collision, unseating his pair of Jawa riders. Animals such as rontos, banthas, dewbacks, jerbas, and eopies are as common a sight in Mos Eisley as landspeeders, skyhoppers, or arriving and departing spacecraft.

10 Renowned in Mos Eisley for his spying aptitude, a long-snouted alien from Kubindi, named Garindan, shadows Luke and Ben as they hastily sell their speeder in order to rendezvous with starship pilots Han Solo and Chewbacca at Docking Bay 94.

9 Partnered with Mark IV repulsorlift patrol droids and armed with BlasTech E-11, DLT-19, and T-21 repeating blasters, squads of stormtroopers search for the fugitive droids, sometimes resorting to house-to-house searches. C-3PO and R2-D2 are forced to hide in the maze of narrow streets to evade capture.

GALACTIC HOTSPOT

Moisture farmers bring their harvests to Mos Eisley only if markets in the capital of Bestine are overly busy. Notoriously open to bribes, customs officials make little attempt to curtail the smuggling of spice, illegal arms, and other proscribed goods that pass through Tatooine on their way to other worlds. Ben Kenobi makes occasional trips to Mos Eisley to learn the latest news about the Empire and the contemptible activities of his former apprentice, Anakin Skywalker—now Darth Vader.

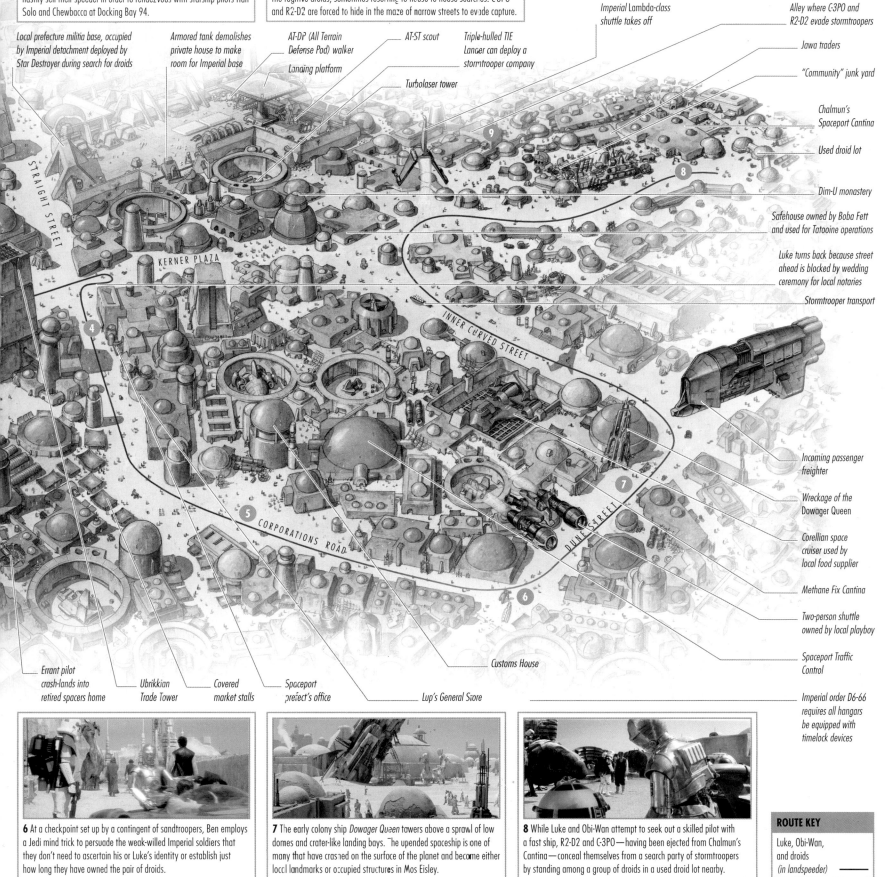

Local prefecture militia base, occupied by Imperial detachment deployed by Star Destroyer during search for droids

Armored tank demolishes private house to make room for Imperial base

AT-DP (All Terrain Defense Pod) walker

Landing platform

AT-ST scout

Turbolaser tower

Triple-hulled TIE Lancer can deploy a stormtrooper company

Imperial Lambda-class shuttle takes off

Alley where C-3PO and R2-D2 evade stormtroopers

Jawa traders

"Community" junk yard

Chalmun's Spaceport Cantina

Used droid lot

Dim-U monastery

Safehouse owned by Boba Fett and used for Tatooine operations

Luke turns back because street ahead is blocked by wedding ceremony for local notaries

Stormtrooper transport

Incoming passenger freighter

Wreckage of the Dowager Queen

Corellian space cruiser used by local food supplier

Methane Fix Cantina

Two-person shuttle owned by local playboy

Spaceport Traffic Control

Imperial order D6-66 requires all hangars be equipped with timelock devices

STRAIGHT STREET

KERNER PLAZA

INNER CURVED STREET

DUNE STREET

CORPORATIONS ROAD

Errant pilot crash-lands into retired spacers home

Ubrikkian Trade Tower

Covered market stalls

Spaceport prefect's office

Lup's General Store

Customs House

---

6 At a checkpoint set up by a contingent of sandtroopers, Ben employs a Jedi mind trick to persuade the weak-willed Imperial soldiers that they don't need to ascertain his or Luke's identity or establish just how long they have owned the pair of droids.

7 The early colony ship *Dowager Queen* towers above a sprawl of low domes and crater-like landing bays. The upended spaceship is one of many that have crashed on the surface of the planet and become either local landmarks or occupied structures in Mos Eisley.

8 While Luke and Obi-Wan attempt to seek out a skilled pilot with a fast ship, R2-D2 and C-3PO—having been ejected from Chalmun's Cantina—conceal themselves from a search party of stormtroopers by standing among a group of droids in a used droid lot nearby.

ROUTE KEY

Luke, Obi-Wan, and droids (in landspeeder) ——

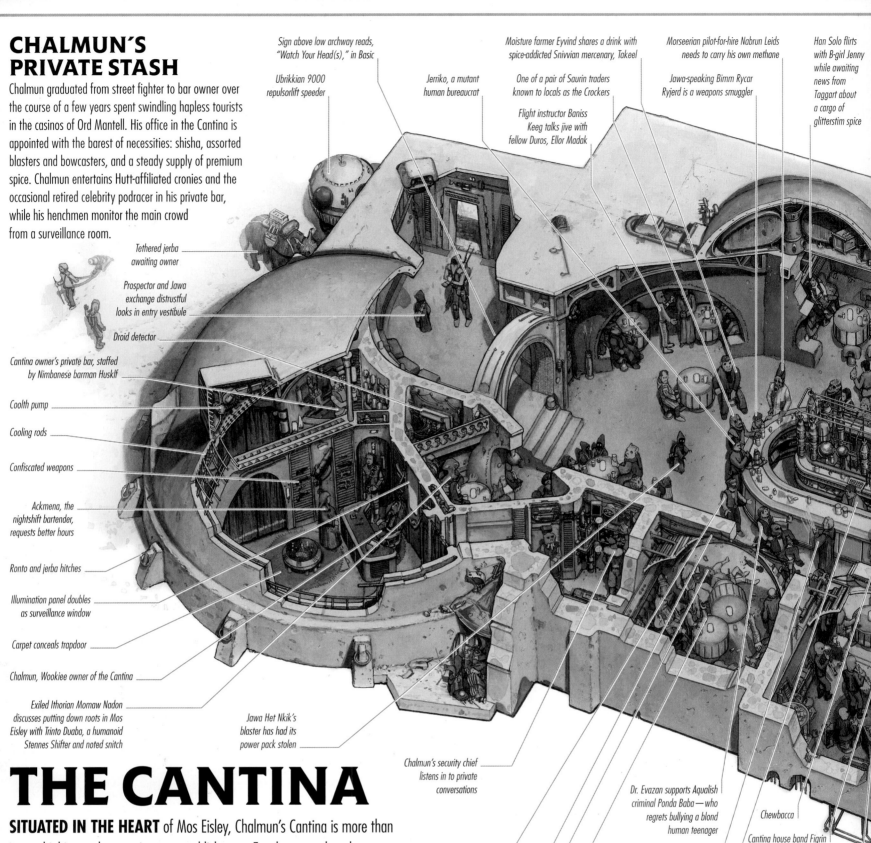

CHALMUN'S PRIVATE STASH

Chalmun graduated from street fighter to bar owner over the course of a few years spent swindling hapless tourists in the casinos of Ord Mantell. His office in the Cantina is appointed with the barest of necessities: shisha, assorted blasters and bowcasters, and a steady supply of premium spice. Chalmun entertains Hutt-affiliated cronies and the occasional retired celebrity podracer in his private bar, while his henchmen monitor the main crowd from a surveillance room.

Tethered jerba awaiting owner

Prospector and Jawa exchange distrustful looks in entry vestibule

Droid detector

Cantina owner's private bar, staffed by Nimbanese barman Husklf

Coolth pump

Cooling rods

Confiscated weapons

Ackmena, the nightshift bartender, requests better hours

Ronto and jerba hitches

Illumination panel doubles as surveillance window

Carpet conceals trapdoor

Chalmun, Wookiee owner of the Cantina

Exiled Ithorian Momaw Nadon discusses putting down roots in Mos Eisley with Trinto Duaba, a humanoid Stennes Shifter and noted snitch

Sign above low archway reads, "Watch Your Head(s)," in Basic

Ubrikkian 9000 repulsorlift speeder

Jerriko, a mutant human bureaucrat

Flight instructor Baniss Keeg talks jive with fellow Duros, Ellor Madak

Moisture farmer Eyvind shares a drink with spice-addicted Snivvian mercenary, Takeel

One of a pair of Saurin traders known to locals as the Crockers

Morseerian pilot-for-hire Nabrun Leids needs to carry his own methane

Jawa-speaking Bimm Rycar Ryjerd is a weapons smuggler

Han Solo flirts with B-girl Jenny while awaiting news from Taggart about a cargo of glitterstim spice

Jawa Het Nkik's blaster has had its power pack stolen

Chalmun's security chief listens in to private conversations

Garouf Lafoe will alert stormtroopers to Obi-Wan's handiwork

Listening wires

Luke Skywalker hits the floor

A Pacithhip, a Devaronian, and an aged Defel meet over a jigger of Merenzane Gold

Dr. Evazan supports Aqualish criminal Ponda Baba—who regrets bullying a blond human teenager

Obi-Wan Kenobi

Droid-hating barman Wuher

Chewbacca

Cantina house band Figrin D'an and the Modal Nodes

Themed bar spigots modeled after head of IG-series of droids

THE CANTINA

SITUATED IN THE HEART of Mos Eisley, Chalmun's Cantina is more than just a drinking and entertainment establishment. For the smugglers, bounty hunters, renegade spacers, and spice handlers who frequent Tatooine's wretched spaceport, it is also office, boardroom, rendezvous, and trading floor. Early pioneers raised the basic structure as a fortification against raids by Sand People, and over time the Cantina has seen use as an armory, a brewery, and a flophouse for vagrants. The current owner, a beige-and-gray-furred Wookiee named Chalmun, bought the building from the Vriichon brothers—Ranat siblings who were running an illegal spice den on the premises. The Vriichons disappeared soon after the sale, fearing perhaps that the grizzled Chalmun would discover the numerous bodies they had buried in the basement.

The droids wait outside the Cantina in the noon heat—Kenobi knows that this is the best time to find the bar crowded with thirsty starpilots.

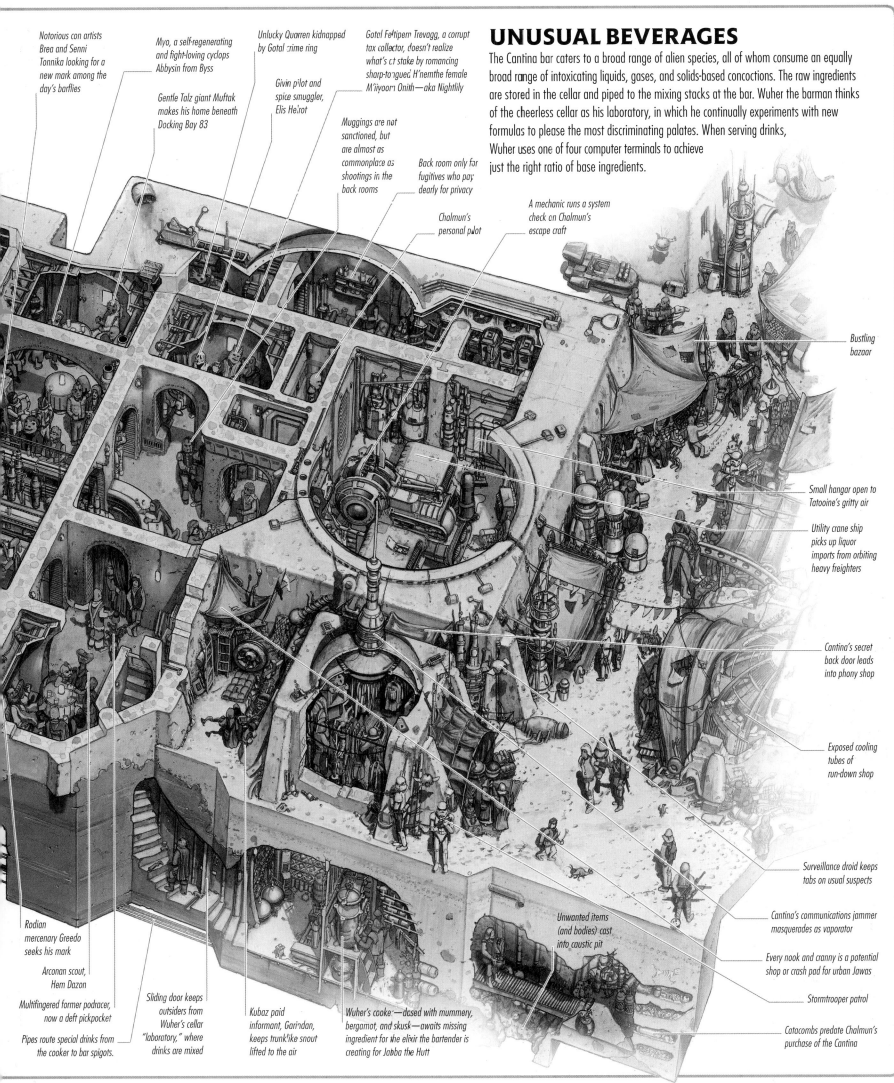

Notorious con artists Brea and Senni Tonnika looking for a new mark among the day's barflies

Myo, a self-regenerating and fight-loving cyclops Abbysin from Byss

Gentle Talz giant Muftak makes his home beneath Docking Bay 83

Unlucky Quarren kidnapped by Gotal crime ring

Givin pilot and spice smuggler, Elis Helrot

Gotal Feltipern Trevagg, a corrupt tax collector, doesn't realize what's at stake by romancing sharp-tongued H'nemthe female M'iiyoom Onith—aka Nightlily

Muggings are not sanctioned, but are almost as commonplace as shootings in the back rooms

Back room only for fugitives who pay dearly for privacy

Chalmun's personal pilot

A mechanic runs a system check on Chalmun's escape craft

UNUSUAL BEVERAGES

The Cantina bar caters to a broad range of alien species, all of whom consume an equally broad range of intoxicating liquids, gases, and solids-based concoctions. The raw ingredients are stored in the cellar and piped to the mixing stacks at the bar. Wuher the barman thinks of the cheerless cellar as his laboratory, in which he continually experiments with new formulas to please the most discriminating palates. When serving drinks, Wuher uses one of four computer terminals to achieve just the right ratio of base ingredients.

Bustling bazaar

Small hangar open to Tatooine's gritty air

Utility crane ship picks up liquor imports from orbiting heavy freighters

Cantina's secret back door leads into phony shop

Exposed cooling tubes of run-down shop

Surveillance droid keeps tabs on usual suspects

Cantina's communications jammer masquerades as vaporator

Every nook and cranny is a potential shop or crash pad for urban Jawas

Stormtrooper patrol

Catacombs predate Chalmun's purchase of the Cantina

Unwanted items (and bodies) cast into caustic pit

Rodian mercenary Greedo seeks his mark

Arconan scout, Hem Dazon

Multifingered former podracer, now a deft pickpocket

Pipes route special drinks from the cooker to bar spigots.

Sliding door keeps outsiders from Wuher's cellar "laboratory," where drinks are mixed

Kubaz paid informant, Garindan, keeps trunklike snout lifted to the air

Wuher's cooker—dosed with mummery, bergamot, and skusk—awaits missing ingredient for the elixir the bartender is creating for Jabba the Hutt

135

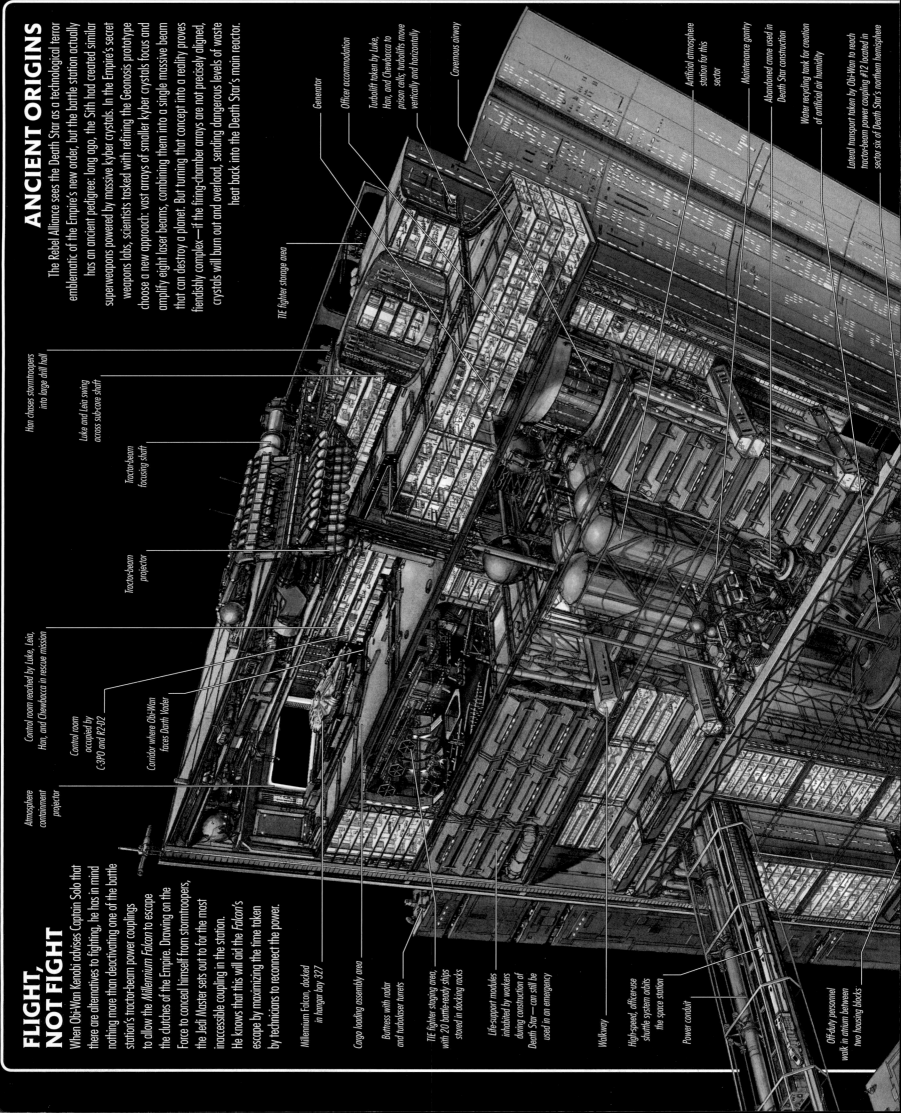

ANCIENT ORIGINS

The Rebel Alliance sees the Death Star as a technological terror emblematic of the Empire's new order, but the battle station actually has an ancient pedigree: long ago, the Sith had created similar superweapons powered by massive kyber crystals. In the Empire's secret weapons labs, scientists tasked with refining the Geonosis prototype choose a new approach: vast arrays of smaller kyber crystals focus and amplify eight laser beams, combining them into a single massive beam that can destroy a planet. But turning that concept into a reality proves fiendishly complex—if the firing-chamber arrays are not precisely aligned, crystals will burn out and overload, sending dangerous levels of waste heat back into the Death Star's main reactor.

FLIGHT, NOT FIGHT

When Obi-Wan Kenobi advises Captain Solo that there are alternatives to fighting, he has in mind nothing more than deactivating one of the battle station's tractor-beam power couplings to allow the *Millennium Falcon* to escape the clutches of the Empire. Drawing on the Force to conceal himself from stormtroopers, the Jedi Master sets out to for the most inaccessible coupling in the station. He knows that this will aid the *Falcon's* escape by maximizing the time taken by technicians to reconnect the power.

Han chases stormtroopers into large drill hall

Luke and Leia swing across sub-core shaft

Tractor-beam focusing shaft

Tractor-beam projector

Control room reached by Luke, Leia, Han, and Chewbacca in rescue mission

Control room occupied by C-3PO and R2-D2

Corridor where Obi-Wan faces Darth Vader

Atmosphere containment projector

TIE fighter storage area

Generator

Officer accommodation

Turbolift taken by Luke, Han, and Chewbacca to prison cells; turbolifts move vertically and horizontally

Cavernous airway

Artificial atmosphere station for this sector

Maintenance gantry

Abandoned crane used in Death Star construction

Water recycling tank for creation of artificial air humidity

Lateral transport taken by Obi-Wan to reach tractor-beam power coupling #12 located in sector six of Death Star's northern hemisphere

Millennium Falcon, docked in hangar bay 327

Cargo loading assembly area

Buttress with radar and turbolaser turrets

TIE fighter staging area, with 20 battle-ready ships stored in docking racks

Life-support modules inhabited by workers during construction of Death Star—can still be used in an emergency

Walkway

High-speed, officer-use shuttle system orbits the space station

Power conduit

Off-duty personnel walk in atrium between two housing blocks

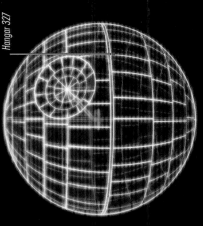

Hangar 327

Disguised as stormtroopers, Han and Luke escort Chewbacca to detention block AA-23, as part of a ploy to rescue Princess Organa.

THE DEATH STAR

THE MOONLET-SIZE superweapon that came to be known as the Death Star had been in the planning stages since before the abrupt outbreak of the Clone Wars. The massive project was funded by a sinister conglomerate of factions, including the Trade Federation, the InterGalactic Banking Clan, the Techno Union, and—more clandestinely—by the beleaguered Republic itself. Its construction began above the Outer Rim world of Geonosis, which was closed to travel except for a few senior Imperial officers, and later depopulated. The battle station's champion, Grand Moff Tarkin, believes its power will terrorize insurgent systems into abandoning the rebel cause, ensuring galactic peace and rendering the quarrelsome Imperial Senate obsolete. Although its destruction of Alderaan shocks the galaxy, the Death Star's own fiery demise above Yavin galvanizes opposition to Palpatine, with new systems joining the rebels or offering covert support.

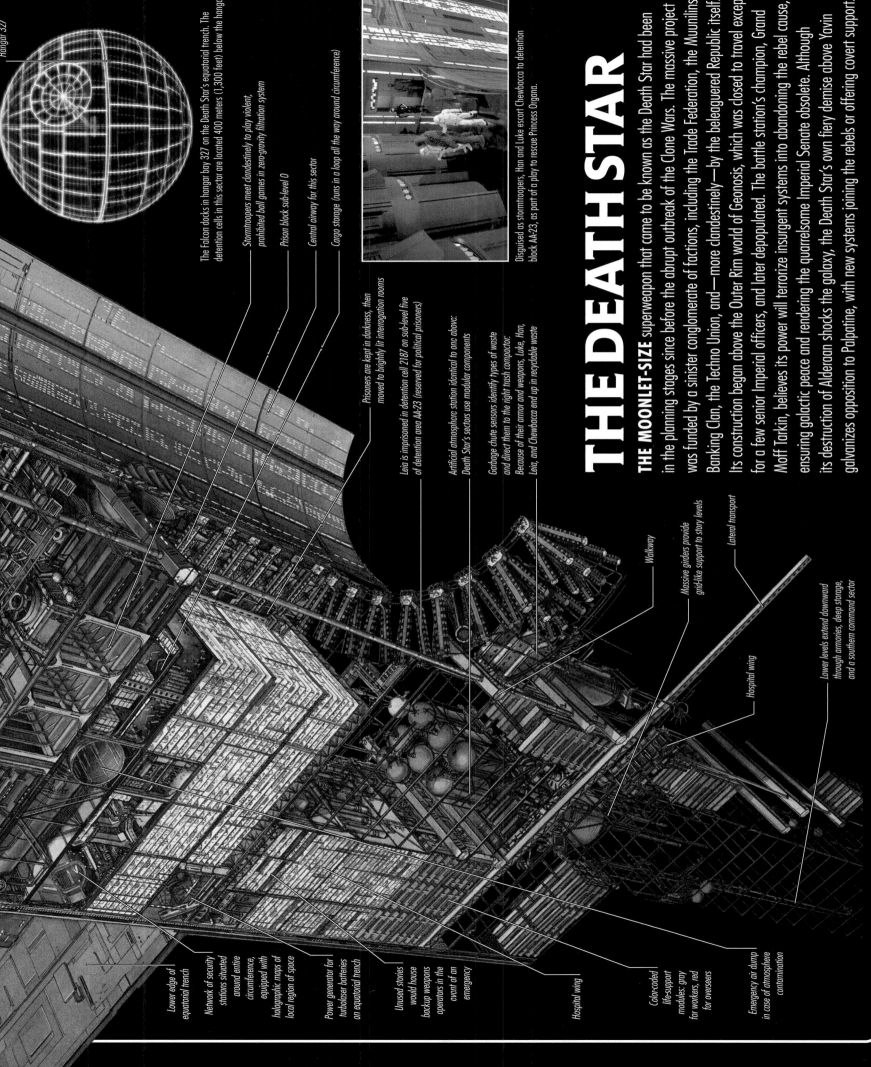

The Falcon docks in hangar bay 327 on the Death Star's equatorial trench. The detention cells in this sector are located 400 meters (1,300 feet) below the hangar.

Stormtroopers meet clandestinely to play violent, prohibited ball games in zero-gravity filtration system

Prison block sub-level 0

Central airway for this sector

Cargo storage (runs in a loop all the way around circumference)

Prisoners are kept in darkness, then moved to brightly lit interrogation rooms

Leia is imprisoned in detention cell 2187 on sub-level five of detention area AA-23 (reserved for political prisoners)

Artificial atmosphere station identical to one above: Death Star's sectors use modular components

Garbage chute sensors identify types of waste and direct them to the right trash compactor. Because of their armor and weapons, Luke, Han, Leia, and Chewbacca end up in recyclable waste

Walkway

Massive girders provide grid-like support to story levels

Lateral transport

Hospital wing

Lower levels extend downward through armories, deep storage, and a southern command sector

Emergency air dump in case of atmosphere contamination

Hospital wing

Color-coded life-support modules: gray for workers, red for overseers

Unused stories would house backup weapons operators in the event of an emergency

Power generator for turbolaser batteries on equatorial trench

Network of security stations situated around entire circumference, equipped with holographic maps of local region of space

Lower edge of equatorial trench

THE GREAT TEMPLE

BLANKETED WITH NEARLY impenetrable vegetation, Yavin 4 is home to countless unique species of plants, animals, and insects, but hosts no intelligent life-forms. The fourth moon of an uninhabitable gas giant, the world had been of interest only to galactic archeologists, who had marveled at the ancient stone temples that rise majestically from its jungles.

These towering, stepped structures are all that remain of the lost civilization of the Massassi. With no sentient population to subdue and no mineral wealth to exploit, Yavin 4 has been overlooked by the Empire and is little known within the wider galaxy. It is for precisely this reason that the resourceful leaders of the Rebel Alliance choose Yavin 4 as their base after having been forced to flee their previous command center on the planet Dantooine.

UNTAMED NATURE

The surrounding jungle of purple-barked Massassi trees resounds with the eerie cries and blood-chilling moans of unseen creatures: woolamanders, lizard crabs, stintaril rodents, and armored eels, among others. Dense thickets of thorny vegetation and unpredictable storms thwart the progress of surveyors and construction engineers. As a result, the rebels stick to the laser-cut access and patrol routes that link the Great Temple to outlying landing zones and the distant power station.

MYSTERIOUS MASONS

Shining like an emerald among the necklace of moons that encircles its gas giant host, Yavin 4 is rich with life and full of mysteries. Little is known of the now-vanished species that crafted the moon's Great Temple except its name: the Massassi. Long ago, this extinct people somehow hewed giant blocks of stone from the moon's crust and transported them many kilometers to locations deemed holy—or perhaps significant for primitive scientific purposes. The rebel pilots and soldiers who now occupy the ancient Massassi ruins can only speculate about what became of their sanctuary's lost builders.

POWER SUPPLY

The functioning of the base is reliant on a power-generating station located two kilometers (1.2 miles) away. Pieced together from turbines and a main reactor stolen from a wrecked Imperial Star Destroyer, the station supplies sufficient power for a protective shield, ion cannons, and other defenses that could hold off an assault from a single large battleship.

Having docked the *Millennium Falcon* at the nearby visitor landing zone, Luke, Han, Leia, and the droids are met by rebel leaders outside the base's impregnable blast door.

Observation and communications room

Tall skylights aligned with equinox and solstice

Turbolift to audience chamber

Massassi-built staircase to observation room at apex

Audience chamber floor filed with translucent precious stones

Water reservoir

Interior of temple clad with sheets of seamed metal

Algae, mosses, and vines resist rebel attempts to blast original rock face clean of vegetation

Luke Skywalker, Han Solo, and Chewbacca march down aisle

Ceremony commemorating destruction of Death Star takes place in audience chamber

Princess Leia, General Dodonna, and other dignitaries stand on ceremonial podium

Holographic memorials to those killed in battle will be placed outside ceremonial hall

Central turbolift cluster

Roughly cut cavities drilled by rebels into straighter sides of original Massassi interior

Anti-personnel cannons

Auxiliary power generators

Temple built with no visible sign of advanced machinery

Command room

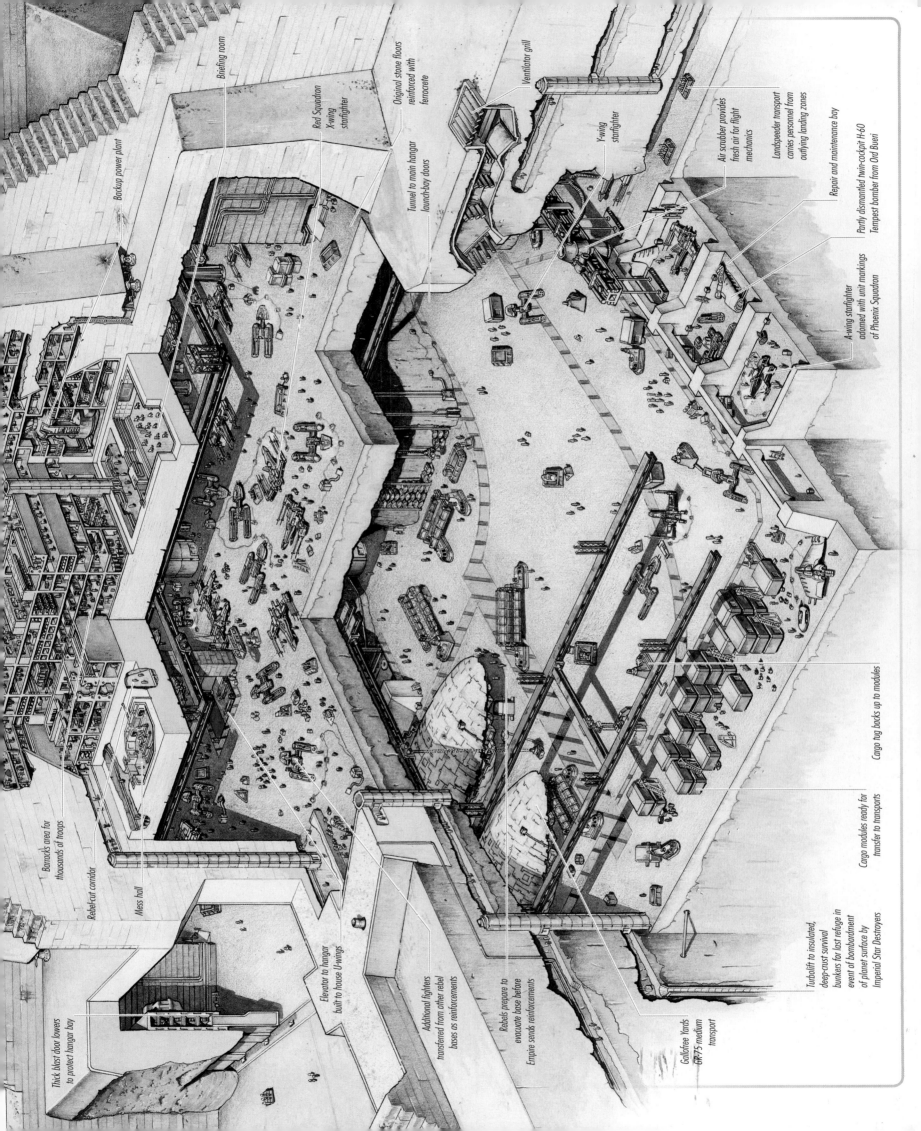

Backup power plant

Briefing room

Red Squadron X-wing starfighter

Original stone floors reinforced with ferrocrete

Ventilator grill

Y-wing starfighter

Air scrubber provides fresh air for flight mechanics

Landspeeder transport carries personnel from outlying landing zones

Repair and maintenance bay

Tunnel to main hangar launch-bay doors

Partly dismantled twin-cockpit H-60 Tempest bomber from Ord Bueri

A-wing starfighter adorned with unit markings of Phoenix Squadron

Thick blast door lowers to protect hangar bay

Barracks area for thousands of troops

Rebel-cut corridor

Mess hall

Elevator to hangar built to house U-wings

Additional fighters transferred from other rebel bases as reinforcements

Rebels prepare to evacuate base before Empire sends reinforcements

Turbolift to insulated, deep-crust survival bunkers for last refuge in event of bombardment of planet surface by Imperial Star Destroyers

Cargo modules ready for transfer to transports

Gallofree Yards GR-75 medium transport

Cargo tug backs up to modules

BATTLE OF HOTH

ALTHOUGH HOTH IS OFTEN CITED as the worst defeat suffered by the Rebel Alliance during the Galactic Civil War, it was not a crushing one. Admiral Ozzel unintentionally granted the rebels time to mount a holding action—and the ensuing organized retreat—by arrogantly bringing the Imperial fleet out of hyperspace too close to Hoth. Darth Vader added to the blunder by being so fixed on capturing Luke Skywalker alive that he ordered his flotilla of Star Destroyers to pursue the *Falcon* rather than hunt down the escaped rebel transports. Moreover, Civil War historians have pointed out that if not for this painful rout, the Alliance might never have risked everything at Endor a year later, where they inflicted a defeat on the Empire from which it never recovered.

1 One of thousands seeded by the Imperial Star Destroyer *Stalker*, an Arakyd Viper probe droid meanders over Hoth's snowfields and glaciers, alert for anomalous energy signatures that might point to Rebel Alliance activity. Its images of the rebel power generator are transmitted back to Imperial officers.

2 In the trenches, Beta Outpost troops commanded by Trey Callum ready their repeating blasters for in-close fighting. Precision targeting by anti-personnel batteries decimates Veers' snowtroopers, buying the rebels more time to evacuate the base and weave their transports through the Star Destroyer blockade.

IMPERIAL GROUND ASSAULT

General Maximillian Veers is tasked with destroying the shield power generator and capturing rather than killing the rebels who survive his assault. Forced to steer clear of the shield perimeter, Imperial landing barges and troop transports set down on the precarious Moorsh Morraine, well north of the heavily fortified mountain base. Having thus surrendered the element of surprise, but augmented with legions of snowtroopers, Veers' contingent of AT-ATs (large, four-legged walkers) and AT-STs (medium bipeds)—dubbed Blizzard Force—begins its inexorable march on the rebel facility.

3 Swiveling on their bases, Golan Arms DF9 anti-artillery batteries hammer away at the advancing walkers, but to no avail. Snowspeeder pilots, too, find their lasers ineffective against the thick armor of the Imperial war machines. Raked by laserfire, Rogue Leader is hit, and Luke's gunner, Dak, is killed.

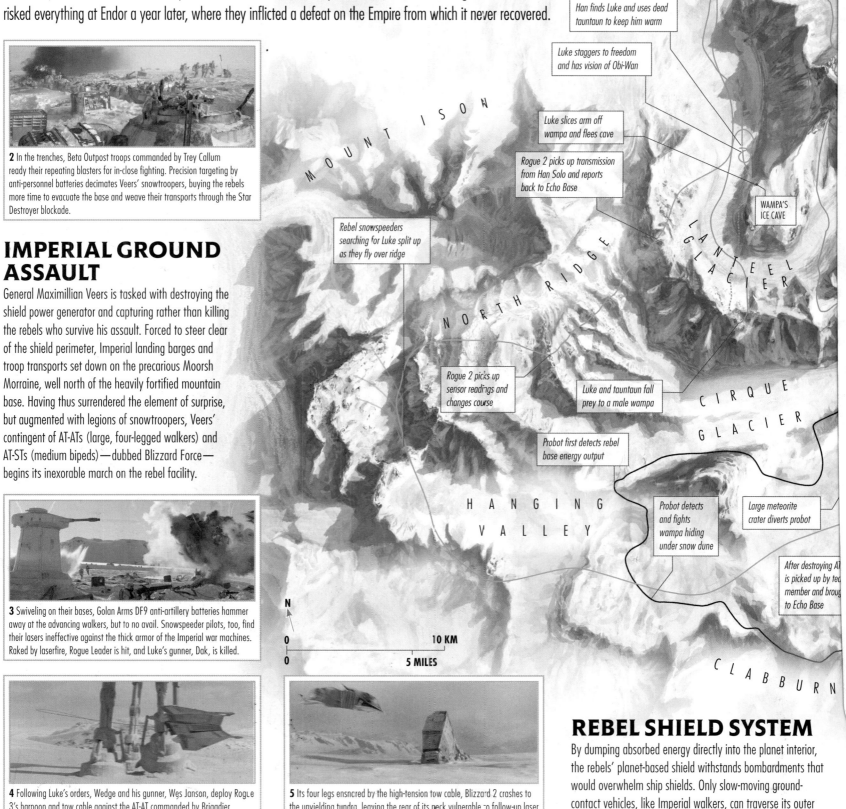

Han finds Luke and uses dead tauntaun to keep him warm

Luke staggers to freedom and has vision of Obi-Wan

Luke slices arm off wampa and flees cave

Rogue 2 picks up transmission from Han Solo and reports back to Echo Base

WAMPA'S ICE CAVE

MOUNT ISON

LANTEEL GLACIER

Rebel snowspeeders searching for Luke split up as they fly over ridge

NORTH RIDGE

Rogue 2 picks up sensor readings and changes course

Luke and tauntaun fall prey to a male wampa

CIRQUE GLACIER

Probot first detects rebel base energy output

HANGING VALLEY

Probot detects and fights wampa hiding under snow dune

Large meteorite crater diverts probot

After destroying A[T] is picked up by te[am] member and broug[ht] to Echo Base

CLABBURN

N

0 — 10 KM
0 — 5 MILES

4 Following Luke's orders, Wedge and his gunner, Wes Janson, deploy Rogue 3's harpoon and tow cable against the AT-AT commanded by Brigadier General Nevar. The dangerous maneuver requires that the cable be wrapped around the legs of a walker, then severed at precisely the right moment.

5 Its four legs ensnared by the high-tension tow cable, Blizzard 2 crashes to the unyielding tundra, leaving the rear of its neck vulnerable to follow-up laser fire. With one walker dispatched, the rebels continue to wage their holding action, but are ultimately overwhelmed by the Empire's durable behemoths.

REBEL SHIELD SYSTEM

By dumping absorbed energy directly into the planet interior, the rebels' planet-based shield withstands bombardments that would overwhelm ship shields. Only slow-moving ground-contact vehicles, like Imperial walkers, can traverse its outer surface. With the projector modules distributed throughout rebel territory, Veers targets the central power generator.

ECHO BASE

AFTER THE EVACUATION of Yavin 4, the Rebel Alliance embarks on a search for a planet or moon to serve as a new secret base of operations. Explorations by Luke Skywalker, Commander Narra, and others lead to the ice planet Hoth, a world so remote as to be off the standard navigational star charts entirely. The command center is constructed over the course of two standard years, under brutal conditions. Rebel engineers and construction crews employ laser ice-cutting equipment to enlarge a series of natural caverns, excavate new ones, and fashion connecting corridors. Designated Echo Base for the cave's strange acoustics, the base is still being constructed when an Imperial probe droid plunges fatefully to Hoth's glacial surface...

Snowspeeders and X-wings are stationed in North Hangar 7. Secret tunnels connect the hangar to several other, smaller, north entrances.

PREPARING FOR THE WORST

While essential for defense, the presence of the shield generator all but guarantees that Echo Base will eventually unmask itself to the Empire. Anticipating that an assault would be launched on the surface of Hoth, General Carlist Rieekan orders that heavy blast doors be installed in the north and south entrances, trenches be excavated on the glacial plains all around the base, and that ground-based anti-personnel batteries be embedded in the mountainside above the principal hangars and in the ice fields between artillery trenches.

Zev Senesca in Rogue 2 snowspeeder

Wedge Antilles and Wes Janson in Rogue 3 snowspeeder

Track for sliding door needs constant lubrication

Luke Skywalker and Dak Ralter in Rogue Leader

Major Dervis' infantry hurry to defensive trenches

Incom T-47 airspeeders modified to function on Hoth

R2-D2 searches for his counterpart

Air boss oversees starfighter launch

"Hobbie" Klivian and Kesin Ommis in Rogue 4 snowspeeder

Routing illuminators guide snowspeeders to launch area

Laser ice-cutter is one of many that enlarged the mountain's caves

Sunlight filters into base through narrow crevasse in the surface ice

Curved transparisteel window overlooks Hangar 7

Millennium Falcon's hyperdrive has yet to be fully repaired

Leia's quarters

EMERGENCY CARE

The Rebel Alliance is careful to provide timely medical support for its valued troops. On Hoth, a well-equipped medical center provides first-rate response and triage for Echo Base's 7,500 combat personnel. Overseen by a medical command officer, the staff of 350 physicians and surgeons, augmented by some 120 specialized droids, remains on call to deal with any emergencies that might arise.

North entrance blast door

Luke's X-wing will be transported to South entrance before last transport leaves

Hangar 7

Elevator to maintenance level

Snubfighter's astromech droid socket

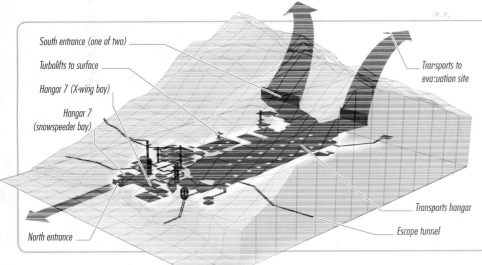

South entrance (one of two)

Turbolifts to surface

Hangar 7 (X-wing bay)

Hangar 7 (snowspeeder bay)

North entrance

Transports to evacuation site

Transports hangar

Escape tunnel

ICE MOUNTAIN HIDE-OUT

Several locations in Hoth's temperate zone were scouted and surveyed before a cavern-hollowed mountain in the southern Clabburn Range was judged suitable to serve as the hidden fortress the rebels had in mind. The Corp of Engineers fashioned interior spaces vast enough to house not only the Alliance's wings of starfighters, but also its tattered fleet of Gallofree Yards transports. Plasmold insulation and armored doors—of a different sort than those used on Yavin 4—help to shelter the base from the ferocity of Hoth's ice storms.

DAGOBAH

NEAR DEATH FROM EXPOSURE to Hoth's sub-zero temperatures, the side of his face crushed by a giant wampa, Luke has a vision of his mentor, Obi-Wan Kenobi. The Jedi Master orders him to go to the Dagobah system to complete his training under the guidance of Kenobi's former instructor, the diminutive Yoda. With a bewildered R2-D2 for companionship, Luke parts with Han and Leia to follow his destined course. Remote from known space routes, shrouded in cloud cover, but emitting massive life-form readings, Dagobah is a gloomy world of swamps and twisted trees, winged predators, and poisonous snakes. Seemingly engulfed by the planet, Luke's X-wing plummets to the surface...

1 Is this a dream or just a bad idea? Luke wonders aloud. His mind as foggy as his new environment, he leaves his crashed starfighter to marinate in the muck of one of Dagobah's black-water bogs and begins to take stock of the inhospitable world to which Obi-Wan has sent him.

2 While Luke can't help feeling that there is something strangely recognizable about haunted Dagobah, there is nothing even remotely familiar about the gnomish green creature who shows up to turn Luke and R2-D2's camp into his private playground.

3 In the creature's cramped dwelling, while torrential rain falls, Luke learns that he has in fact found Yoda. But the ancient Jedi Master and a ghostly Obi-Wan Kenobi disagree about whether Luke will be able to surrender his yearning for adventure and be properly trained in the ways of the Force.

4 Under Yoda's sometimes mystifying tutelage, Luke learns to perform superhuman tasks and will his body to levitate objects—including the astromech. With Yoda clasped to his back, Luke runs, leaps, and somersaults through Dagobah's riotous jungle, his strength flowing from the Force.

6 Yoda demonstrates to Luke that "size matters not," when he telekinetically rescues Luke's sinking X-wing from the grasp of the sticky bog. Disappointed with Luke, Yoda explains that the youth's failed attempt was due to his inability to believe in his own potential and the power of the Force.

5 Deep within the cave-like root system of a colossal gnarltree—a domain of thick-bodied snakes and quick-tongued sleens—Luke has a precognitive vision of the true relationship with his evil adversary, Darth Vader. Strong with the dark side, the cave contains no more than what Luke has taken with him.

7 A vision of Han and Leia imperiled on a city in the clouds persuades Luke to abbreviate his training and leave Dagobah—despite Yoda's admonition that, by doing so, Luke will likely destroy all for which Han and Leia have fought and suffered.

Gnarltree bridge over lagoon inlet

Yoda gathers galla seeds and sohli bark from areas surrounding his home

Spring-fed sweet water lagoon

Yoda's house

R2-D2 peers through the window of Yoda's dwelling

Yoda often gathers yarum seeds from forest, avoiding the sharp webs spun by butcherbugs

Parasitic blackvine forms natural bridges

Entrance to uncharted cave complex

Cargo cranes and gantries

Extensive cargo storage bays

Personnel carrier

Gallofree medium transport Dutyfree is escorted off-planet by Luke Skywalker and Wedge Antilles

Tauntaun ready room

Cargo modules bound for transports

Transport bridge

Power generator

Last transport to leave the base, Bright Hope, is loaded with hundreds of wounded soldiers from the battlefield

Principal reactor cowl of transport

Gallofree Yards GR-75 medium transports are equipped with more engines than civilian-use GR-45 models, for increased power

Lower-level ventilation shaft

Y-wing receives charge through power umbilical

Y-wing prep bays

X-wings being readied to escort transports into orbit

LIVESTOCK

At first, Hoth appeared to be almost devoid of large animals—which suited the rebels well. In fact, the ice world is home to a surprising variety of hardy species that have adapted to the harsh environment, including tauntauns and their chief predators, wampas. The latter are too ferocious to be domesticated, but tauntauns prove to be a great asset to the rebels while their X-wings and snowspeeders are undergoing special modifications. Hundreds of the reptilian "snow lizards" are rounded up and corralled inside the base, where their natural food of lichen and moss is carefully cultivated. Eventually, the creatures are trained for use as pack animals and patrol mounts.

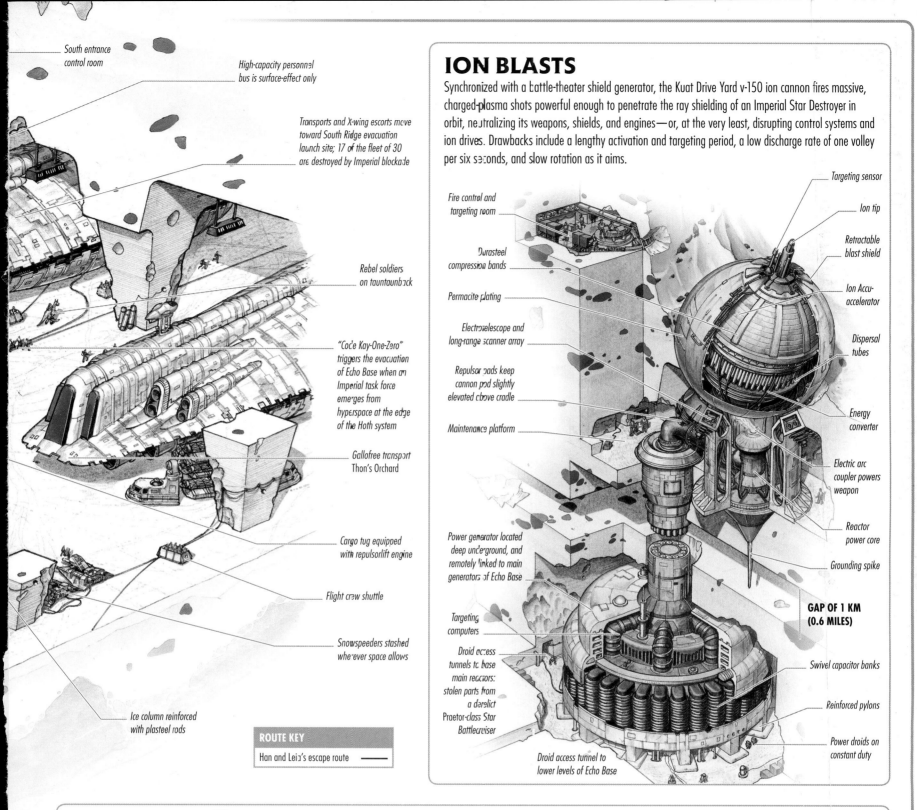

South entrance
control room

High-capacity personnel
bus is surface-effect only

Transports and X-wing escorts move
toward South Ridge evacuation
launch site; 17 of the fleet of 30
are destroyed by Imperial blockade

Rebel soldiers
on tauntaunback

"Code Kay-One-Zero"
triggers the evacuation
of Echo Base when an
Imperial task force
emerges from
hyperspace at the edge
of the Hoth system

Gallofree transport
Thon's Orchard

Cargo tug equipped
with repulsorlift engine

Flight crew shuttle

Snowspeeders stashed
wherever space allows

Ice column reinforced
with plasteel rods

ION BLASTS

Synchronized with a battle-theater shield generator, the Kuat Drive Yard v-150 ion cannon fires massive, charged-plasma shots powerful enough to penetrate the ray shielding of an Imperial Star Destroyer in orbit, neutralizing its weapons, shields, and engines—or, at the very least, disrupting control systems and ion drives. Drawbacks include a lengthy activation and targeting period, a low discharge rate of one volley per six seconds, and slow rotation as it aims.

Fire control and
targeting room

Durasteel
compression bands

Permacite plating

Electrotelescope and
long-range scanner array

Repulsor pads keep
cannon pod slightly
elevated above cradle

Maintenance platform

Power generator located
deep underground, and
remotely linked to main
generators of Echo Base

Targeting
computers

Droid access
tunnels to base
main reactors:
stolen parts from
a derelict
Praetor-class Star
Battlecruiser

Droid access tunnel to
lower levels of Echo Base

Targeting sensor

Ion tip

Retractable
blast shield

Ion Accu-
accelerator

Dispersal
tubes

Energy
converter

Electric arc
coupler powers
weapon

Reactor
power core

Grounding spike

**GAP OF 1 KM
(0.6 MILES)**

Swivel capacitor banks

Reinforced pylons

Power droids on
constant duty

Cargo crane pivot

Armored plating protects mostly hollow vessel

Forward communications array

Lateral sensor

Loading arm

Rotating cargo-pod offloader

16-module capacity
quad cargo carousel

Cargo tug

Hoisted containers glide
on magnetic holding rails

Magnetic containment
shield safeguards cargo

Lateral main
engine fuel
tank

Detachable crew/
passenger module

Landing gear

MEDIUM TRANSPORT

Little more than armored shells, the 90 meter (300 feet)-long Gallofree Yards transports are perfectly suited to the needs of the Rebel Alliance because of the relative ease of their loading and unloading process, their enormous cargo capacity, and their ability to land directly on the surface of a planet or moon. In transit, the GR-75's modular cargo pods are suspended from magnetic rails and kept in place by a powerful magnetic containment field. The ships were sold to the Alliance at a bargain price, and used chiefly for transporting weapons, raw materials, food, fuel, and spare parts, though a few Gallofrees were retrofitted for personnel transport by adapting the interiors to accommodate sealed passenger pods.

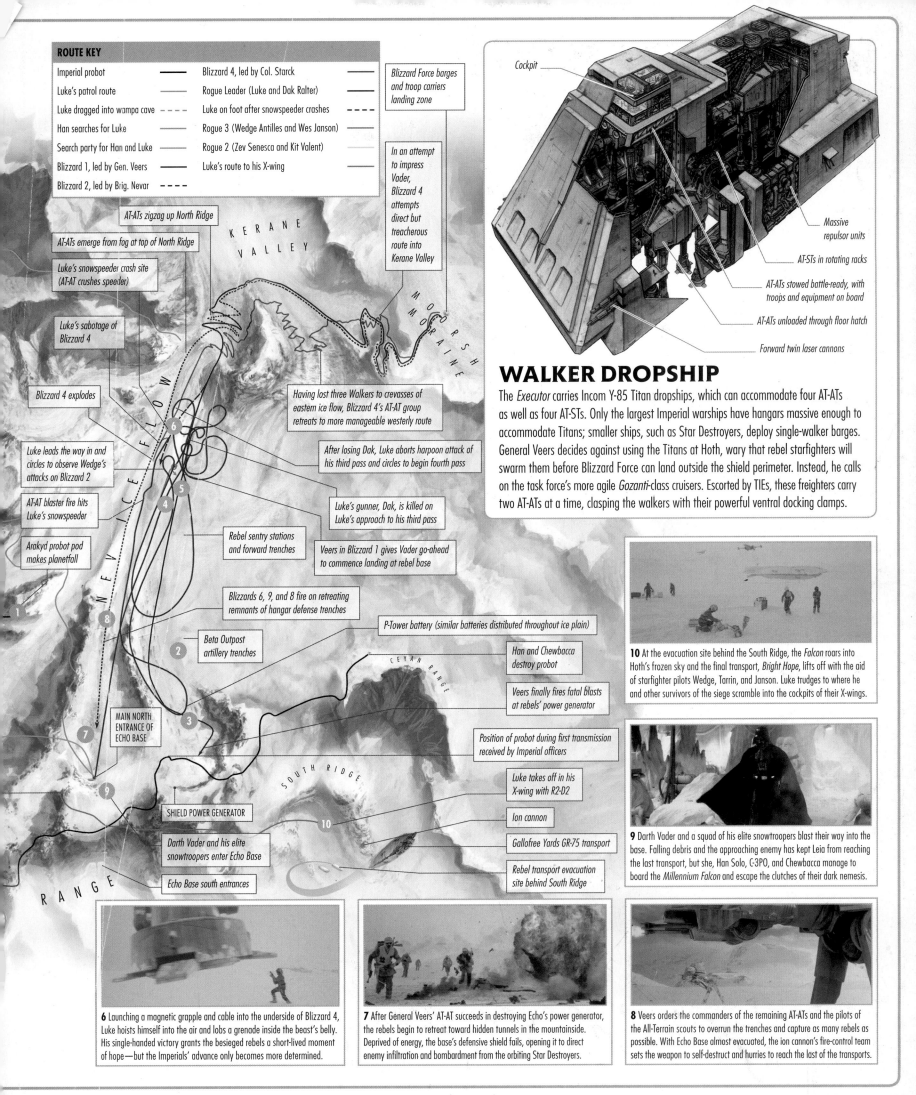

ROUTE KEY

Imperial probot	——————	Blizzard 4, led by Col. Starck	——————
Luke's patrol route	——————	Rogue Leader (Luke and Dak Ralter)	——————
Luke dragged into wampa cave	– – – –	Luke on foot after snowspeeder crashes	– – – –
Han searches for Luke	——————	Rogue 3 (Wedge Antilles and Wes Janson)	——————
Search party for Han and Luke	——————	Rogue 2 (Zev Senesca and Kit Valent)	——————
Blizzard 1, led by Gen. Veers	——————	Luke's route to his X-wing	——————
Blizzard 2, led by Brig. Nevar	– – – –		

KERANE VALLEY

MOORSH MORAINE

AT-ATs zigzag up North Ridge

AT-ATs emerge from fog at top of North Ridge

Luke's snowspeeder crash site (AT-AT crushes speeder)

Luke's sabotage of Blizzard 4

Blizzard 4 explodes

In an attempt to impress Vader, Blizzard 4 attempts direct but treacherous route into Kerane Valley

Blizzard Force barges and troop carriers landing zone

Having lost three Walkers to crevasses of eastern ice flow, Blizzard 4's AT-AT group retreats to more manageable westerly route

Luke leads the way in and circles to observe Wedge's attacks on Blizzard 2

After losing Dak, Luke aborts harpoon attack of his third pass and circles to begin fourth pass

AT-AT blaster fire hits Luke's snowspeeder

Luke's gunner, Dak, is killed on Luke's approach to his third pass

Arakyd probot pod makes planetfall

NEV ICE FLOW

Rebel sentry stations and forward trenches

Veers in Blizzard 1 gives Vader go-ahead to commence landing at rebel base

Blizzards 6, 9, and 8 fire on retreating remnants of hangar defense trenches

Beta Outpost artillery trenches

P-Tower battery (similar batteries distributed throughout ice plain)

CEYAN RANGE

Han and Chewbacca destroy probot

Veers finally fires fatal blasts at rebels' power generator

MAIN NORTH ENTRANCE OF ECHO BASE

Position of probot during first transmission received by Imperial officers

SOUTH RIDGE

Luke takes off in his X-wing with R2-D2

SHIELD POWER GENERATOR

Ion cannon

Gallofree Yards GR-75 transport

Darth Vader and his elite snowtroopers enter Echo Base

Rebel transport evacuation site behind South Ridge

Echo Base south entrances

RANGE

WALKER DROPSHIP

The *Executor* carries Incom Y-85 Titan dropships, which can accommodate four AT-ATs as well as four AT-STs. Only the largest Imperial warships have hangars massive enough to accommodate Titans; smaller ships, such as Star Destroyers, deploy single-walker barges. General Veers decides against using the Titans at Hoth, wary that rebel starfighters will swarm them before Blizzard Force can land outside the shield perimeter. Instead, he calls on the task force's more agile *Gozanti*-class cruisers. Escorted by TIEs, these freighters carry two AT-ATs at a time, clasping the walkers with their powerful ventral docking clamps.

Cockpit

Massive repulsor units

AT-STs in rotating racks

AT-ATs stowed battle-ready, with troops and equipment on board

AT-ATs unloaded through floor hatch

Forward twin laser cannons

10 At the evacuation site behind the South Ridge, the *Falcon* roars into Hoth's frozen sky and the final transport, *Bright Hope*, lifts off with the aid of starfighter pilots Wedge, Tarrin, and Janson. Luke trudges to where he and other survivors of the siege scramble into the cockpits of their X-wings.

9 Darth Vader and a squad of his elite snowtroopers blast their way into the base. Falling debris and the approaching enemy has kept Leia from reaching the last transport, but she, Han Solo, C-3PO, and Chewbacca manage to board the *Millennium Falcon* and escape the clutches of their dark nemesis.

6 Launching a magnetic grapple and cable into the underside of Blizzard 4, Luke hoists himself into the air and lobs a grenade inside the beast's belly. His single-handed victory grants the besieged rebels a short-lived moment of hope—but the Imperials' advance only becomes more determined.

7 After General Veers' AT-AT succeeds in destroying Echo's power generator, the rebels begin to retreat toward hidden tunnels in the mountainside. Deprived of energy, the base's defensive shield fails, opening it to direct enemy infiltration and bombardment from the orbiting Star Destroyers.

8 Veers orders the commanders of the remaining AT-ATs and the pilots of the All-Terrain scouts to overrun the trenches and capture as many rebels as possible. With Echo Base almost evacuated, the ion cannon's fire-control team sets the weapon to self-destruct and hurries to reach the last of the transports.

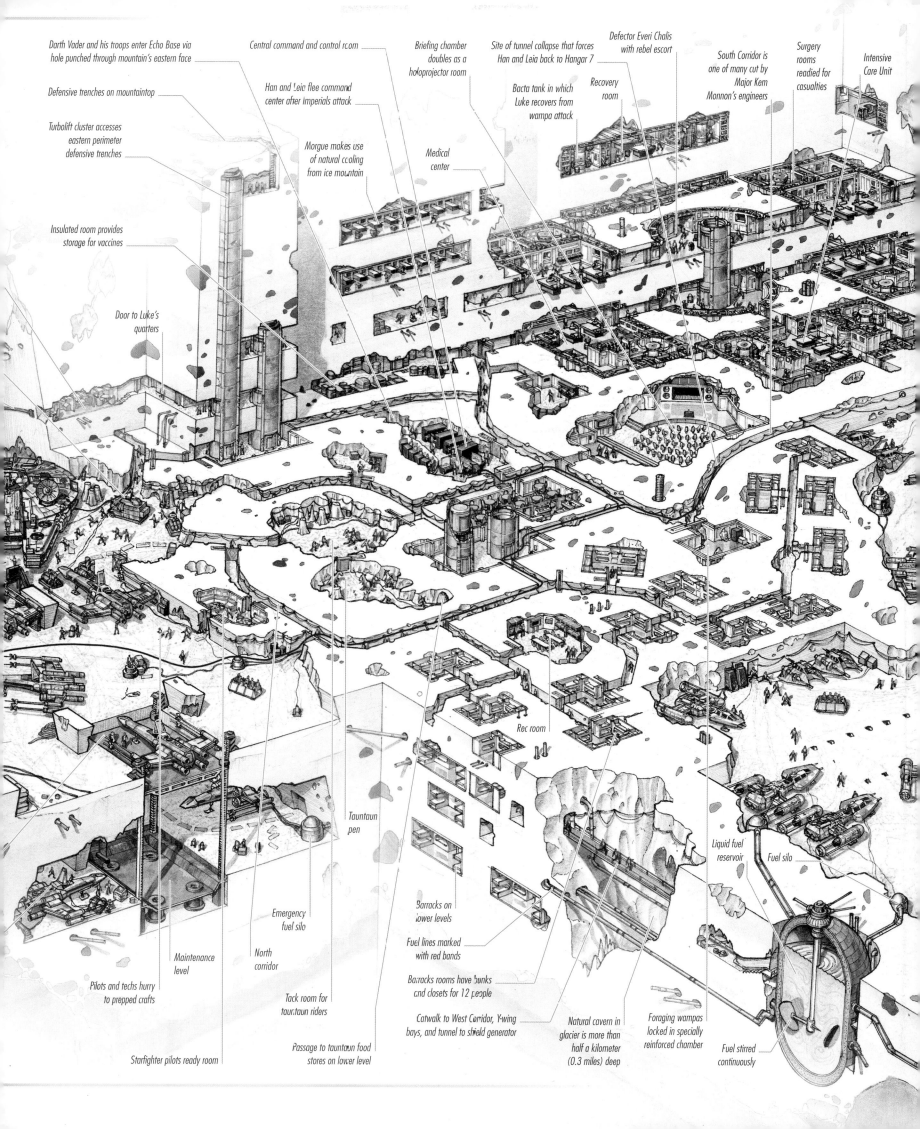

Darth Vader and his troops enter Echo Base via hole punched through mountain's eastern face

Central command and control room

Briefing chamber doubles as a holoprojector room

Site of tunnel collapse that forces Han and Leia back to Hangar 7

Defector Everi Chalis with rebel escort

South Corridor is one of many cut by Major Kem Monnon's engineers

Surgery rooms readied for casualties

Intensive Care Unit

Defensive trenches on mountaintop

Han and Leia flee command center after Imperials attack

Bacta tank in which Luke recovers from wampa attack

Recovery room

Turbolift cluster accesses eastern perimeter defensive trenches

Morgue makes use of natural cooling from ice mountain

Medical center

Insulated room provides storage for vaccines

Door to Luke's quarters

Rec room

Liquid fuel reservoir

Fuel silo

Tauntaun pen

Barracks on lower levels

Fuel lines marked with red bands

Pilots and techs hurry to prepped crafts

Maintenance level

North corridor

Emergency fuel silo

Tack room for tauntaun riders

Barracks rooms have bunks and closets for 12 people

Catwalk to West Corridor, Y-wing bays, and tunnel to shield generator

Natural cavern in glacier is more than half a kilometer (0.3 miles) deep

Foraging wampas locked in specially reinforced chamber

Fuel stirred continuously

Starfighter pilots ready room

Passage to tauntaun food stores on lower level

EPISODE V
THE EMPIRE STRIKES BACK

It is a dark time for the Rebellion. Although the Death Star has been destroyed, Imperial troops have driven the Rebel forces from their hidden base and pursued them across the galaxy.

Evading the dreaded Imperial Starfleet, a group of freedom fighters led by Luke Skywalker has established a new secret base on the remote ice world of Hoth.

The evil lord Darth Vader, obsessed with finding young Skywalker, has dispatched thousands of remote probes into the far reaches of space....

DISMAL AND DANGEROUS

Dagobah's bogs and lagoons are home to a host of creatures, including the swamp slug, which pulverizes its prey between thousands of tiny grinding teeth; the stealthy dragonsnake, whose razor-sharp claws are strong enough to incise alloy; and the quick-striking scrange, which uses its tusked tail to make short work of any creature that wanders into its reach. Smaller, but equally deadly, is the butcherbug, which spins slicing webs, and the morp, whose venom causes paralysis.

STRONG IN THE FORCE

During the Clone Wars, the Force spirit of Qui-Gon Jinn contacted Yoda, instructing the Jedi Master to travel to Dagobah in secret. Qui-Gon explained that the swamp planet was one of the purest places in the galaxy, made strong in the Force by its abundant life. There, Qui-Gon began to instruct Yoda in the mysteries of the Cosmic Force and the Jedi Master experienced a vision of the Sith's triumph. After Order 66, Yoda sought refuge on Dagobah, learning how to retain his consciousness after death.

Luke confronts vision of Vader

Rusting remnants of Yoda's escape pod

Many petrified gnarltrees

Entire shoreline of peninsula is quicksand

Luke leaves Yoda to reach cave entrance

Entrance to cave located in immense gnarltree hollow

Luke swings across boggy inlet using tree vines

Good area for finding paludial fungi "yogurt plants"

Trees weighed down with heavy nests built by jubba birds using mud scooped up from Dragonsnake Bog

DRAGONSNAKE BOG

Enormous, predatory dragonsnake lurks just beneath bog waters

Luke's X-wing landing trajectory causes swathe of broken branches

Luke's training area

R2-D2 is swallowed by dragonsnake and spat out again

X-wing lands on edge of Dragonsnake Bog

Yoda levitates Luke's X-wing from the bog and places it onto dry land

Luke's temporary camp

R2-D2 lands on firm ground after being spat out by dragonsnake

ROUTE KEY

R2-D2's swamp walk	———
Luke walks to a clearing and sets up camp	———
Yoda takes Luke and R2-D2 back to his dwelling	———
Luke's training circuit	———
Luke in the cave	- - -

YODA'S HOUSE

HAND-BUILT OF MUD, gnarltree wattle, and stones, Yoda's house sits in the embrace of a giant gnarltree, atop a moss-covered knoll at the edge of a sweet water lagoon. The tiny dwelling comprises a sitting room, kitchen, and small sleeping loft, as well as windows and skylights with panes that may have been forged from precious gems—or perhaps from the transparisteel viewports of an abandoned escape pod. When Luke is invited inside, he practically wears the miniature house like a shell. But Yoda is only amused by the young man's head-bumping attempts to make himself comfortable.

For a young starfighter pilot who has spent months on Hoth eating only self-warming rations, a bowl of rootleaf stew should taste like high cuisine.

Bitter fruit from stickle tree

Large galla seeds

Luke's drying flight suit

Handcrafted chimney

Tindersticks for stove

Simmering rootleaf stew

Dried dung-patties used as fuel in fireplace

The Jedi Master opines that "wars not make one great"

Walking stick made from gimer twig—in his old-age, Yoda chews on the bark to release its natural anesthetic

Assorted roots, fruits, berries, and nuts for use in cooking

Tree-stump table arrayed with tasty dishes

Wattle-and-daub construction

Vines, leaves, and roots cover exterior of cottage

Non-venomous vine snakes share space with Yoda

Low-fire clay tiles grouted with mortar

Escape pod's hydraulic oil cooler acts as foot-cleaning mat

Front entry incorporates nozzle system of a Republic-era escape pod

AN UNCLUTTERED LIFE

Just another life-form among the snakes and spiders that share his home—and the bogwings, dragonsnakes, spotlight sloths, and butcherbugs that inhabit the swamps—Yoda spends part of each day foraging for food and paying keen attention to the life cycles of Dagobah's exotic creatures. Hobbling about on his gimer stick, the diminutive 900-year-old Jedi Master roams the shores of the mist-shrouded bogs searching out herbs, spices, paludial fungi, and fruits to flavor his rootleaf stews and flower petal salads. In a sense, Yoda lives the life he might have led had he not become a Jedi.

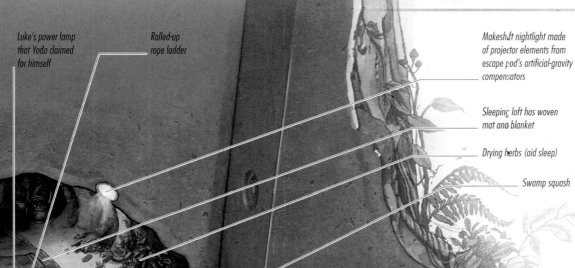

Luke's power lamp that Yoda claimed for himself

Rolled-up rope ladder

Makeshift nightlight made of projector elements from escape pod's artificial-gravity compensators

Sleeping loft has woven mat and blanket

Drying herbs (aid sleep)

Swamp squash

A SECRET PURPOSE

Yoda knew of Dagobah long before he chose it to be his place of self-exile. While it might appear that in so doing he sentenced himself to a life of seclusion, self-denial, and hardship, or that he was seeking only to place himself far from the Emperor's reach, he had a deeper motive in mind. Without distractions, or any means of leaving Dagobah to confront the Emperor or Darth Vader on his own, Yoda has been able to devote the years of his exile to pondering ancient Jedi texts, meditating on the deepest mysteries of the Force, and using his Jedi skills to communicate with Obi-Wan Kenobi and other exiles. He also monitors the children of Anakin Skywalker, patiently awaiting the day they might help restore balance to the Force.

Sink fed by water drawn from sluice

Backstrap-loomed cloth

Luminous stone used for glowlamp

Tools, machete, spade, and digging spikes for uncovering edible roots

Box holds keepsakes, ancient texts, and Yoda's lightsaber

Growth rings in the oldest gnarltree roots that act as cottage frame

A fretful R2-D2 peeps inside dwelling

Burrows made by silver-nape beetles

Salvaged deck-plating forms sturdy, waterproof foundation to house

Mud mixed with tree resin to complete water proofing of walls and floors

Luke not sure just what he has gotten himself into

Local twigs and grasses reinforce plaster

Rug made of spotlight sloth fur

BEGUILING ENVIRONMENT

The Force was strong on Dagobah even before Yoda arrived. While he could have drawn on the Force to raise a home as elegant as the Jedi Temple on Coruscant, he instead fabricated a primitive abode that makes Obi-Wan's house on Tatooine seem palatial by comparison. Yoda's hut looks as if it could be reduced to rubble by one of Dagobah's torrential rainstorms, and in fact it does fall into ruin soon after his death. In the same way that Yoda uses the Force and the planet's natural defenses to discourage visitors from investigating Dagobah, he can also draw on the power inherent in Dagobah to hold the hut together.

CLOUD CITY

FOUNDED BY ECCENTRIC INDUSTRIALIST Lord Ecclessis Figg of Corellia, Cloud City was originally known as Floating Home Mining Colony. Hovering at some 59,000 kilometers (37,000 miles) from Bespin's core, the installation is designed to extract rare tibanna gas from the lower atmosphere of the planet, which is then processed and packaged for shipment off-world. The facility is small by galactic standards, with its administrator, Lando Calrissian, hoping to turn a profit while avoiding scrutiny from the Mining Guild and the Empire. In recent years Lando has invited casinos to Cloud City, hoping to line his own pockets while providing further cover for the tibanna gas business.

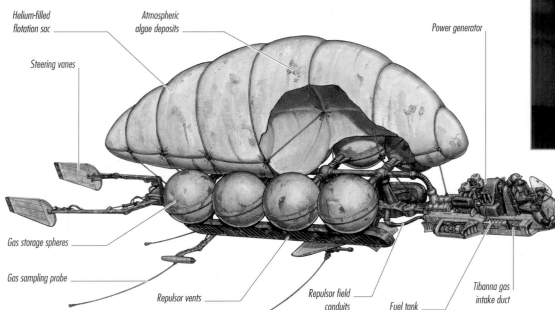

Helium-filled flotation sac

Atmospheric algae deposits

Power generator

Steering vanes

Gas storage spheres

Gas sampling probe

Repulsor vents

Repulsor field conduits

Fuel tank

Tibanna gas intake duct

CHASING GAS STORMS

Gas prospectors have navigated Bespin's breathable upper atmosphere for many generations, and Cloud City still employs a legion of these freelance daredevils to pinpoint lush pockets of spin-sealed Tibanna. Piloting their own jury-rigged craft through the clouds, prospectors seek to locate and exploit fresh eruptions of tibanna gas before the major contractors. Gas storms on Bespin are highly volatile and unpredictable, and, though the prospectors accept the risks for the sake of the sizeable profits, some pursuits are decidedly deadly.

FLOATING PARTNERSHIPS

Cloud City shares Bespin's extraordinary skies with smaller refineries. Kept aloft by massive repulsorlift generators, these mobile, automated facilities can re-orient themselves to draw tibanna from newly discovered pockets of gas. In general, however, these refineries handle surpluses from larger installations like Cloud City.

FRESH AIR

Constructed from materials mined from the Bespin System's innermost planet, Miser, Cloud City rises atop the 16 kilometer (10 mile)-wide mining structure. Its five million residents and visitors inhabit the planet's breatheable upper atmosphere, known as the "Life Zone," which is replenished and shielded from the noxious lower atmosphere by a layer of airborne algae.

WATCH THE SKIES

With mining operations and tourism running unabated throughout Bespin's long year, the need for security is great. Stringent visa procedures are in place, and unidentified vessels are detected and intercepted long before they reach any of the docking platforms. A shield generator protects Cloud City from near-space bombardment and/or laser fire, but routine vigilance is overseen by the Wing Guard, which uses twin-pod cloud cars for patrol and emergency actions. These two-person fliers are equipped with blaster cannons and can sustain an average speed of 1,500 kph (930 mph). Employing both repulsorlifts and ion engines, the atmospheric airspeeders are also used as pleasure craft.

UNEASY REMINDER

The upper levels of Cloud City are designed to showcase the planet's two-hour-long sunsets and natural beauty. The white synthstone of Leia's chamber pays homage to the style of the planet Alderaan, the home of Lord Figg's wife. But this reminder of her destroyed planet does nothing to put Leia at ease. Instead, it only heightens her sense that all is not right on Cloud City.

CARBONITE STORAGE REPULSOR SLED

Bespin Motors' carbonite sled is intended for use in conjunction with a carbon-freeze chamber for the safe transport of exotic gases that exist at high pressure, such as tibanna. Tibanna is used in starship weaponry, hyperdrives, and as a coolant around the gravito-active elements of repulsorlifts. Inside the sled's control frame, a quantity of gas is suspended within a super-strong block of carbonite. Lord Vader decides to use Han Solo as a test subject for the storage of a humanoid within carbonite. By this process, Vader hopes to immobilize his son, Luke Skywalker, for transport to the Emperor. As he is lowered into the freezing chamber, Han is injected to induce hibernation before carbonite infuses and solidifies throughout his body.

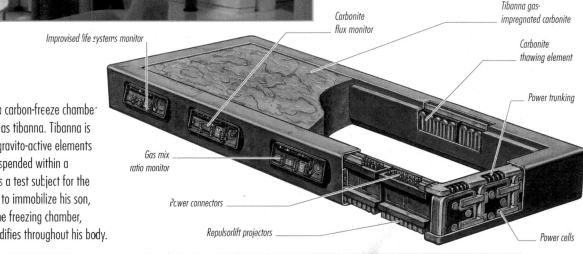

Improvised life systems monitor

Carbonite flux monitor

Tibanna gas-impregnated carbonite

Carbonite thawing element

Power trunking

Gas mix ratio monitor

Power connectors

Repulsorlift projectors

Power cells

Vestibule turbolifts
and passageways to
tibanna repositories

Transport shuttle
tunnel to warehouses

Hangar for repulsorlift
maintenance vehicles

Sensor panels around shaft
regulate low air pressure needed
to maintain unrefined tibanna

Support cable
anchor points

Narrow transportation
tunnel connects processing
vane to rest of facility

HARD-PRESSED WORKERS

The monotonous and sometimes dangerous work of mining and
processing tibanna gas is performed by Ugnaughts—porcine humanoids
native to the planet Gentes—who reside in the floating metropolis's
labyrinth of humid, red-lighted work corridors.

Single-track conveyor alternately
transports empty carbon-block frames
into vane and filled blocks out

High-tensile
support cables

PROCESSING VANE

DEEP INSIDE THE BELLY of Cloud City, Darth Vader takes
advantage of one of the airborne facility's gigantic gas-processing
vanes for his own evil ends. He makes sinister use of a carbon-freeze
chamber—where tibanna gas is admixed with carbonite for flash-
freeze preservation—by having Han Solo encased in carbonite and
placed in the custody of bounty hunter Boba Fett. The Dark Lord
then battles Luke Skywalker onto a sensor balcony suspended over
a vast reactor shaft, in which tibanna is stored at low pressure before
purification and stabilization. Luke is finally sucked out of the shaft
through a network of gas-exhaust pipes and ends up dangling from
the underbelly of Cloud City, desperately clutching a weather vane.

Processing vane (area
enlarged, right) situated
on side of reactor shaft

City level

Gas exhaust port into
which Luke is sucked

Tibanna block warehouse
and conveyors

Transport
docking bays

Tractor beam arrays
line underbelly of pod

Ring of repulsorlifts holds city aloft

Weather/climate sensor vane

Heavily shielded main power
converter and distribution node

SPIN-SEALED RICHES

Generators located along Cloud City's underbelly
emit tractor beams that converge below the
reactor bulb to create an energy funnel. This
funnel mines tibanna from Bespin's lower
atmosphere at depths of more than 23,000
kilometers (14,200 miles). The gas passes via an
aperture in the underside of the reactor bulb (1)
to the reactor stalk (2) and into smaller reactor
shafts (3), where it filters into processing vanes.
The manufactured gas outperforms the energy
produced by competing gases in starcraft
weaponry and hyperdrives.

Tibanna gas shoots up reactor
stalk and is ducted into reactor
shafts at top for processing

Power conduits and
converters line side of stalk

Ring of ducts around reactor
bulb allows mined gases to
enter reactor stalk from
aperture in underside of bulb

Only just managing to keep ahold of the teetering sensor balcony in the reactor shaft, Luke refuses
to accept Vader's offer of an alliance—or his revelation that he is in fact Luke's father.

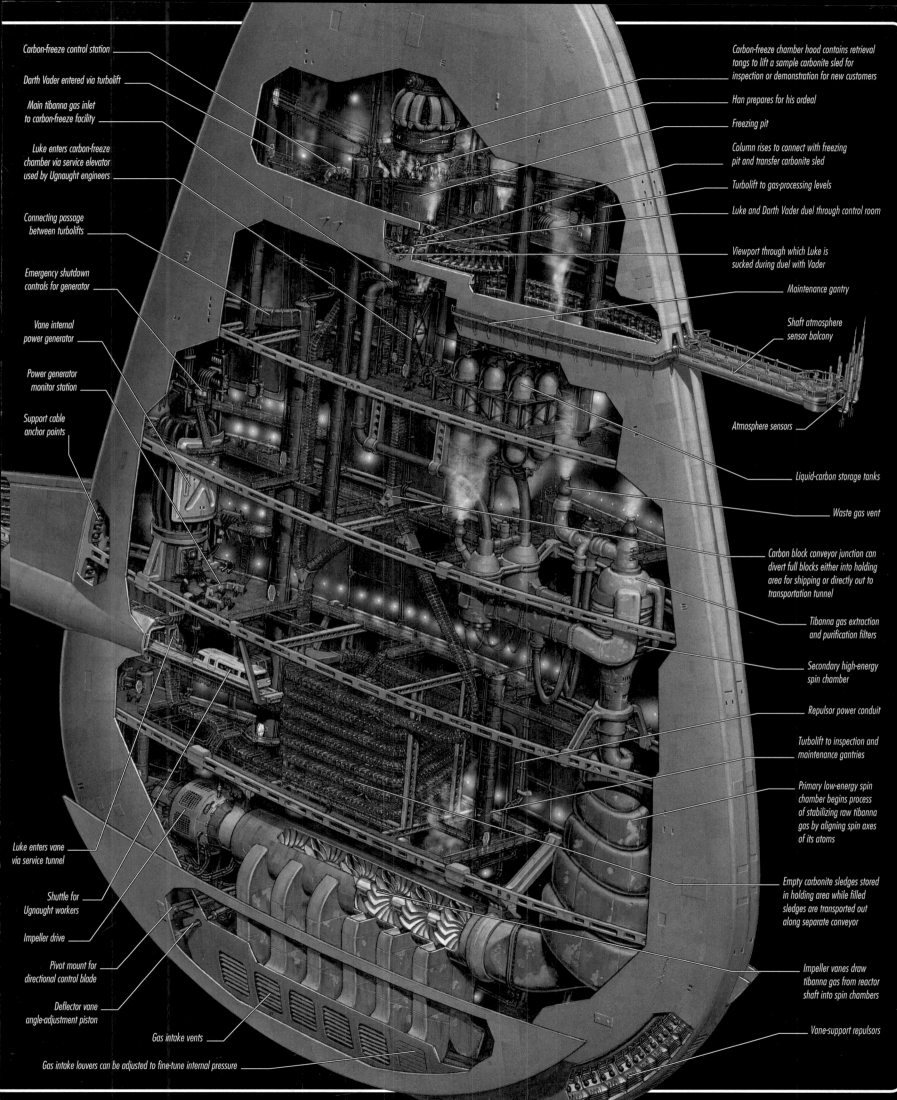

Carbon-freeze control station

Darth Vader entered via turbolift

Main tibanna gas inlet to carbon-freeze facility

Luke enters carbon-freeze chamber via service elevator used by Ugnaught engineers

Connecting passage between turbolifts

Emergency shutdown controls for generator

Vane internal power generator

Power generator monitor station

Support cable anchor points

Luke enters vane via service tunnel

Shuttle for Ugnaught workers

Impeller drive

Pivot mount for directional control blade

Deflector vane angle-adjustment piston

Gas intake vents

Gas intake louvers can be adjusted to fine-tune internal pressure

Carbon-freeze chamber hood contains retrieval tongs to lift a sample carbonite sled for inspection or demonstration for new customers

Han prepares for his ordeal

Freezing pit

Column rises to connect with freezing pit and transfer carbonite sled

Turbolift to gas-processing levels

Luke and Darth Vader duel through control room

Viewport through which Luke is sucked during duel with Vader

Maintenance gantry

Shaft atmosphere sensor balcony

Atmosphere sensors

Liquid-carbon storage tanks

Waste gas vent

Carbon block conveyor junction can divert full blocks either into holding area for shipping or directly out to transportation tunnel

Tibanna gas extraction and purification filters

Secondary high-energy spin chamber

Repulsor power conduit

Turbolift to inspection and maintenance gantries

Primary low-energy spin chamber begins process of stabilizing raw tibanna gas by aligning spin axes of its atoms

Empty carbonite sledges stored in holding area while filled sledges are transported out along separate conveyor

Impeller vanes draw tibanna gas from reactor shaft into spin chambers

Vane-support repulsors

155

EPISODE VI
RETURN OF THE JEDI

Luke Skywalker has returned to his home planet of Tatooine in an attempt to rescue his friend Han Solo from the clutches of the vile gangster Jabba the Hutt.

Little does Luke know that the GALACTIC EMPIRE has secretly begun construction on a new armored space station even more powerful than the first dreaded Death Star.

When completed, this ultimate weapon will spell certain doom for the small band of rebels struggling to restore freedom to the galaxy....

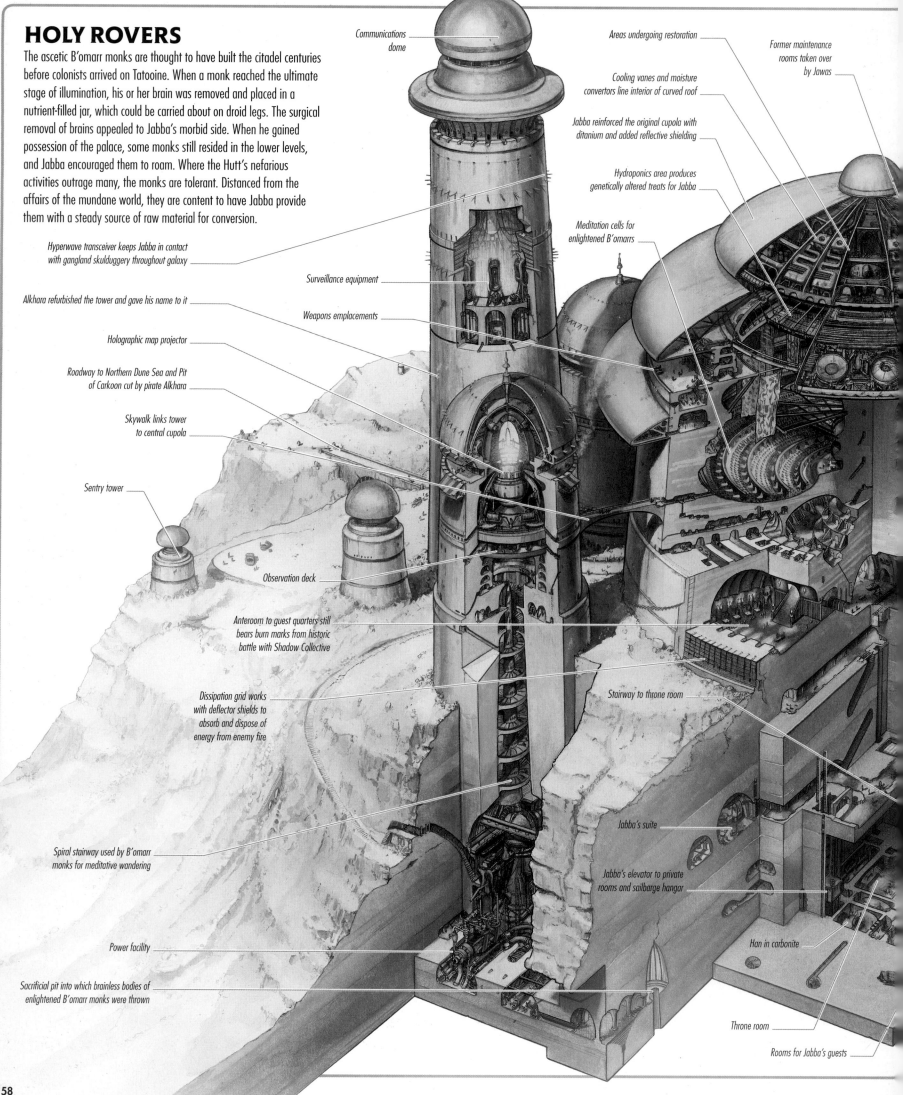

HOLY ROVERS

The ascetic B'omarr monks are thought to have built the citadel centuries before colonists arrived on Tatooine. When a monk reached the ultimate stage of illumination, his or her brain was removed and placed in a nutrient-filled jar, which could be carried about on droid legs. The surgical removal of brains appealed to Jabba's morbid side. When he gained possession of the palace, some monks still resided in the lower levels, and Jabba encouraged them to roam. Where the Hutt's nefarious activities outrage many, the monks are tolerant. Distanced from the affairs of the mundane world, they are content to have Jabba provide them with a steady source of raw material for conversion.

Communications dome

Areas undergoing restoration

Former maintenance rooms taken over by Jawas

Cooling vanes and moisture convertors line interior of curved roof

Jabba reinforced the original cupola with ditanium and added reflective shielding

Hydroponics area produces genetically altered treats for Jabba

Meditation cells for enlightened B'omarrs

Hyperwave transceiver keeps Jabba in contact with gangland skulduggery throughout galaxy

Surveillance equipment

Alkhara refurbished the tower and gave his name to it

Weapons emplacements

Holographic map projector

Roadway to Northern Dune Sea and Pit of Carkoon cut by pirate Alkhara

Skywalk links tower to central cupola

Sentry tower

Observation deck

Anteroom to guest quarters still bears burn marks from historic battle with Shadow Collective

Stairway to throne room

Dissipation grid works with deflector shields to absorb and dispose of energy from enemy fire

Jabba's suite

Jabba's elevator to private rooms and sailbarge hangar

Spiral stairway used by B'omarr monks for meditative wandering

Power facility

Han in carbonite

Sacrificial pit into which brainless bodies of enlightened B'omarr monks were thrown

Throne room

Rooms for Jabba's guests

THIEVES AND MURDERERS

The bandit Alkhara was the first outsider to appropriate the B'omarr monastery for his own use. Among his legendary misdeeds, Alkhara had the members of a local police garrison murdered; he then, in turn, slaughtered the Sand People who had carried out the crime, thus initiating a blood feud between Tusken Raiders and settlers that exists to this day. Alkhara remained at the citadel for 34 years, before being driven off Tatooine by Jabba the Hutt.

SAIL BARGE HANGAR

Jabba is ferried across Tatooine in signature sail barges and skiffs designed by the Ubrikkian Corporation, but commissioned by architect Derren Flet. When it came to designing dungeons for the palace, however, Flet didn't fare nearly as well — he was executed for failing to take into account the number of beings Jabba would imprison, or the full extent of the Hutt's depravity.

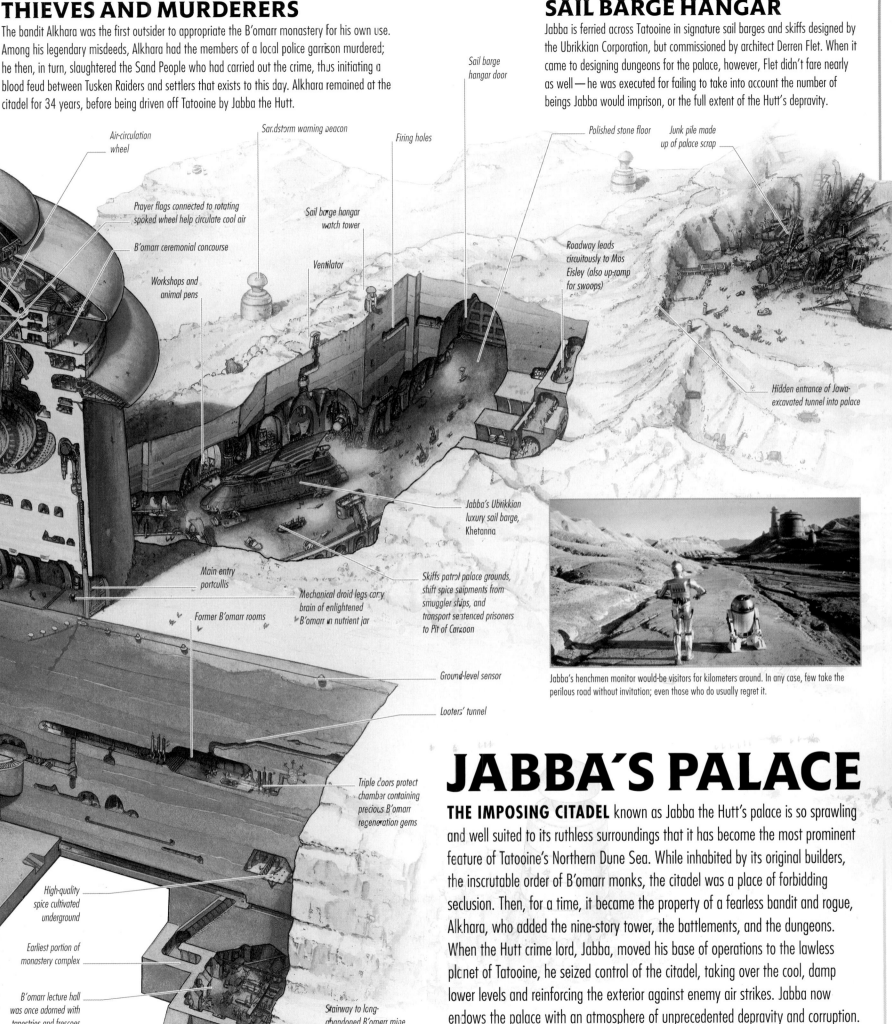

Air-circulation wheel

Prayer flags connected to rotating spoked wheel help circulate cool air

B'omarr ceremonial concourse

Workshops and animal pens

Sandstorm warning beacon

Sail barge hangar watch tower

Ventilator

Firing holes

Sail barge hangar door

Polished stone floor

Junk pile made up of palace scrap

Roadway leads circuitously to Mos Eisley (also up-ramp for swoops)

Hidden entrance of Jawa-excavated tunnel into palace

Jabba's Ubrikkian luxury sail barge, Khetanna

Main entry portcullis

Mechanical droid legs carry brain of enlightened B'omarr in nutrient jar

Former B'omarr rooms

Skiffs patrol palace grounds, shift spice shipments from smuggler ships, and transport sentenced prisoners to Pit of Carkoon

Ground-level sensor

Looters' tunnel

Triple doors protect chamber containing precious B'omarr regeneration gems

Jabba's henchmen monitor would-be visitors for kilometers around. In any case, few take the perilous road without invitation; even those who do usually regret it.

High-quality spice cultivated underground

Earliest portion of monastery complex

B'omarr lecture hall was once adorned with tapestries and frescoes

Stairway to long-abandoned B'omarr mine

JABBA'S PALACE

THE IMPOSING CITADEL known as Jabba the Hutt's palace is so sprawling and well suited to its ruthless surroundings that it has become the most prominent feature of Tatooine's Northern Dune Sea. While inhabited by its original builders, the inscrutable order of B'omarr monks, the citadel was a place of forbidding seclusion. Then, for a time, it became the property of a fearless bandit and rogue, Alkhara, who added the nine-story tower, the battlements, and the dungeons. When the Hutt crime lord, Jabba, moved his base of operations to the lawless planet of Tatooine, he seized control of the citadel, taking over the cool, damp lower levels and reinforcing the exterior against enemy air strikes. Jabba now endows the palace with an atmosphere of unprecedented depravity and corruption.

JABBA'S THRONE ROOM

JABBA THE HUTT'S FONDNESS FOR murky underground places and theatricality leads him to convert a portion of the former B'omarr monastery into a presence, or throne, room, which he fills with his corrupt associates, cut-throat recruits, and sycophantic followers. At his command, the strains of music waft through the spicy air; dancers of exotic species gyrate across the stone floor; smugglers or weapons merchants who cross him are humiliated and thrown to the ferocious rancor beast—or a bounty hunter and his prisoner are admitted for audience.

THE HUTT'S HOUSE BAND

Made up of veteran local banders, the Max Rebo Band plays regularly for Jabba the Hutt, appearing at his palace or in his townhouse in Mos Eisley. The band's core consists of Max, Droopy McCool, and Sy Snootles; for high-profile gigs, Max supplements this ensemble, drawing on the talents of Joh Yowza, Barquin D'an, Doda Bodonawieedo, and Rappertunie, as well as drummers, backup singers, and dancers.

CORRUPT COURT

Only the most notorious smugglers and bounty hunters are allowed to consort openly in the throne room—those who have proved themselves adept at murder, mayhem, or crimes of high standing. Those of junior reputation room the vast palace, forced to make do with entertaining Jabba's subordinates, and are afforded less respect than Jabba's chief droids. It is into this intimidating atmosphere that Princess Leia, disguised as bounty hunter Boushh, enters.

LATE EVENING

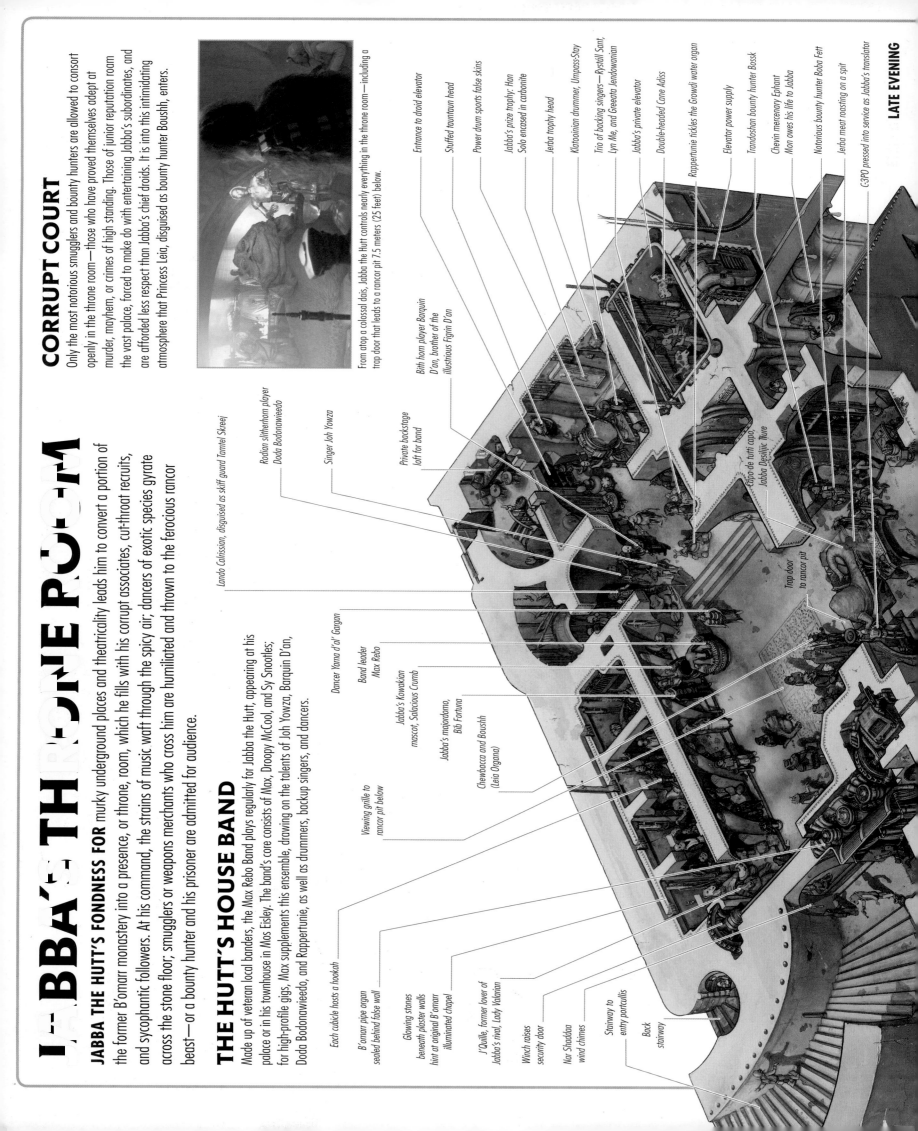

Entrance to droid elevator
Stuffed tauntaun head
Power drum sports false skins
Jabba's prize trophy: Han Solo encased in carbonite
Jerba trophy head
Klatooinian drummer, Umpass-Stay
Trio of backing singers—Rystáll Sant, Lyn Me, and Greeata Jendowanian
Jabba's private elevator
Double-headed Cane Adiss
Rappertunie tickles the Growdi water organ
Elevator power supply
Trandoshan bounty hunter Bossk
Chevin mercenary Ephant Mon owes his life to Jabba
Notorious bounty hunter Boba Fett
Jerba meat roasting on a spit
C-3PO pressed into service as Jabba's translator

From atop a colossal dais, Jabba the Hutt controls nearly everything in the throne room—including a trap door that leads to a rancor pit 7.5 meters (25 feet) below.

Bith horn player Barquin D'an, brother of the illustrious Figrin D'an

Rodian slitherhorn player Doda Bodonawieedo

Singer Joh Yowza

Private backstage loft for band

Lando Calrissian, disguised as skiff guard Tamtel Skreej

Capo de tutti capo, Jabba Desilijic Tiure

Trap door to rancor pit

Dancer Yarna d'al' Gargan

Band leader Max Rebo

Jabba's Kowakian mascot, Salacious Crumb

Jabba's majordomo, Bib Fortuna

Chewbacca and Boushh (Leia Organa)

Viewing grille to rancor pit below

Each cubicle hosts a hookah

B'omarr pipe organ hint at sealed behind false wall

Glowing stones beneath plaster walls

J'Quille, former lover of Jabba's rival, Lady Valarian

Winch raises security door

Nar Shaddaa wind chimes

Stairway to entry portcullis

Back stairway

B'omarr original illuminated chapel

Doda Bodonawieedo

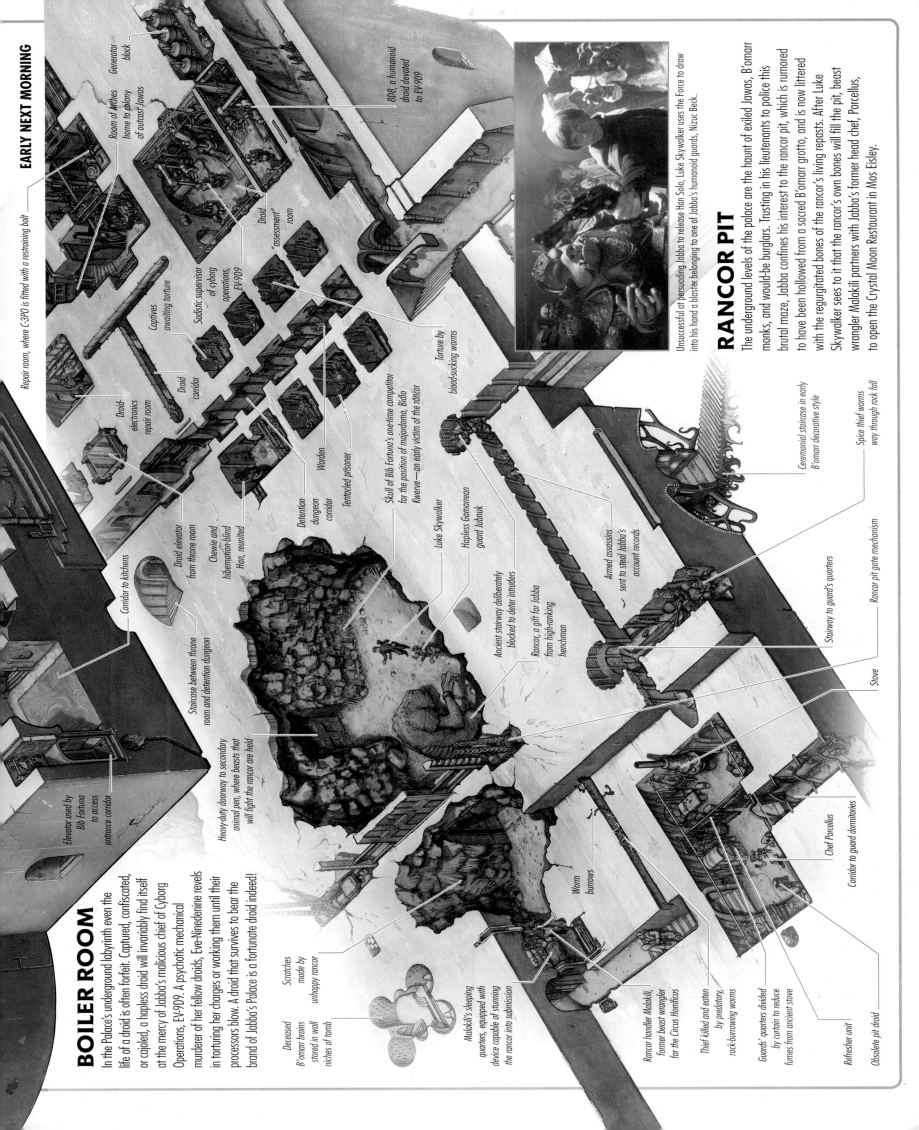

Repair room, where C-3PO is fitted with a restraining bolt

Generator block

Room of Arches home to colony of outcast Jawas

808, a humanoid droid devoted to EV-9D9

Droid electronics repair room

Captives awaiting torture

Sadistic supervisor of cyborg operations, EV-9D9

Droid "assessment" room

Droid corridor

Warden

Detention dungeon corridor

Tentacled prisoner

Torture by bloodsucking worms

Skull of Bib Fortuna's one-time competitor for the position of majordomo, Bidlo Kwerve—an early victim of the rancor

Luke Skywalker

Hapless Gamorrean guard Jubnuk

BOILER ROOM

In the Palace's underground labyrinth even the life of a droid is often forfeit. Captured, confiscated, or cajoled, a hapless droid will invariably find itself at the mercy of Jabba's malicious chief of Cyborg Operations, EV-9D9. A psychotic mechanical murderer of her fellow droids, Eve-Ninedenine revels in torturing her charges or working them until their processors blow. A droid that survives to bear the brand of Jabba's Palace is a fortunate droid indeed!

Corridor to kitchens

Droid elevator from throne room

Chewie and hibernation-blind Han, reunited

Staircase between throne room and detention dungeon

Elevator used by Bib Fortuna to access entrance corridor

Heavy-duty doorway to secondary animal pen, where beasts that will fight the rancor are held

Deceased B'omarr brains stored in wall niches of tomb

Scratches made by unhappy rancor

Malakili's sleeping quarters, equipped with device capable of stunning the rancor into submission

Rancor handler Malakili, former beast wrangler for the Circus Horrificus

Thief killed and eaten by predatory, rock-burrowing worms

Worm burrows

Rancor, a gift for Jabba from high-ranking henchman

Ancient stairway deliberately blocked to deter intruders

Armed assassins sent to steal Jabba's account records

Guards' quarters divided by curtain to reduce fumes from ancient stove

Refresher unit

Obsolete pit droid

Corridor to guard dormitories

Chef Porcellus

Stove

Rancor pit gate mechanism

Stairway to guard's quarters

Ceremonial staircase in early B'omarr decorative style

Spice thief worms way through rock fall

Unsuccessful at persuading Jabba to release Han Solo, Luke Skywalker uses the Force to draw into his hand a blaster belonging to one of Jabba's humanoid guards, Nizuc Beck.

RANCOR PIT

The underground levels of the palace are the haunt of exiled Jawas, B'omarr monks, and would-be burglars. Trusting in his lieutenants to police this brutal maze, Jabba confines his interest to the rancor pit, which is rumored to have been hollowed from a sacred B'omarr grotto, and is now littered with the regurgitated bones of the rancor's living repasts. After Luke Skywalker sees to it that the rancor's own bones will fill the pit, beast wrangler Malakili partners with Jabba's former head chef, Porcellus, to open the Crystal Moon Restaurant in Mos Eisley.

BATTLE OF ENDOR

WHILE IT COSTS THE REBEL ALLIANCE many lives, Bothan spies furnish the following intelligence: the Empire is constructing a second Death Star near the isolated Forest Moon of Endor. The Alliance has to strike before the facility is operational—but the Bothans also report that the Death Star is protected by a massive defensive shield projected from a generator and dish network located on the surface of the Forest Moon. Thus, a desperate plan is hatched. Entrusting the *Millennium Falcon* to Lando Calrissian and Sullustan navigator Nien Nunb, Luke, Han, Leia, and a team of commandos travel to Endor in a stolen Imperial shuttle, intent on destroying the shield installation.

1 Thanks to an old but serviceable Imperial code, the shuttle is allowed to land on the Forest Moon. The commandos set out for the shield-generator bunker, but are forced to engage a handful of Imperial scouts on speeder bikes. When two of the scouts flee, Luke and Leia take up the pursuit.

2 The 200-kph (124-mph) chase takes Luke and Leia on a zigzagging course through Endor's forest of mighty trees. Two more Imperials join the pursuit and Luke leaps onto the back of one of the bikes. He hurls the pilot into a tree, then drops back to deal with the second pair of scouts.

THE AFTERMATH OF VICTORY

The explosion of the second Death Star sends a rain of meteoric debris toward the Forest Moon, but the rebel fleet is able to deploy shields and tractor beams to deflect debris away from their strike team on the surface. The morning after the battle, rebel forces scramble to destroy an Imperial base on the far side of the moon. Within days, the Alliance is battling Imperial forces on a number of fronts, as moffs and Imperial commanders seek to carve out power in a rapidly fragmenting Empire.

Leia swoops down from treetops, firing at scout trooper with her blasters

Luke leaps off his speeder bike and uses his lightsaber to slice control vanes off scout trooper's bike as it passes

Luke's speeder bike hits tree

Scout trooper hits tree

Scout trooper begins firing at Leia

Leia falls from her speeder and is discovered by Wicket

Scout trooper looks back to see explosion of Leia's speeder bike before crashing into tree

Ewok trap

Lake Sui, home to Ewok stilt villages

Bright Tree Village

3 Thrown from her speeder bike, Leia regains consciousness to discover that she has company: a furry Endor native, whose crude spear is taller than he is. After sharing rations with the Ewok, and allying with him to dispatch two more Imperial scouts, Leia accompanies Wicket to Bright Tree Village.

4 Chewbacca inadvertently leads Luke, Han, R2-D2, and himself into an Ewok net trap. The astromech's circular saw arm cuts effortlessly through the net, only to drop the prisoners to the ground and directly into captivity, at the hands—and spears—of Teebo, Paploo, and other Ewoks.

5 Deprived of their weapons, Luke, Han, Chewbacca, and the two droids are marched to Bright Tree Village high above the forest floor. Much to Han's dismay, the Ewoks treat C-3PO with reverential respect, having taken him for a deity—even though the droid's programming prohibits impersonation.

Ewok army and rebels cross strait of Lake Marudi using Ewok-made rope bridge

N
0   1 KM
0   1 MILE

9 As the Ewoks deploy crude weapons against the Imperial troops—catapults, hang gliders, and pouches of burning lizard oil—Han and Leia try frantically to reopen the blast door that has sealed the bunker. As Imperial AT-STs are being toppled by rocks and logs, Ewoks are felled by cruel blaster fire.

IMPERIAL INSTALLATION

Landing platforms serve as touchdown decks for shuttles and craft of similar sizes, and as loading gantries for AT-ATs. The columnar legs of the modular platform house turbolifts, and the deck features a tractor beam emitter, multiple floodlights, and twin landing-zone target circles.

Corridors link loading gantries and turbolift shafts

Turbolift

Tractor beam emitter

Leia pulls up into treetops

Scout trooper hits tree after blaster strike from Luke

Luke drops behind scout troopers, while Leia continues behind the lead trooper

Two additional scout troopers pull in behind Luke

Above-ground Imperial shield projector—the underground power generator complex spans an area 70 kilometers (43 miles) in diameter

8 Rebel commandos infiltrate the installation via the rear entrance of the control bunker. Unaware that they have done just as the Emperor predicted, they are soon surrounded by stormtroopers. Outside the bunker, C-3PO acts as a momentary diversion, while the Ewoks prepare to launch a counter-offensive.

SPECIAL OPERATIONS

The Pathfinders, a renowned Alliance special forces unit, play a key role in helping destroy the shield generator, an assault that leaves the second Death Star vulnerable to attack by rebel starfighters. Among those decorated for valor are Major Bren Derlin, who leads the commando team at Endor, and General Crix Madine, the Imperial defector largely responsible for planning the raid.

Imperial turbolaser outpost at which Luke surrenders

Rebels land close to turbolaser tower outpost under guise of being parts and technical crew

Luke jumps over to scout trooper's bike and pushes trooper off

Luke and Leia on single speeder bike pull up alongside rear scout trooper bike

Extent of battle between rebel/Ewok army and Imperial forces

Rear entrance to shield generator bunker

Chewbacca shoots escaping scout trooper

Scout trooper camp

Imperial landing platform

Landing platform overlook

6 With Han about to be roasted over a fire, Luke uses the Force to levitate C-3PO and his wooden throne over the heads of Ewok shaman, Logray, and Bright Tree Village chief, Chirpa. At C-3PO's command, Han, Luke, and R2-D2 are released from captivity and able to reunite with Leia.

7 Having sensed the presence of his son, Darth Vader arrives by shuttle at the landing platform for the massive shield generator installation, its perimeter safeguarded by Imperial war machines, including AT-AT walkers and AT-ST scouts.

ROUTE KEY

Route	
Leia, Luke, Han, Chewbacca, C-3PO, R2-D2, and troops of rebel strike-team squad head toward shield generator bunker, via scout trooper camp	———
Luke and Leia set off on single speeder bike	- - -
Scout trooper 1	———
Scout trooper 2	———
Luke hijacks scout trooper 2's speeder bike	———
Leia (solo) on speeder bike	═══
Scout trooper 3	———
Scout trooper 4	———
Luke's route back to Han, Chewbacca, and the droids at scout trooper camp	———
Han, Luke, Chewbacca, and the droids search for Leia, are captured by Ewoks, and end up in the Ewok village	———
Rebel strike-team squad head to shield generator bunker	———
Wicket takes Leia to Ewok village	———
Luke's route to Imperial post, where he surrenders	———
Luke is carried to Imperial Landing Platform by AT-AT	———
Han, Leia, Chewbacca, droids, and army of Ewoks trek to rendezvous with squad at shield generator	———

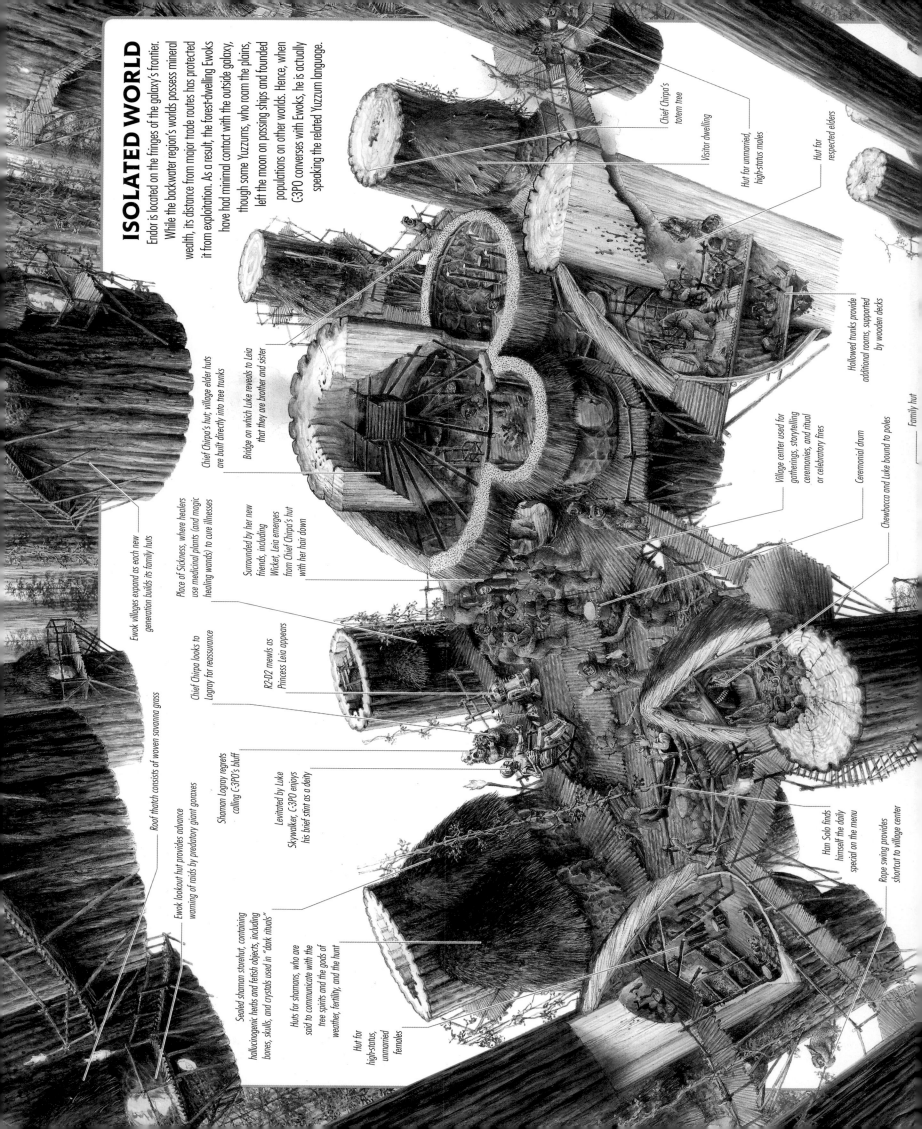

ISOLATED WORLD

Endor is located on the fringes of the galaxy's frontier. While the backwater region's worlds possess mineral wealth, its distance from major trade routes has protected it from exploitation. As a result, the forest-dwelling Ewoks have had minimal contact with the outside galaxy, though some Yuzzums, who roam the plains, left the moon on passing ships and founded populations on other worlds. Hence, when C3PO converses with Ewoks, he is actually speaking the related Yuzzum language.

Chief Chirpa's totem tree

Visitor dwelling

Hut for unmarried, high-status males

Hut for respected elders

Hollowed trunks provide additional rooms, supported by wooden decks

Chief Chirpa's hut; village elder huts are built directly into tree trunks

Bridge on which Luke reveals to Leia that they are brother and sister

Village center used for gatherings, storytelling ceremonies, and ritual or celebratory fires

Ceremonial drum

Chewbacca and Luke bound to poles

Family hut

Place of Sickness, where healers use medicinal plants (and magic healing wands) to cure illnesses

Surrounded by her new friends, including Wicket, Leia emerges from Chief Chirpa's hut with her hair down

Han Solo finds himself the daily special on the menu

Rope swing provides shortcut to village center

Ewok villages expand as each new generation builds its family huts

Chief Chirpa looks to Logray for reassurance

R2-D2 mewls as Princess Leia appears

Roof thatch consists of woven savanna grass

Ewok lookout hut provides advance warning of raids by predatory giant goraxes

Shaman Logray regrets calling C-3PO's bluff

Levitated by Luke Skywalker, C-3PO enjoys his brief stint as a deity

Sealed shaman storehut, containing hallucinogenic herbs and fetish objects, including bones, skulls, and crystals used in "dark rituals"

Huts for shamans, who are said to communicate with the tree spirits and the gods of weather, fertility, and the hunt

Hut for high-status, unmarried females

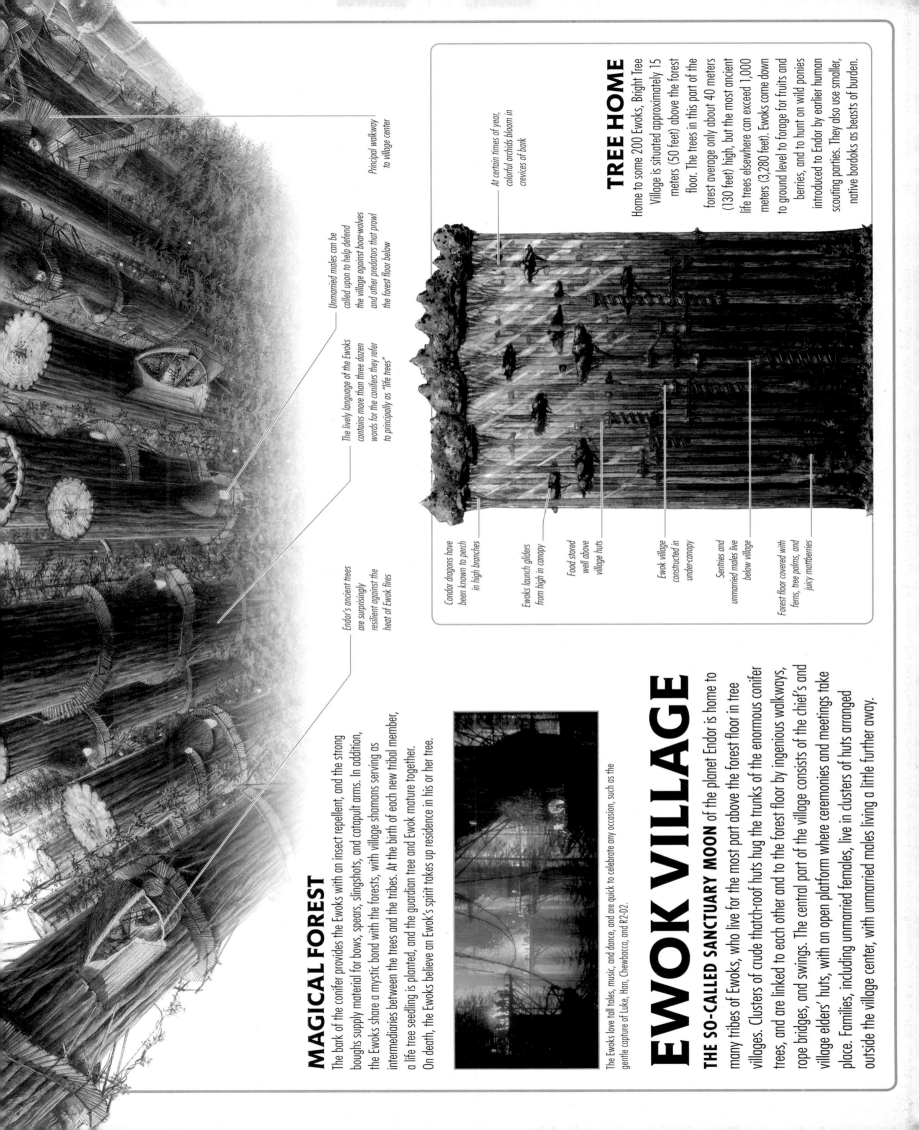

TREE HOME

Home to some 200 Ewoks, Bright Tree Village is situated approximately 15 meters (50 feet) above the forest floor. The trees in this part of the forest average only about 40 meters (130 feet) high, but the most ancient life trees elsewhere can exceed 1,000 meters (3,280 feet). Ewoks come down to ground level to forage for fruits and berries, and to hunt on wild ponies introduced to Endor by earlier human scouting parties. They also use smaller, native bordoks as beasts of burden.

At certain times of year, colorful orchids bloom in crevices of bark

Condor dragons have been known to perch in high branches

Ewoks launch gliders from high in canopy

Food stored well above village huts

Ewok village constructed in under-canopy

Sentries and unmarried males live below village

Forest floor covered with ferns, tree palms, and juicy mattberries

Unmarried males can be called upon to help defend the village against boar-wolves and other predators that prowl the forest floor below

The lively language of the Ewoks contains more than three dozen words for the conifers they refer to principally as "life trees"

Principal walkway to village center

MAGICAL FOREST

The bark of the conifer provides the Ewoks with an insect repellent, and the strong boughs supply material for bows, spears, slingshots, and catapult arms. In addition, the Ewoks share a mystic bond with the forests, with village shamans serving as intermediaries between the trees and the tribes. At the birth of each new tribal member, a life tree seedling is planted, and the guardian tree and Ewok mature together. On death, the Ewoks believe an Ewok's spirit takes up residence in his or her tree.

Endor's ancient trees are surprisingly resilient against the heat of Ewok fires

The Ewoks love tall tales, music, and dance, and are quick to celebrate any occasion, such as the gentle capture of Luke, Han, Chewbacca, and R2-D2.

EWOK VILLAGE

THE SO-CALLED SANCTUARY MOON of the planet Endor is home to many tribes of Ewoks, who live for the most part above the forest floor in tree villages. Clusters of crude thatch-roof huts hug the trunks of the enormous conifer trees, and are linked to each other and to the forest floor by ingenious walkways, rope bridges, and swings. The central part of the village consists of the chief's and village elders' huts, with an open platform where ceremonies and meetings take place. Families, including unmarried females, live in clusters of huts arranged outside the village center, with unmarried males living a little further away.

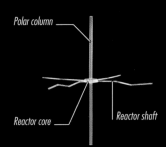

1 The primary stage focused on assembling components necessary for construction of the main reactor core—approximately one-tenth the diameter of the entire structure—and the immense cylindrical polar column, which served to distribute power and stabilize the Death Star's rotational capabilities. A quartet of reactor shafts—bent 15 degrees in five places—extended outward to what would be the station's circumference, two of them emerging exactly at the equator. Capacitor panels were layered around the reactor core.

Polar column

Reactor core

Reactor shaft

Command bridge located above lens, or dish, and patterned after bridge of original Death Star

Polar cap

Superlaser

Equatorial regions

2 Subsidiary shafts were added to both the polar column and the four reactor shafts. (Some of these would later be used by rebel starfighters to reach the surface of the station.) The equatorial, or "waistband," regions were constructed next, as they contained important docking facilities and the thrusters that rotated the station.

Superlaser lens focuses tributary beams into primary beam of devastating, planet-destroying power

3 With the core and equatorial systems in place, construction crews next prioritized the building of the primary weapon. Only Vader and a few of the Emperor's advisors grasped that Palpatine's plan in leaving so much of the base unfinished was to deceive the Alliance into thinking that the superlaser would not be operational when the rebels launched their attack.

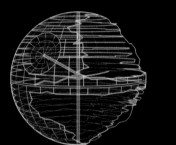

4 As had been confirmed during development of the original Death Star, construction advanced most efficiently when the working surface allowed sufficient space for the greatest possible number of self-replicating construction droids. This was Moff Jerjerrod's justification for filling the station's interior in a piecemeal manner.

Docking ring for starships to moor at tower; smaller vessels, like Imperial shuttles, link via "umbilical" air tube

Sensors and communications arrays in summit

BASE OF OPERATIONS

Rising from the Death Star II's north pole, the Emperor's 100-story isolation tower was anchored to the station well before his arrival. This structure is surrounded by the greatest concentration of anti-starfighter gun emplacements, placed at intervals of as little as a few hundred meters, and all with improved fire control. Emperor Palpatine's Throne Room occupies one spoke of the penultimate story's quadripartite structure.

Imperial Guards stationed throughout the tower at all times

Laser cannons girdle crown

Circular viewports overlook weapons-studded city sprawls that surround the tower

Sleep chamber linked to medical diagnosis computers to monitor the Emperor's health

Receiving area, where Palpatine conspires and dictates his twisted thoughts on political power

Emperor's Throne Room

Other than to conduct routine maintenance, droids are not permitted in the upper tower

Holographic map of Galactic Empire indicates planets or star systems that are to be subjugated or punished

DEATH STAR II

SECRETLY CONSTRUCTED IN ORBIT around the remote Forest Moon of Endor, the second Death Star is over 160 kilometers (100 miles) in diameter—even larger than its destroyed predecessor. Like the original Death Star, its purpose is to terrorize planets and systems in league with the Rebel Alliance with a ruthless demonstration of power. But this superweapon also has another purpose: to act as bait to lure the rebels to their doom. The Emperor believes that the end of the Rebellion is at hand, but it is the second Death Star that is doomed—and the Emperor along with it.

In place of the two meter (6.5 feet)-wide thermal exhaust port targeted by the rebels at Yavin 4, the second Death Star possesses millions of millimeter (0.04 inch)-sized heat-dispersion tubes extending over the entire surface, each equipped with emergency baffle mechanisms to block excess-power surges

Artificial gravity is localized throughout Death Star: in surface decks (the "city sprawl") gravity is directed toward the core, allowing gun crews to stand "on" the surface of the globe; in stacked inner decks, it is directed north to south

Areas immediately above and below equatorial trench are heavily armored

Equatorial trench contains nested hierarchy of lesser trenches, along with docking bays secured by atmospheric containment fields

Surface "city sprawls" are linked to internal air circulation shafts and contain a high density of towers and surface weapons emplacements

Convoys of spaceships constantly supply construction crews with building materials

Construction droids work on future housings for hyperdrive motivator units

Active construction sites illuminated by sparks from countless welding droids; arc lights allow human crews to supervise operations

Construction droids work on future fuel-storage area

Arrays of temporary repulsorlift generators fill engineering sectors

Incomplete, the station reveals the axisymmetric planar structure of decks and shell-like structure of quadanium outer skin

Quarters for shell-construction crews and energy replenishment stations for labor droids

DESTRUCTIVE MIGHT

The Death Star II is not parked in a naturally synchronous orbit above the Forest Moon, so remaining over one point on the moon's surface requires a considerable uplift force against Endor's gravity. Initially, the station was supported by a repulsorlift field projected from the same ground facility that would eventually supply the station with its defensive shield. Tales told by Ewok shamans relate that the extra weight on the moon's crust had dramatic side effects, including massive groundquakes, land that shifted and buckled, and lakes that spilled out of their natural basins. After crushing the Rebel Alliance, the Emperor plans to send massive fleets to the Alliance-sympathetic worlds of Chandrila and Mon Cala, blockading both planets until the battle station's completion. The subsequent obliteration of these rebel hotbeds, Palpatine is certain, will prevent future insurgents from ever daring to challenge Imperial rule again.

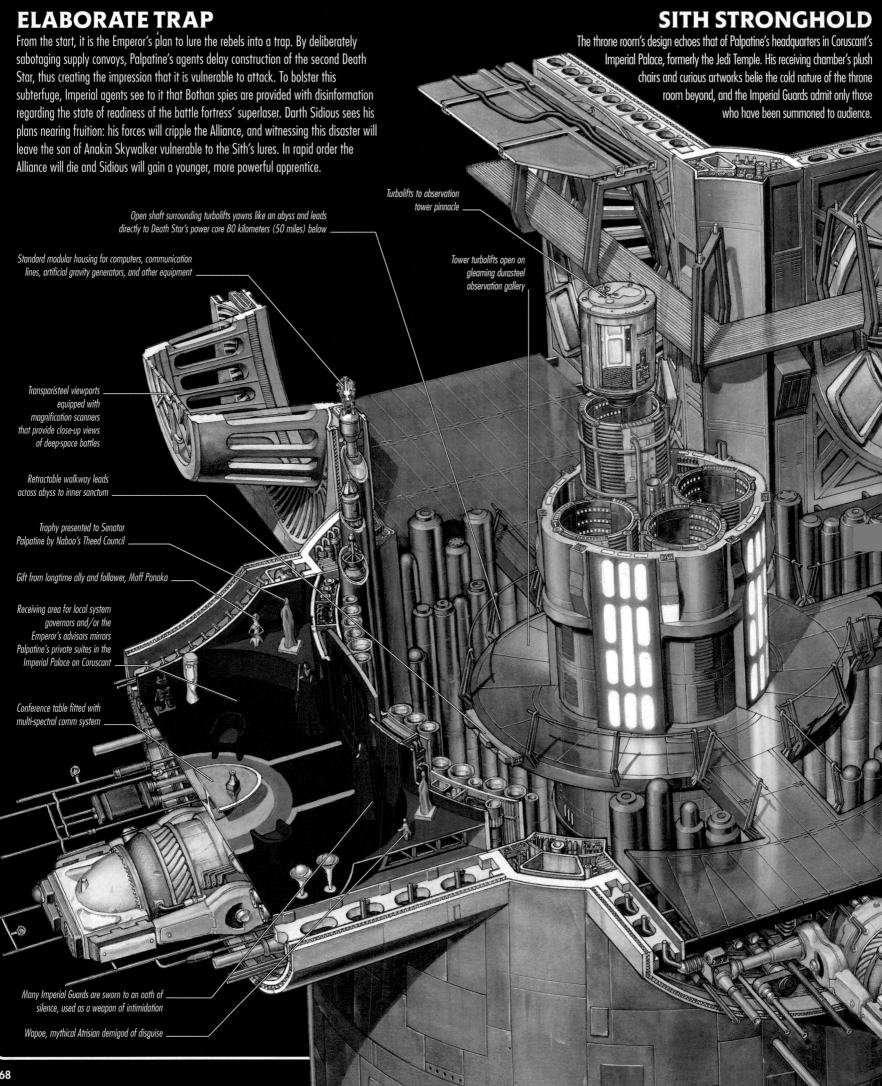

ELABORATE TRAP

From the start, it is the Emperor's plan to lure the rebels into a trap. By deliberately sabotaging supply convoys, Palpatine's agents delay construction of the second Death Star, thus creating the impression that it is vulnerable to attack. To bolster this subterfuge, Imperial agents see to it that Bothan spies are provided with disinformation regarding the state of readiness of the battle fortress' superlaser. Darth Sidious sees his plans nearing fruition: his forces will cripple the Alliance, and witnessing this disaster will leave the son of Anakin Skywalker vulnerable to the Sith's lures. In rapid order the Alliance will die and Sidious will gain a younger, more powerful apprentice.

SITH STRONGHOLD

The throne room's design echoes that of Palpatine's headquarters in Coruscant's Imperial Palace, formerly the Jedi Temple. His receiving chamber's plush chairs and curious artworks belie the cold nature of the throne room beyond, and the Imperial Guards admit only those who have been summoned to audience.

Turbolifts to observation tower pinnacle

Open shaft surrounding turbolifts yawns like an abyss and leads directly to Death Star's power core 80 kilometers (50 miles) below

Standard modular housing for computers, communication lines, artificial gravity generators, and other equipment

Tower turbolifts open on gleaming durasteel observation gallery

Transparisteel viewports equipped with magnification scanners that provide close-up views of deep-space battles

Retractable walkway leads across abyss to inner sanctum

Trophy presented to Senator Palpatine by Naboo's Theed Council

Gift from longtime ally and follower, Moff Panaka

Receiving area for local system governors and/or the Emperor's advisors mirrors Palpatine's private suites in the Imperial Palace on Coruscant

Conference table fitted with multi-spectral comm system

Many Imperial Guards are sworn to an oath of silence, used as a weapon of intimidation

Wapoe, mythical Atrisian demigod of disguise

Viewscreens display results of exterior scans and interior views throughout entire battle station, as well as tactical schematics, blueprints, and other data

Shield projector rings encircle each viewport

Interrogation and restraint grappling equipment

Tower is adaptation of standard Imperial mooring tower for large ships, with additional shielding

In keeping with Emperor's unadorned robes and cowl, throne itself is a simple, swivel-mount contour chair

The lustrous dais, or audience platform, is open underneath

Duty posts for Imperial Guards were unused prior to and during the Battle of Endor

Visual feeds to viewscreen

Deflector shield power conduits

Luke hid beneath dais until Vader realized Leia is his daughter

Collapsed portion of catwalk—its suspension supports severed by Darth Vader's hurled lightsaber

The Emperor joins the assault on Luke

Luke's lightsaber

Bolts of Sith lightning shoot from Darth Sidious' crooked fingers

Luke Skywalker is prepared to die for love of his father

His mechanical right hand sacrificed to Luke's lightsaber, a humbled Darth Vader struggles with what it will mean to allow his only son to succumb to the Emperor's merciless attack

The shielded hull of the 100-story tower is impregnable to attack by starfighters or even capital ships

Shield generator

The Emperor's throne room tower rises from the second Death Star's north pole and is defended by a larger-than-usual concentration of turbolaser turrets.

EMPEROR'S LAIR

THE THRONE ROOM is Emperor Palpatine's command center and seat of power aboard the second Death Star. With its gleaming decks, exposed superstructure, and shadowy recesses, it is both intimidating and menacing. While the climactic Battle of Endor rages outside, Palpatine descends from his dais to teach Luke Skywalker a lesson about the power of the dark side. Convinced that his mastery of events is assured, the Emperor fails to realize that Darth Vader's final act will not only turn defeat to victory for the hard-pressed Rebel Alliance, but also create balance in the Force.

EXECUTOR COMMAND TOWER

RAISED ON A THICK STALK above the *Executor's* dorsal technoscape, the 285 meter (935 feet)-wide command tower is practically a ship in its own right. It houses a profusion of vital components, including shield generators, communications systems, and sensor arrays, as well as officers' quarters, briefing rooms, and escape pods for the vessel's upper-echelon commanders. Just above the centerline of its forward face sits the command bridge. Standing on the bridge of this gigantic warship, its commander can call on almost unimaginable power, in the process embodying both the glory and wrath of the Empire.

Crewmen stationed at consoles below the Executor's command bridge walkway toil under the withering scrutiny of Lord Vader.

Command tower

FATAL FLAW

With its gleaming command walkway and two meter (seven feet)-tall transparisteel viewports, the *Executor's* bridge provides unobstructed views of quarries and kills. The ship's shielding—driven by the power of its massive reactor—makes such displays of Imperial arrogance possible. Yet the vessel is not impregnable. At Endor, pounded mercilessly by the capital ships of the Rebel Alliance flotilla, the ship's shields fail. At that moment, the rebels are able to strafe the command tower—and with the *Executor's* navigation suite in ruins and defensive guns losing coordination, a careening A-wing destroys the bridge.

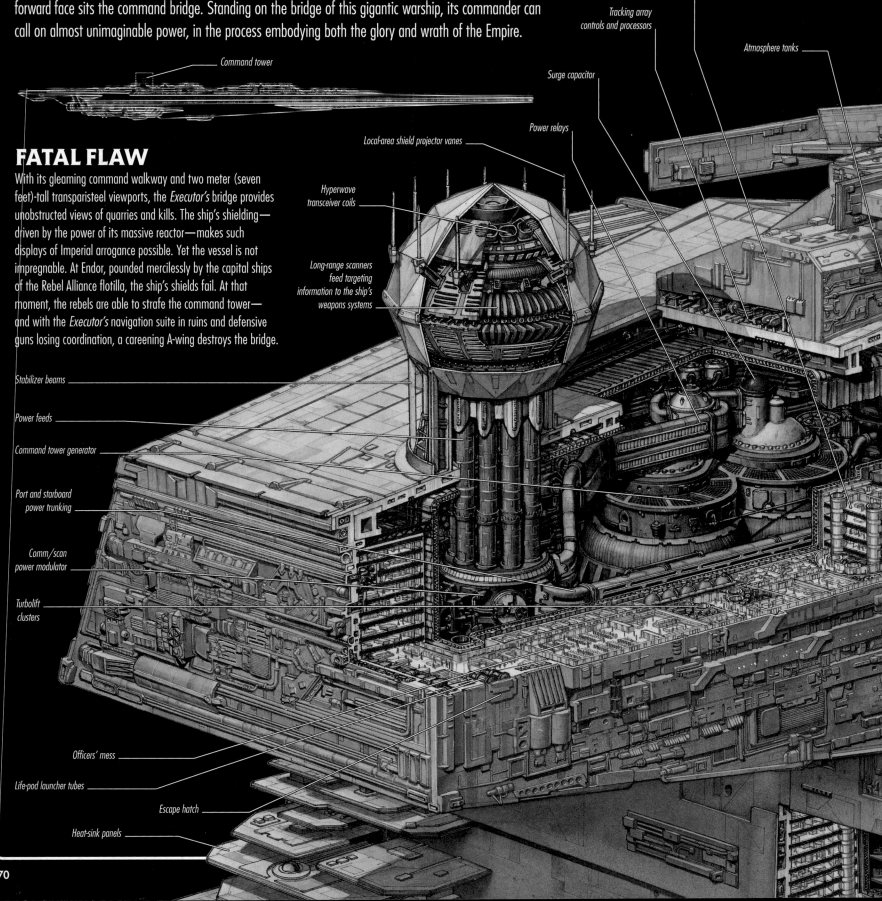

Bridge tower's main computer deck

Tracking array controls and processors

Atmosphere tanks

Surge capacitor

Power relays

Local-area shield projector vanes

Hyperwave transceiver coils

Long-range scanners feed targeting information to the ship's weapons systems

Stabilizer beams

Power feeds

Command tower generator

Port and starboard power trunking

Comm/scan power modulator

Turbolift clusters

Officers' mess

Life-pod launcher tubes

Escape hatch

Heat-sink panels

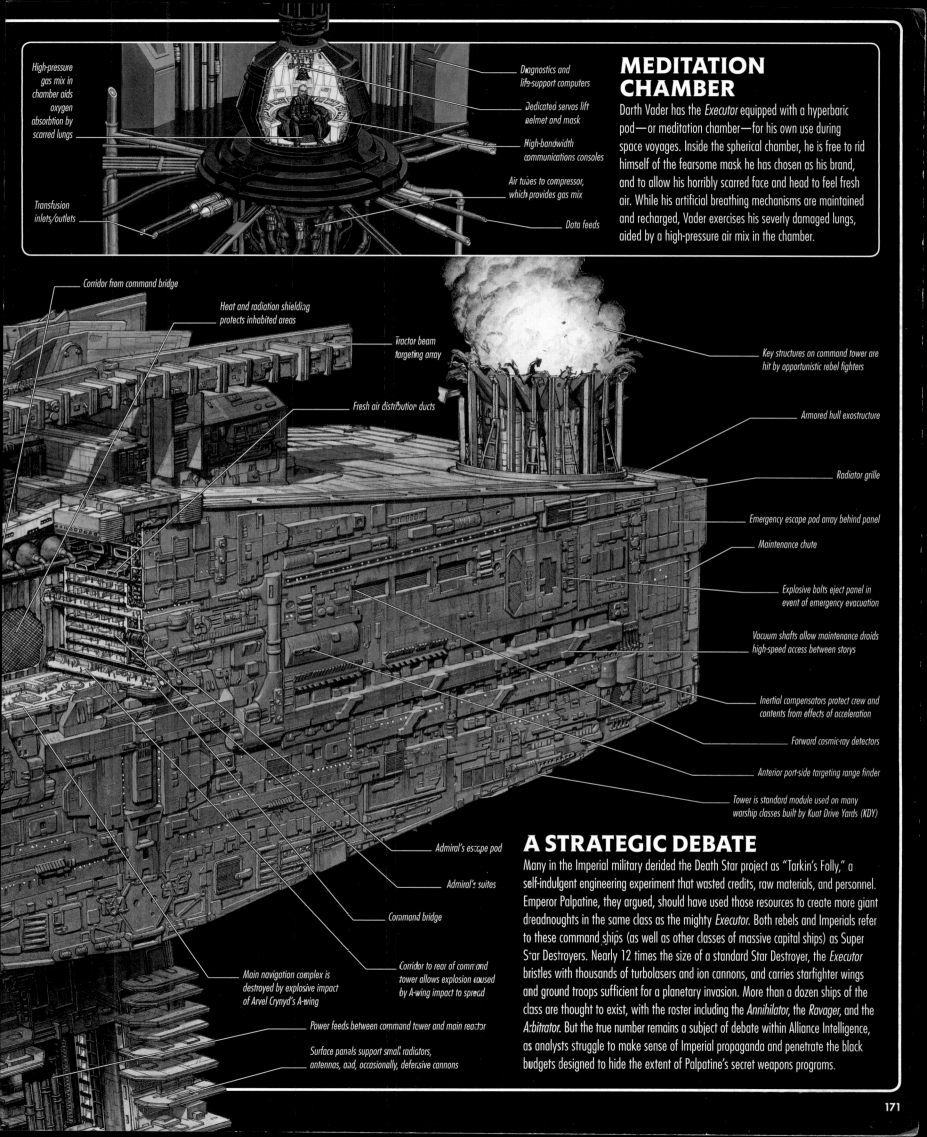

MEDITATION CHAMBER

Darth Vader has the *Executor* equipped with a hyperbaric pod—or meditation chamber—for his own use during space voyages. Inside the spherical chamber, he is free to rid himself of the fearsome mask he has chosen as his brand, and to allow his horribly scarred face and head to feel fresh air. While his artificial breathing mechanisms are maintained and recharged, Vader exercises his severly damaged lungs, aided by a high-pressure air mix in the chamber.

High-pressure gas mix in chamber aids oxygen absorbtion by scarred lungs

Transfusion inlets/outlets

Diagnostics and life-support computers

Dedicated servos lift helmet and mask

High-bandwidth communications consoles

Air tubes to compressor, which provides gas mix

Data feeds

Corridor from command bridge

Heat and radiation shielding protects inhabited areas

Tractor beam targeting array

Fresh air distribution ducts

Key structures on command tower are hit by opportunistic rebel fighters

Armored hull exostructure

Radiator grille

Emergency escape pod array behind panel

Maintenance chute

Explosive bolts eject panel in event of emergency evacuation

Vacuum shafts allow maintenance droids high-speed access between storys

Inertial compensators protect crew and contents from effects of acceleration

Forward cosmic-ray detectors

Anterior port-side targeting range finder

Tower is standard module used on many warship classes built by Kuat Drive Yards (KDY)

Admiral's escape pod

Admiral's suites

Command bridge

Main navigation complex is destroyed by explosive impact of Arvel Crynyd's A-wing

Corridor to rear of command tower allows explosion caused by A-wing impact to spread

Power feeds between command tower and main reactor

Surface panels support small radiators, antennas, and, occasionally, defensive cannons

A STRATEGIC DEBATE

Many in the Imperial military derided the Death Star project as "Tarkin's Folly," a self-indulgent engineering experiment that wasted credits, raw materials, and personnel. Emperor Palpatine, they argued, should have used those resources to create more giant dreadnoughts in the same class as the mighty *Executor*. Both rebels and Imperials refer to these command ships (as well as other classes of massive capital ships) as Super Star Destroyers. Nearly 12 times the size of a standard Star Destroyer, the *Executor* bristles with thousands of turbolasers and ion cannons, and carries starfighter wings and ground troops sufficient for a planetary invasion. More than a dozen ships of the class are thought to exist, with the roster including the *Annihilator*, the *Ravager*, and the *Arbitrator*. But the true number remains a subject of debate within Alliance Intelligence, as analysts struggle to make sense of Imperial propaganda and penetrate the black budgets designed to hide the extent of Palpatine's secret weapons programs.

EPISODE VII
THE FORCE AWAKENS

Luke Skywalker has vanished. In his absence,
the sinister FIRST ORDER has risen from the ashes
of the Empire and will not rest until Skywalker,
the last Jedi, has been destroyed.

With the support of the REPUBLIC, General Leia
Organa leads a brave RESISTANCE. She is
desperate to find her brother Luke and gain his help
in restoring peace and justice to the galaxy.

Leia has sent her most daring pilot on a secret
mission to Jakku, where an old ally has
discovered a clue to Luke's whereabouts....

JAKKU

A FORLORN WORLD on the edge of settled space, Jakku is a bleak desert globe notable as the site of the Empire's last stand a year after its defeat at Endor. With the battle going against them, Imperial warships used tractor beams to lock onto New Republic foes, dragging them down to the surface. A generation later, these wrecks form the Graveyard of Ships, picked over by scavengers searching for technology to salvage. Besides scavengers, Jakku is home to religious orders craving solitude, conspiracy theorists peddling wild tales about lost Imperial secrets, and desperate beings seeking to start new lives or escape past misdeeds.

GRAVEYARD OF SHIPS

The Graveyard is an eerie place, with shattered ships protruding from the sand like silent sentinels, surrounded by the bleached bones of their long-dead crews. The wrecks range from the vast bulk of the mighty Super Star Destroyer *Ravager*, lying broken on its back, to the scattered remains of countless starfighters. Jakku's scavengers lead a perilous existence inside the cavernous hulls, searching for intact components amid razor-sharp metal, spilled toxins, cracked reactors, and unexploded munitions.

TUANUL VILLAGE

Tuanul village is built on top of a massive rock mesa

KELVIN RAVINE

NAMENTHE'S CRATER

Ghtroc-690 crash site

Vertically buried starship known to scavengers as "The Spike"

Wreck of Super Star Destroyer Ravager

Wreck of Imperial Star Destroyer Inflictor

ROUTE KEY

Poe's route
Finn's route
BB-8's route
The Pilgrims' Road
Rey's route from home to Graveyard
Rey's route from Graveyard to Niima
Millennium Falcon's escape route

Wreck of New Republic Star Cruiser Freedom's Dawn

Wreck of Imperial Star Destroyer Interrogator

FERESSEE'S POINT

REY'S HOME

THE SITTER

CARBON RIDGE

1 Tuanul village is attacked by First Order forces looking for clues to the location of Luke Skywalker. They capture Resistance pilot Poe Dameron, and massacre the villagers.

2 Deep inside the wreck of a crashed Star Destroyer, a scavenger named Rey finds a valuable capacitor bearing, and adds it to her haul of tech to trade at Niima Outpost.

3 Having finished scavenging for the day, Rey returns from Niima Outpost to the wrecked Imperial walker that she calls home, and eats her evening meal.

4 Poe Dameron's droid, BB-8, escaped the massacre at Tuanul, and has made his way to the dunes near Rey's house. Rey rescues him from a surly Teedo scavenger.

Poe gets a ride with a Blarina scavenger named Naka Iit

BLOWBACK TOWN

5 Stormtrooper-turned-deserter Finn's stolen TIE fighter crashes onto the unstable sands of the Sinking Fields. Finn leaves the smoldering wreckage and walks south-east.

SINKING FIELDS

KELVIN RIDGE

Finn first sees Niima Outpost from this ridge

6 Finn and Rey first encounter each other at Niima Outpost, and shortly afterward are chased by stormtroopers looking to seize BB-8 and capture Finn.

NIIMA OUTPOST

Dunes of the Graveyard give way to salt flats around Niima Outpost

OLD MERU'S

7 Rey, Finn, and BB-8 steal a dilapidated freighter called the *Millennium Falcon* from Unkar Plutt, and are chased by First Order TIE fighters, but finally escape from Jakku.

Unkar Plutt's trading stall, nicknamed the "Concession Stand"

Bazaar established by Niima the Hutt

Constable's office

Spaceport gate is based on traditional Hutt architecture

The Millennium Falcon

Quadjumper

NIIMA OUTPOST

Jakku's largest settlement is Niima Outpost, named for a long-dead Hutt crime lord. Niima consists of a bazaar, a spaceport that is little more than a fence and a few rigs for refueling, and the stall of Unkar Plutt. The hulking Crolute junk boss keeps a tight hold on the market for tech salvaged from the Graveyard of Ships, trading meal rations to scavengers in exchange for their finds.

REY'S HOME

REY HAS MADE a home for herself in a toppled Imperial walker in Jakku's Goazon Badlands. The downed AT-AT has been stripped of its valuable components and now serves as shelter for the capable scavenger. Rey lives in the troop compartment, which is simultaneously her kitchen, bedroom, and workroom. To defend against intruders, she has welded the AT-AT's hatches shut, coming and going through the auxiliary hatch in the walker's belly. Buried sensors alert her to visitors, but Jakku's scavengers mostly stay away, wary of traps she's reportedly installed in her home and her willingness to use the quarterstaff she carries for self-defense.

Troop seating

Lamps crafted from nightwatcher-worm casings by Tuanul village artisan

Salvaged Y-wing flight computer

Hammock woven by Rey as a child

Rey has welded this escape hatch shut

Rey's speeder

Battle damage covered by curtain

Speeder garage formed from empty engine compartment

Auxiliary belly hatch serves as front door

Stove

Electroshock traps rigged to entrance passage

Solar array crafted from TIE fighter parts

Eksoan power generator links to homemade solar array

CASUALTY OF WAR

While in Imperial service, the AT-AT Rey now calls home was designated Hellhound 2, and formed part of the military complement of the Star Destroyer *Interrogator*. Rey discovered this information in the craft's troop manifest, but has never found any sign of what happened to the stormtroopers, pilots, or their commanders—they, like so many others, were apparently casualties of the chaotic Battle of Jakku decades earlier. Rey has salvaged fuel cells from the AT-AT's laser-cannon energizer and from two wrecked speeder bikes, then wired them to scavenged TIE solar panels. This homemade power system feeds her home's generator, though the cobbled-together system requires constant maintenance.

SCAVENGER'S WORK

While at home, Rey spends most of her time at her workbench. She prefers cleaning and refurbishing parts here to using Unkar Plutt's washing tables in Niima Outpost because the junk boss charges for the use of his facilities. By working at home, Rey can gain more portions in exchange for her salvage, lessening Unkar's power over her. Rey's work area also includes an old Y-wing computer that she uses to study ship schematics, run flight simulations, and practice alien languages and droidspeak.

Rey reacts angrily when she discovers a Teedo capturing an astromech near her home. Jakku's Teedos have always respected her territory and kept out of it. Rey knows if she doesn't protest this one's intrusion, she'll soon have problems.

Top hatch with cryptographic lock protects head, where Rey keeps her most valuable items

Teedo

Water barrels (hidden to prevent theft)

Cooling unit for perishables

AT-AT pilot control panel

Medium blaster cannon

Class II heavy laser cannon

Fuel storage

Motion sensors hidden in pile of junk

Neck is crushed and impassable

Valuable parts from ankle drive motors salvaged and traded with Unkar Plutt

Knee joint cover

As well as its remote location, Rey chose Hellhound 2 as her home because its heat shielding has remained largely intact. This allows her to work within its interior without being cooked by the heat of a Jakku day.

Rey likes to rest in shade created by AT-AT's foot

Terrain sensors in foot have been removed and repurposed as motion sensors

After eating a meager meal of rations and inspecting the AT-AT's systems, Rey allows herself a few minutes to sit in the cool evening. Soon it will be time to return to her workbench. But for a little while, she lets herself dream, imagining that tomorrow will be the day that she escapes Jakku.

Scavenged rebel pilot's helmet

MAZ'S CASTLE

THE GALAXY HAS no shortage of strange watering holes, but Maz Kanata's fortress might be the strangest. The diminutive Maz Kanata has welcomed visitors to her home on the planet Takodana for centuries, offering them a safe haven from galactic quarrels. Maz offers her visitors food and drink, room and board, medical assistance, repairs to droids and starships, loans and appraisals, entertainment, and information. Her castle also serves as a hub for deal-making, with everyone from pirates and smugglers to information brokers and diplomats striking agreements at her tables. Deals are witnessed and sealed by MD-8D9, an ancient protocol droid who enforces the castle's rules and ensures that Maz gets her cut of any bargain struck within her halls.

THE RULES

Visitors to the castle will notice a simple warning posted in numerous galactic languages: NO FIGHTING. Those who violate this principal commandment will find themselves turned away the next time they visit, and Maz has a long memory. The castle's other rules are unwritten but passed down to new visitors: one night's food, drink, and shelter are free to all, with no questions asked. After that, you have to pay—and cheaters may find themselves rethinking their lives in Maz's dungeons. Maz has seen galactic regimes rise and fall, and insists on keeping Takodana neutral ground as conflicts engulf the galaxy beyond her castle's walls.

"DON'T STARE"

Maz's castle is an overwhelming place for new arrivals. Musicians, poets, and artists take turns on the stage; laughter, boasts, and curses rise from the gambling tables as sabacc cards are thrown down and chance cubes tumble; and the kitchens conjure up cuisine and grog suitable for countless species' digestive systems. And that's just the public spaces of the castle: away from prying eyes, pirate captains search for brave young deckhands, explorers and fortune-hunters barter secret hyperspace routes, and those seeking illegal solutions to underworld problems find no shortage of helpers. Meanwhile, spies of every affiliation gather information for their masters.

STORIES AND SECRETS

Maz sees every visitor as a source of stories, delighting in the experiences of grizzled war heroes and wide-eyed young dreamers alike. Her castle's storehouses and vaults overflow with objects that have piqued her interest over the centuries: antique weapons wielded by lost heroes, indecipherable poems from extinct species, icons of vanished religions, and maps to dead worlds. Maz protects objects that speak to her, guided by a certainty that one day her relics will call out to other searchers.

Ancient power generators in tower collect energy from Takodana's storms

Laboratory rented by Thromba and Laparo, Frigosian cryptosurgeons— Maz prefers not to ask what they use it for

Maz's quarters

Maz's library and private museum

Castle communications center and control room

Hyperwave transceiver

Sensors scan low orbit for incoming ships

Maz's private hangar contains her ship, the Epoch Swift

Private casinos

Rumors of strange beasts in the surrounding forests keep guests within the castle walls

Prayer flags hung by deep-space explorers

Statue of Maz is a (relatively) recent addition to the castle, a gift from a former husband

Private banquet hall

Maz's office

Observation deck

Main kitchen, staffed by Strono "Cookie" Tuggs

Bar/serving counter

Storage room

Castle sub-level

Crypt containing Luke Skywalker's lightsaber

...mium guest suites

Castle's lowest level is largely untouched since time of Jedi occupation

Sealed crypt containing remains of fallen Jedi

Holding cell for those who break Maz's rules

Ancient defensive passageways

Guest dormitories

Water filtration system and brewery

Spa and sauna

Flags include podracing pennants and Mandalorian war banners

Han, Rey, Finn, and BB-8 walk toward castle entrance

FIRST ORDER ASSAULT

Maz's castle is built on the site of an ancient battle between the Jedi and the Sith. For centuries the powers of the galaxy have respected its neutrality, sparing its stone halls and soaring towers from war. In its determination to annihilate the New Republic and destroy the Resistance, the First Order ignores this tradition, sending TIE fighters to blast the castle to rubble. Standing among her shocked guests, Maz calmly vows to clean up the mess and continue as she always has.

RESISTANCE BASE

REBEL PILOTS DISCOVERED D'Qar shortly before the Battle of Endor, but the remote planet only housed a small Alliance outpost during the Galactic Civil War. Seeking a home for her new Resistance movement, Leia Organa remembered D'Qar and sent engineers to expand the facility. Much of the base is underground, with the jungle planet's thick foliage hiding the facility from the air and sensor countermeasures concealing power leaks and other evidence of its presence. Remembering the Alliance's near-extinction on Hoth, Leia has insisted on portable equipment that can be evacuated ahead of an attacking First Order fleet.

The Resistance base's resemblance to the famed rebel headquarters on Yavin 4 appeals to Leia and the other rebel veterans on her staff.

Sturdy earthworks protect upper hangars

Ventilation shaft

Medcenter staffed by Doctor Kalonia

Base command center with holographic command interface

Command center entrance concealed in ruins

Memorial wall in base records names of Resistance personnel lost in conflict

Subterranean maintenance hangars used for major refits and storage

Personnel quarters

Upper hangars used for simple repairs and loading of ordnance

LIVING WORLD

D'Qar lacks intelligent life but teems with other varieties: huge trees rise from its steamy jungles, great flocks of avians darken the skies, and the night is alive with the howls of creatures and the thrum of insects. The base occupies a small footprint, both to avoid detection and to keep from disturbing the harmony of this lush refuge. The jungle is relentless, with fast-growing tree roots squeezing through seams in base corridors and chambers. Leia finds such intrusions strangely comforting: nature continues to thrive even as the galaxy descends into conflict.

Hangar elevator lowers ship to maintenance level

Poe Dameron's customized T-70 X-wing, Black One

REBELS ONCE MORE

After the Battle of Endor, Princess Leia Organa was hailed as a rebel hero. But she soon found herself shut out of the New Republic she had fought to restore. Her protests about disarming the fleet were dismissed as paranoia, while her warnings about the First Order's intentions were derided as warmongering. Convinced that a new darkness threatened the galaxy, Leia gathered former Alliance compatriots—many of them also sidelined by a new generation of New Republic leaders—and formed the Resistance.

D'Qar vegetation had to be cleared when base was first reoccupied

Mountain conceals observation post

Long-range sensor tower

Hyperwave transceiver

The Millennium Falcon

Pipeline from deep-level fuel reservoir

Encrypted nav-beacon

Vober Dand, Chief of Ground Logistics Division

Portable power generator

Boxes contain starship components for rapid repairs

Sensor jamming array masks base's sensor signature

Proton torpedoes ready for loading

Jury-rigged speeders are used to transport personnel and munitions

Command center and primary weapon firing control

Assembly chamber where Kylo Ren and General Hux contact Supreme Leader Snoke

Rostrum from which Hux addresses First Order personnel

Banner with First Order symbol

Parade ground/landing platform

A FATEFUL ORDER

The First Order's Supreme Leader Snoke is infuriated when he learns that BB-8 and the map to Luke Skywalker will likely soon be in the hands of the Resistance. Eager to prevent Skywalker's return, Snoke agrees to General Hux's proposal to unveil the Starkiller by destroying the New Republic capital of Hosnian Prime. Hux predicts this vicious attack will cripple the New Republic and force the Resistance to respond, revealing its hidden base of operations and giving the Starkiller its next target.

Addressing a rally at Starkiller Base's command center, General Hux declares that the last day of the Republic is at hand, and the galaxy's star systems will soon bow to the First Order.

Main hangar

TIE fighters in conveyor mechanism to parade ground level

Interrogation room where Rey is held

Stormtrooper barracks

Firing shaft field regulators

Officers' quarters

Maintenance hangar

Firing shaft funnels dark energy in controlled breach of containment field

FIERCE MACHINE

The Starkiller weapon draws on decades of secret Imperial research into harnessing the potential of dark energy. A collector on one side of the planet gathers dark energy from a host star and redirects it into the planetary core. There, this energy is bound by a containment field created by a combination of the planet's magnetic field and unique crystal substructure, and artificial forces regulated by a thermal oscillator. A breach is then opened in the field, funneling the dark energy into a shaft on the planet's other side. This escaping energy takes a form of an astonishingly powerful beam that tunnels through hyperspace itself, its lethal force undiminished even after traveling halfway across the galaxy. A planet is a barely adequate vessel for containing such terrifying power; even the Starkiller's normal operations destabilize the crust of its host, breeding groundquakes and atmospheric disturbances that boil up into vicious storms.

The dark energy collection process is awe-inspiring to witness—vast sheets of flame are drawn down into the planet's core, and smoke and steam rise into the sky from the region around the collector.

STARKILLER BASE

IN THE DEPTHS of the galaxy's Unknown Regions, far from the wary gaze of New Republic politicians and Resistance probes, the First Order has transformed an entire planet into a terrifying superweapon. The Starkiller harnesses the limitless potential of the universe's dark energy to send a lance of destructive power halfway across the galaxy at speeds far faster than light. With this weapon at its command, the First Order can destroy entire star systems without traveling across the stars or warning its enemies that an attack is imminent. This gives the First Order a strategic advantage in seeking control of the galaxy that the Death Stars' architects never dared imagine.

Triple-barreled defensive turbolaser turret

Massive containment field generators are built into planet's solidified mantle at regular intervals

Containment field in modified planetary core

Planet's unique crystal substructure helps contain power of weapon

Thermal oscillator

Sensor arrays in oscillator shaft constantly monitor conditions within the field

FIRST ORDER MILITARY

FOR MANY YEARS, the First Order has been secretly amassing a vast military, waiting patiently for the day when it could launch a devastating surprise attack and destroy its enemies. That day has now come. Across the Unknown Regions, stormtroopers prepare for battle and fleets of warships gather. With the New Republic deluded into thinking the First Order poses no threat, the forces of the First Order stand poised to conquer an unsuspecting galaxy.

LEGIONS REBORN

The First Order's stormtroopers are not the poorly trained garrison troops that made up large parts of the Imperial army. Constantly drilled and indoctrinated from birth, these are soldiers at the peak of effectiveness. They are equipped with the finest weaponry and have been taught to regard the New Republic with a hatred bordering on the fanatical. The creation of new stormtroopers clearly violates the Galactic Concordance treaty between the New Republic and First Order, but by the time the Republic realizes it has been deceived, it will be far too late.

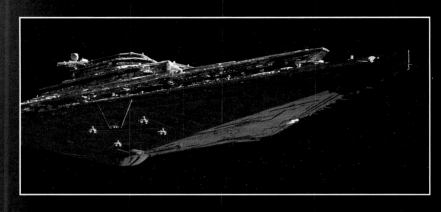

STAR DESTROYERS

The First Order made the construction of new shipyards within the Unknown Regions a priority, and within a relatively short time these yards were producing huge new capital ships. While the fleet does not rival the Old Empire in terms of numbers, the ships themselves are a significant improvement. The *Resurgent*-class, as they have been named, are much larger than an Imperial Star Destroyer, carry more starfighters and stormtroopers, have improved defenses, and utilize advanced kyber crystal-augmented weaponry. They outgun anything in the New Republic fleet by a considerable margin.

ASSAULT LANDERS

First Order strategists argue that the Empire's use of shuttles as troop transports was at best a compromise, and its lack of dedicated assault landers was a serious flaw that resulted in unnecessary casualties. To rectify this, the First Order uses an advanced lander designed from the outset for combat drops into hostile territory. The Atmospheric Assault Lander (AAL) is more heavily shielded and armored than an Imperial shuttle, and can land and deploy its troops far more rapidly.

STARKILLER BASE

The crowning achievement of the First Order is Starkiller Base. This immense, planet-scale facility is half military command center and half superweapon. Construction has taken many years and consumed vast resources, but the base is now ready for its terrifying unveiling to the wider galaxy. With a single shot, the Starkiller has the power to destroy the entire New Republic government and military command, leaving the First Order free to sweep to its inevitable—and crushing—victory.

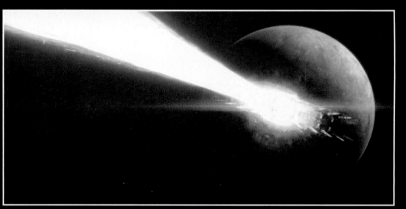

TIE FIGHTERS

Although more advanced versions of TIE fighter, like the TIE Interceptor, had entered production by the time the Empire fell, the First Order believed that the original TIE design held ample opportunities for upgrades. Sienar-Jaemus Fleet Systems, a First Order-controlled successor to the infamous Sienar Fleet Systems, was given the task. The addition of shields and more efficient components transformed the TIE into the TIE/fo—a far more versatile and capable fighter. To complement it, the First Order also commissioned a more powerful variant, featuring a heavy weapons turret, two pilots, and a hyperdrive system. This fighter, dubbed the TIE/sf, is reserved for the use of elite Special Forces personnel.

Rey and Finn watch
confrontation between
Han and Kylo

Han Solo confronts
Kylo Ren on bridge
over oscillator shaft

Dent caused by
ineffective proton
torpedo impact

Control vanes in oscillator's interior
regulate the containment field,
allowing it to hold back the forces
inside the planet

Communications relay allows
oscillator to be controlled remotely
from base command center

TIE/sf space
superiority fighter

Resistance pilots have
been told to expect at
least 80% casualties

STOLEN WORLD

Starkiller Base was once a remote and mysterious world
known only to a handful in the galaxy. During the time of
the Empire it had been used as a source of kyber crystals for
use in the Death Stars' superlasers. Before fleeing into the
Unknown Regions, the founders of the First Order secured
research logs from the secret Imperial labs that had tested
these experimental weapons. Its location revealed, the world
became the heart of a new secret empire, with the First Order
harvesting its kyber crystals for use in its war machine before
turning the planet itself into a mobile weapons platform.

Oscillator cooling system

Sensor feeds from deep-level
monitoring systems in
oscillator shaft

Dampening chambers absorb
harmful spikes of dark energy
moving up shaft from planet core

PERILOUS PLAN

The Resistance attack on Starkiller Base exploits weaknesses in the weapon's construction. First, Han Solo approaches at supralight speeds in the *Millennium Falcon*, slipping through the planet's energy shield. It takes Han's phenomenal instincts as a pilot—and a fair measure of Corellian luck—to survive this perilous passage. Han, Chewie, and Finn then target the shield control room, forcing Captain Phasma to bring the shields down so the Resistance's X-wings can attack the weapon's thermal oscillator. But the oscillator's armored housing proves impervious to aerial bombardment; only after Chewie uses detonators to blow a hole through the housing is the oscillator vulnerable to Poe Dameron's attack run. With the oscillator destroyed, Starkiller Base's containment field ruptures, causing the freed dark energy to shatter the planet and engulf its fragments.

Surrounding region is constantly patrolled by snowtroopers

Armored housing built to withstand any attack

Defensive turbolasers mounted on casing unleash a wall of laser bolts at attacking ships

Black Leader engaging TIEs of "Tarkin's Revenge" fighter wing

Trench system holds conduits that link thermal oscillator to containment field generators

Entry to oscillator is controlled remotely as an additional security measure

Anti-ship missile batteries

Poe uses this trench as cover for his final attack run

Thermal oscillator sits in center of vast trench network

KEY TO THE WEAPON

A complex network of generators maintains the containment field inside Starkiller Base's planetary core, linked by conduits in a web of surface trenches. Keeping this field continuously intact would require massive amounts of energy and generate waste heat that would overload the system. Instead, the field oscillates, with each generator cycling on and off as needed. The hexagonal thermal oscillator is the heart of this system, monitoring conditions in the containment field and thermally regulating the generators to preserve stability. When the thermal oscillator is destroyed, the containment field weakens and then fails catastrophically.

Oscillator shaft is hundreds of kilometers deep

INDEX

Managing Art Editor Ron Stobbart
Art Director Lisa Lanzarini
Publisher Julie Ferris
Publishing Director Simon Beecroft

For Lucasfilm
Senior Editor Frank Parisi
Image Archives Tim Mapp
Art Director Troy Alders
Story Group Leland Chee, Pablo Hidalgo,
Matt Martin, and Rayne Roberts

Inside the Worlds of Star Wars Trilogy © & TM 2004 LUCASFILM LTD.

A catalog record for this book is available from the Library of Congress.

ISBN 978-1-4654-5272-6

DK books are available at special discounts when purchased in bulk for sales
promotions, premiums, fund-raising, or educational use. For details, contact:
DK Publishing Special Markets, 345 Hudson Street, New York, New York 10014
SpecialSales@dk.com

Printed and bound in China

A WORLD OF IDEAS:
SEE ALL THERE IS TO KNOW
www.dk.com
www.starwars.com